Julie Bindel is a freelance journalist, broadcaster and feminist activist. She is the co-founder of the law reform organisation Justice For Women. She is named, in the World Pride Power List, as one of the most influential lesbian and gay people in the world. *Straight Expectations* is her first book

'Julie Bindel's writing is always sharp, often entertaining and rarely less than controversial. Even where our views diverge profoundly, I welcome her voice in a world where too few are ready to truly put their beliefs up for public scrutiny.'

Stella Duffy

'As gay rights become more enshrined in law than ever before, Julie Bindel offers a timely reminder of how we got here – and what we lost along the way.'

Paul Burston

'I always read Julie Bindel because I know her writing is routinely lucid, compelling and fearless. Her unafraid examination of modern life is always thought-provoking (and sometimes just provoking).'

Rose George

'Julie Bindel is a lesbian for lesbians to be proud of. She makes us laugh, cry, think and debate. Read this book and do all of those.'

Beatrix Campbell

STRAIGHT EXPECTATIONS

What Does It Mean to Be Gay Today?

Julie Bindel

guardianbooks

Published by Guardian Books 2014

2 4 6 8 10 9 7 5 3 1

First published in Great Britain in 2014 by

Guardian Books
Kings Place, 90 York Way
London N1 9GU

www.guardianbooks.co.uk

A CIP catalogue record for this book is available from the British Library

ISBN 978-1783-56000-4

Cover design by Two Associates

Typeset by seagulls.net

Printed in England by CPI Group (UK) Ltd, Croydon CR0 4YY

CONTENTS

INTRODUCTION

The past decade has seen a seismic shift in the legislation affecting lesbians and gay men. In March 2014, when this book was written, the first same-sex weddings took place in Britain, nearly 10 years after the passing of the Civil Partnership Act 2004. This means that gay men and women can now marry legally for the first time on British soil and convert civil partnerships into marriages.

Adoption rights have also undergone significant change in the last decade. Prior to 2005 same-sex couples who wished to adopt a child would find themselves in a difficult position, as only one partner was legally entitled to adopt. Not only that but if one half of a lesbian couple used a sperm donor and gave birth to a baby, the other half would have no legal rights unless she was able to adopt the child. Similarly, if a gay male couple wished to have a baby together, only the partner with a biological connection was recognised as a father. Thankfully, as we see in chapter 5, legislation relating to the new gay family has now changed for the better.

In July 2010, in another groundbreaking decision, the supreme court ruled that a lesbian or gay person who flees to the UK to escape persecution may be recognised as a refugee if they 'face a well-founded fear of persecution' in their country of origin. This is life-altering legislation for lesbians and gay men who flee countries such as Uganda, Jamaica and Nigeria, and who in the past were routinely refused asylum and disbelieved by the authorities.

There have also been noteworthy cultural changes during the past decade. In 2013 *Tatler* threw a party to celebrate and 'normalise' high-society lesbians. In the same year Olympic medallist Tom Daley announced that he was in a relationship with a man. Suddenly, it seems, homosexuality is 'fashionable'.

With all these legal and social changes, there is definitely a mood in the UK of exhilaration and victory. Legislatively, nothing now separates lesbians and gay men from heterosexuals. In the space of a few decades it appears we have gone from shame to same. The bigotry of yesteryear, when we were viewed as freaks and corrupting influences, has seemingly been replaced by a seat at the table of normality. When I tell younger lesbians and gay men what it was like for me as an out lesbian in the 1970s – the threats, assaults, social exclusion and enforced isolation – they tell me how lucky they are that they were born after most of the battle towards full acceptance has been won.

But has it?

However positive these changes are for many lesbians and gay men in the UK today, the fact remains that anti-gay bigotry still rages in the public domain, as witnessed during the parliamentary and media debate on same-sex marriage that has taken place in recent years. In private life, too, there is still a long way to go. As we will learn later in the book, the swath of legislative change does not necessarily reflect shifting cultural attitudes; in some areas, there is still much work to be done. Anti-gay language is rife in schools, and more than half of school-age lesbian, gay or bisexual students have experienced direct bullying. Hate crime towards lesbians and gay men remains as prevalent as ever, and the closet is still heaving with sporting figures, lesbian actors and folk in small towns and villages across the UK.

In addition, there is also a sense that by gaining legislative rights, we have perhaps lost a part of our gay identity. While it is staggering to look back at the time I came out in 1977, as a 15-year-old, and compare it to today, it is almost more staggering to realise that as well as the pride I feel at being part of a vital gay liberation movement that has achieved huge advances, I also feel a bitter disappointment at how we have lost our way as a community. When I speak to young lesbians and gay men, some in their teens, as I have while researching this book, I marvel at how different their experiences are compared to my own. But even as a young woman, coming out in a climate of hate and prejudice, I never wanted to be 'like them'. I wanted straight people to see me as a whole human being. My ambition, as a young and passionate lesbian feminist, was to put a rocket up the backside of heterosexuality and to have straight people question the notion of 'normality'. We wanted to challenge the status quo head-on. For a while we did just that, but in recent years the gay community has gone from being critical of the status quo to begging to be a part of it.

However, when the bigots are gunning against the changes that have enabled lesbians and gay men to marry, join the armed forces, have babies and raise a family, I find myself in an awkward position. As an out and proud lesbian lucky enough to have a platform from which to speak, I want to use that privilege effectively. I want to say to younger gay people: 'Look at me. I came out into the most horrendous anti-lesbian bigotry and yet I survived.' I do not want to then see the confusion and distaste in their eyes as I begin to pull apart some of the so-called gains of the past 40-plus years and denounce them as mere shortcuts to an easier life.

It is extremely challenging to argue a point that you *know* is radical when parts of it are shared by closed-minded chauvinists with an opposing agenda. When I say that as a feminist I do not want children, there are always bigots ready to agree with why I should not procreate, confusing my choice with their morality. If I complain that lesbians and gay men should not be joining the unequal and anti-feminist institution of marriage, voices apparently agree that we should not be *allowed* to. If I proclaim loudly that being a lesbian can be a positive alternative for women who feel trapped by the expectations imposed by heterosexuality, I am told by my gay sisters and brothers that by suggesting we have any control whatsoever over our sexual orientation, I am giving strength to those religious zealots who wish to see us all 'cured'.

What, as a woman who lives and breathes politics and tends not to follow the party line, do I do now?

I write a book. And during the course of writing that book, I seek to listen and learn from those lesbians and gay men with views that oppose mine, to challenge myself and see if I start to shift my opinions from those I began to develop from the time I came out, and in the process hopefully gain a deeper understanding of the values and political strategies adopted by the vast majority.

To do this, I had to ask as many people as possible, both gay and straight, about their lives and beliefs. As well as directly interviewing as wide a range of people as I could, I also disseminated two online surveys.

In total, between August 2013 and October 2013, 5,492 participants completed the survey aimed at those identifying themselves as 'other than heterosexual' and 4,036 the one for those who do not identify themselves as lesbian or gay (of which 90 per cent self-identified as heterosexual). From these 9,528 responses – one of the largest surveys of its type – I have been able to gain a broad understanding of modern gay issues and concerns.

This book will examine the contemporary lesbian and gay rights movement and consider how and why it is so fundamentally different from the time I became involved in it, back in the late 1970s. I'll be looking at such areas as bigotry, the causes of same-sex attraction, the relationship between lesbians and gay men, the rise of alternative families, the interface between capitalism and gay culture, and how far we have come and what still needs to be achieved. I include interviews with some of the key players, references to arguments, theories, ideas and activism, quotes from my extensive surveys and my own personal views and experiences of being an out lesbian for more than three decades. This is not a historical trawl through the gay liberation movement, or a round-up of its significant moments. This book will reflect the lesbian and gay world as seen through my eyes, and, of course, through those of the people who will help to tell my story.

So where does the gay nation stand as we adapt to the changes, challenges and conflicts of this brave new world? How should we react to the evolution of public opinion? What does the future hold for the next generation of lesbians and gay men? And just what does it mean to be gay nowadays? These were the questions I was asking as I set out on my journey to discover the state of the lesbian and gay nation today.

CHAPTER 1
THE STATE OF THE NATION

Timeline of key events in the gay political calendar since 1957

1957 The Wolfenden Committee publishes its report, in which it recommends that consensual homosexual behaviour between men over the age of 21 should be decriminalised except in the armed forces. Three years later the Homosexual Law Reform Society holds its first public meeting, attended by 1,000 people.

1966 Almost 10 years after Wolfenden, Leo Abse introduces the Sexual Offences bill with support from Roy Jenkins, the then Labour home secretary, and homosexuality is finally decriminalised with the passing of the Sexual Offences Act 1967.

1974 Maureen Colquhoun becomes Labour MP for Northampton North. Rumours begin to circulate about her sexuality. Colquhoun comes out in autumn 1977 as 'gay and proud of it'. However, her local constituency disapproves of this, and the party refuse to support her (although they claim to have deselected her as a candidate due to her poor performance). Local party chairman Norman Ashby says in the aftermath: 'She was elected as a working wife and mother … This business has blackened her image irredeemably.'[1]

1980 The Criminal Justice (Scotland) Act 1980 decriminalises homosexual acts 'in private' between two men over 21 years of age in Scotland.

1981 George Morton, Labour MP for Manchester Moss Side, is not deposed by his local party in spite of being arrested for gross indecency (consensual gay sexual behaviour). He is quoted as being pointedly unapologetic about the 'feelings that gave rise' to his arrest.

1982 The Sexual Offences Act 1982 decriminalises homosexual acts 'in private' between two men over 21 years of age in Northern Ireland.

1983 During the 1983 byelection, members of the Liberal party join in anti-gay attacks on Labour candidate Peter Tatchell.

1984 Newly elected Labour MP Chris Smith comes out. The opening line to his speech to a crowd in Rugby is: 'My name is Chris Smith, I'm the Labour MP for Islington South and Finsbury, and I'm gay.' Far from being vilified, as Colquhoun was, he receives a standing ovation.

1987 Margaret Thatcher, the prime minister, is quoted as saying: 'Children who need to be taught to respect traditional moral values are being taught that they have an inalienable right to be gay.'

1988 As a result of the extreme anti-gay bigotry brought about by misinformation about the HIV/Aids crisis – namely that it was a 'gay disease' that could be spread by non-sexual as well as sexual contact – Section 28 caused the addition of Section 2A to the Local Government Act 1986 (affecting England, Wales and Scotland, but not Northern Ireland). It became law on 24 May 1988. This amendment made it illegal for local authorities to 'promote homosexuality' in state schools, perpetuating the idea that homosexuality destroys traditional family values. The picture book *Jenny Lives with Eric and Martin* is found in an Inner London Education Authority teachers' centre and creates a media storm. Lesbian, gay, bisexual and transgender (LGBT) issues and anti-gay bullying in schools are largely ignored, as the majority of teachers believe that they are not allowed to intervene under the new law.

In the same year, Labour declares that gay men and lesbians 'must have the same freedom from discrimination and prejudice and the same freedom to live their lives as other people'.

1989 The campaign group Stonewall is formed.

1994 Conservative MP Edwina Currie introduces an amendment to the Criminal Justice Bill seeking to make the age of consent for homosexual acts 16 rather than 21. The amendment is defeated, but the gay male age of consent is later reduced to 18. No age of consent is set for lesbians.

1997 Angela Eagle, Labour MP for Wallasey, becomes the first MP to come out (voluntarily) as a lesbian while in parliament.

The Labour MP for Enfield Southgate Stephen Twigg becomes the first openly gay MP to be elected to the House of Commons.

1998 The Labour Lord Alli becomes the first openly gay member of the House of Lords.

2000 The Labour government ends the policy of disallowing homosexuals in the armed forces and, in February, attempts to repeal Section 28 under the Local Government Act 1988. It is opposed and defeated by the House of Lords, especially the Conservative party, led by Lady Young.

The House of Commons forces through the Sexual Offences (Amendment) Act 2000, lowering the age of consent for homosexuals to 16, without the Lords voting it through.

2002 Alan Duncan becomes the first Conservative MP to come out voluntarily.

2003 Section 28 is repealed as part of the Local Government Act 2003.

2005 Two laws come into effect: the Adoption and Children Act (passed 2002) allows same-sex couples to adopt children, and the Civil Partnership Act (passed 2004) affords 'same-sex couples the right to formalise their relationships and claim the same benefits as married heterosexual couples'.

2006 Margot James is elected local councillor for the Brompton ward of Kensington and Chelsea; she is already out as a lesbian when elected, and goes on to become the first out Tory lesbian MP when she is elected to the constituency of Stourbridge in 2010. David Borrow, Labour MP for South Ribble, becomes the first MP to have a civil partnership.

2009 David Cameron apologises on behalf of the Conservative party for introducing Section 28 (in spite of the fact he had accused Tony Blair, the then prime minister, of being 'anti-family' and wanting the 'promotion of homosexuality in schools' during the first attempts of repeal back in 2000, when Cameron was still an unelected Conservative party member).

That was then, and this is … how?

For those below the age of 60, the idea that same-sex encounters between men were once punishable by prison seems as strange as women being denied the vote. The monumentally significant change in the law brought about by the Wolfenden report of 1957, which eventually received royal assent on 27 July 1967, when homosexuality was decriminalised, proved to be a watershed in the history of gay liberation.

The comments of Roy Jenkins, then home secretary, during the parliamentary debate reflected the general views of the government when he said: 'Those who suffer from this disability carry a great weight of shame all their lives.'

Today, of course, homosexuality is no longer classified as a mental disorder or a disability within the medical profession, and the shame has been largely shifted from the shoulders of gays and on to those of the bigots who despise, and actively seek to blight, our lives.

Today, gays are once again in the news, but now it is because we have won the right to marry each other. The debates – in the media, student debating societies, pubs, homes and parliament – on whether marriage should be extended to include same-sex couples brought much bigotry out into the open. Hardline religious folk argued that marriage is meant for heterosexual couples who wish to procreate, and the anti-gays likened us to bestial creatures participating in pretend and unnatural relationships.

To counter these arguments, gay rights groups and individuals argued that lesbians and gay men are the same as heterosexuals – that we are respectable, decent and law-abiding. As a result, perhaps, the campaign for equal marriage was won without us taking to the streets with placards or chaining ourselves to railings.

However, a number of us do not consider that being allowed to marry like heterosexuals signifies the end of anti-gay bigotry in the UK. While such a sedate success might seem like a victory, as a lifelong radical lesbian who has fought for liberation from the confines of heterosexuality, I have been vocal about my dismay at the state of our movement today and despair of how different it is from the late 1970s. All our problems are not solved – far from it. There is still anti-gay bullying in schools and the workplace, there is a lack of decent representation in the media, and physical and verbal attacks still occur in the streets. According to the surveys that inform this book, 78 per cent of gay men and lesbian respondents had experienced prejudice during their lifetime, with more than a quarter of them suffering physical assault.

Gay liberationists used to set the agenda for change, but now our enemies do. As a response to Christian bigots arguing that we can be converted to heterosexuality, a seemingly growing number of gay men and lesbians claim that we are born gay, despite there being no credible evidence to support this. Many who hold this view argue that none of us would opt to be gay if we could help it, again despite evidence to the contrary, as we shall see in chapter 3. Our entire identity is being reduced to a fictional genetic quirk, and those of us who switch from being happily straight to lesbian or gay are dismissed as bisexual, confused or curious.

Indeed, almost 40 years since homosexuality was removed from the list of recognised mental disorders, scientists persist in searching for a biological cause, refusing to consider whether sexuality and sexual desire could be social constructs, not biologically or genetically determined.

Throughout the 1970s and early 1980s – the heyday of the gay liberation movement – the heady excitement of challenging the orthodoxy of heterosexuality attracted even the shy and apolitical to its cause. Today, however, many gay men and lesbians have moved into a more conservative approach and argue that being gay is not something to be proud of, just something you do, and that being tolerated as opposed to overthrowing bigotry is good enough. Their attitude seems to be that we must not upset the apple cart by demanding anything more than gay marriage and to be left alone.

But I feel that we have regressed as a movement and been swallowed up by the status quo, while swallowing it ourselves. We begged for an invitation to the party instead of continuing to throw a better one ourselves. Instead of improving upon the nuclear family, we have decided that it was what we wanted all along. The majority have been happy to eat at the same table as heterosexual society, not caring that all of us are just being given crumbs to feed on, straight and gay alike. We have not just replicated a system that oppresses women and curtails men, but expanded and strengthened it. Once we were secure in the knowledge, and happy to tell people, that devoting a life to bringing up babies in an overpopulated world was a waste of energy and an indulgence in narcissism. Now we are all becoming married with kids and breeding like everyone else.

Perhaps all we ever wanted was a place at the table rather than to take a pickaxe to the polished teak? Maybe all that shouting and banner-waving on public demonstrations, with slogans such as 'Two, four, six, eight, is your missus really straight?' aimed at the sneering straight boys, were necessary at the time, but now that we have 'equality' it is no longer so. How have we reached this point? As we cross from the picket line to the picket fence, I reckon it is time to take a long, hard look at what we have achieved and just how much we have left behind. In order to understand our current position, it's useful to look back at the history of the gay liberation movement and see how gay men and women responded differently to the challenges of overcoming prejudice in the turbulent era of the 1970s and 1980s.

The Gay Liberation Front (GLF)

Things were certainly different in the early days. The first meeting of the GLF was called in October 1970, and just 19 people attended. Subsequent meetings saw rapid expansion, with the group growing out of meeting places and developing a national workshop and a commune-based structure along the lines of Maoist-influenced consciousness-raising groups. The GLF attracted alternative folk, both gay men and lesbians, who liked to cause a rumpus and challenge the consensus.

United by a common goal, gay male and lesbian liberation activists rejected the medical model of homosexuality as sickness, successfully campaigning to have homosexuality removed from the list of mental illness diagnoses. They proclaimed: 'Gay is good' – not: 'Please don't mind us being gay' – and believed that anti-gay oppression was the result of (straight) male dominance. For these radical activists, feminism and gay liberation were inevitably connected, and one could not be achieved without the other.

Homosexual oppression and the oppression of women were both seen to result from the imposition of what were called 'sex roles'. Political activists of the left in this period were profoundly social-constructionist in their approach. Thus both gay liberationists and feminists saw sex roles, which would probably now be called 'gender roles', as being politically constructed to ensure male dominance, and reinforced as a result of it. Women were relegated to the female sex role of the private sphere, nurturing and being concerned with beautifying the body in order to be an appropriate sex object. Lesbians were persecuted because they challenged the female sex role of sexual passivity and the servicing of men, and because they removed the man from the head of the traditional adult household. Gay men were persecuted because they challenged the male sex role, which, as well as requiring nominally masculine behaviour, was founded upon heterosexuality and sexual intercourse with women.

So fundamental was the early GLF opposition to marriage that it was emphasised by Jill Tweedie, an influential opinion columnist for the *Guardian*, in a positive piece about gay liberation: 'Gay Lib does not plead for the right of homosexuals to marry. Gay Lib questions marriage.'[2]

At first gay men were broadly supportive of the feminist cause. After all, the oppression of gay men was seen to be a reflection of the oppression of women, so sex roles were a problem for gay men too. The GLF believed, as I do still, that the oppression of gay men stems from the oppression of women, and that some forms of gay male sexual practice, such as cruising and effeminacy, are the results of oppression, rather than inevitable and authentic forms of gay behaviour.

As Peter Tatchell, an early member of the GLF and lifelong gay activist, explained to me: 'We saw ourselves as part of a revolutionary movement, not just against what we now call homophobia, biphobia and transphobia but also against sexism. We were very strongly aligned with the women's liberation movement and did a lot of joint actions, particularly around the Miss World contest.'

The GLF agenda was about a change in society, rather than assimilating and adapting to it. One of its slogans was: 'Innovate, don't assimilate.' The common social view was that homosexuality was a problem and the early liberationists threw that back in the straight people's faces, saying: 'No, it's society's attitudes, laws and values that are the problem.' The goal was a new sexual democracy where people could love and have sex with who they wanted without fear of prejudice, discrimination or violence.

Sexism and gay liberation

The gay male and lesbian alliance proved to be short-lived. Either the men's commitment to women's liberation politics was not sustainable or there were only a minority who prioritised it. In 1973 the majority of lesbians involved in the GLF in the UK walked out en masse, sick of the sexism they were experiencing from their gay 'allies', something I will explore in more detail in chapter 4.

The GLF wasn't the only gay liberation group to suffer a rift at this time: several helplines that had been set up to give information and support to lesbians and male gays also experienced division. 'Most lesbians also walked out of [Gay] Switchboard, Icebreakers and Friend in 1977 to found Lesbian Line,' says Lisa Power, former policy director at the Terrence Higgins Trust. 'I remember because I was the second lesbian who rejoined Switchboard, towards the end of 1979.'

For her oral history of the London GLF, *No Bath but Plenty of Bubbles*, Power interviewed men and women who had been involved in the early 1970s gay liberation. One man, Tim Clark, explained that the men were united by all the sexual activity that took place between them. 'And by and large they [lesbians] were excluded from the mass sex that the men were having, which acted as a bond.'[3] One lesbian interviewee supported the idea that the men and women were divided over the men's determination to see their sexual practice as the very stuff of liberation: 'What caused trouble between the men and women was that so many of the men wanted to talk about cottaging [sex in public toilets] in the meetings.'[4]

By the time I met lesbian feminists in 1979, the story of the GLF split had already become the stuff of legend. The radical lesbians who moved away from mixed groups began to work towards a utopia that would lead to the liberation of all women and would provide an opportunity for heterosexual women to consider their options. The idea was that the entire system of patriarchy would be dismantled, and lesbian feminists would be instrumental in liberating all women and girls from this tyranny.

From dreams of liberation to the age of equality

In the late 1980s a politics of gay equal rights activism began to develop, which some gay liberationists saw as deradicalising and undermining the movement for radical social change. It was not necessarily desirable simply to be equal members of an unjust society.

Sasha Roseneil, professor of sociology at Birkbeck, University of London, came out as a lesbian in 1982, aged 15. Roseneil described to me the excitement she felt the following year on arriving at Greenham, the women's peace camp set up by political activists to protest nuclear weapons. 'One day I got arrested and was sitting in a holding pen. I asked someone if there were lesbians on the camp and they looked at me in such a way as if to say: "Of course!" It was a life-changing moment.'

Roseneil, along with me and other radical lesbian feminists, spent much of her time critiquing heterosexuality, promoting lesbianism as a positive alternative and challenging gay men's sexism back in the 1980s. That decade, therefore, saw both a growing equal rights movement for many gay activists alongside a more revolutionary agenda pursued by radical feminists, although gay male politics remained the dominant force. However, things were to change for both groups towards the end of the decade.

Then came Section 28

In 1988 the government introduced Section 28, a pernicious piece of legislation that stipulated a local authority should not 'intentionally promote homosexuality or publish material with the intention of promoting homosexuality' or 'promote the teaching in any maintained school of the acceptability of homosexuality as a pretended family relationship'. In retrospect, this was a significant moment. This was when the voices with the most traction in the lesbian and gay community decided to abandon radicalism in favour of the politics of equality. Eschewing the radical tactics of its predecessors, the gay rights movement threw away the placards and became placatory, asking for nothing more than the opportunity to blend into the background. Rather than take a radical approach in campaigning against Section 28, gay rights moved off into another direction. The rot had set in.

The response of gay men to Section 28 tended to focus on the argument that schoolchildren are assigned their gay identity at birth, so it is unfair to punish them for their biological destiny. This argument was taken to its furthest conclusion by a 1988 piece that appeared in the London listing magazine *City Limits* entitled 'The Road to Auschwitz'. Written by a gay man, the article outlined the potential negative consequences of Section 28. The heading quite rightly caused offence to some Jewish activists because they considered it an inappropriate analogy: grotesque as it is to prevent teachers from discussing gay issues and identity in class, it is not quite the same as being confined to a camp with the threat of extermination. The author's intention was to compare the Jewish experience to that of lesbians and gay men by arguing that gays, like Jews, cannot help being born into their identity, and that the effects of the legislation would be similar to the fate met by Jewish people at the hands of the Nazis. Despite the flaws in this argument – what of those of us who happily choose to be gay? – this became the dominant gay party line.

Many lesbians, however, responded rather differently to Section 28. While gay men made speeches asking to be tolerated because they meant no harm and were 'born that way', the girls demanded respect and recognition by pulling a series of stunts designed to ensure that the government and public would take notice.

In February 1988 three lesbians smuggled rope into the public gallery in the House of Commons and abseiled into the chamber shouting: 'Lesbians are out!' In the kerfuffle that followed, with several House of Lords ushers attempting to apprehend the protesters, two of the lesbians managed to simply walk out of the chamber.

A month later I was part of a gang that locked itself into a model house at the Ideal Home Exhibition. It was Mother's Day and the action mocked the idea that lesbians were 'pretend mothers', as stated by the Thatcherite propaganda. When we occupied the house and shut the doors, I remember one of the male security guards asking, in puzzlement: 'How can lesbians be mothers?' We laughed and someone shouted 'There's a lesbian in every woman' as we uncurled a banner reading: 'An ideal home has two lesbians in it and no men!'

In the month that Section 28 became law, four women invaded the BBC studio in Shepherd's Bush and handcuffed themselves to the newsreader's chair during a TV broadcast of *The Six O'Clock News*. Their muffled shouts and thumps could be heard in the background. Those were the days of protest and passion; we were not apologetic sops asking to be tolerated.

One good thing to come out of Section 28 and the related return to 'family values' by the Thatcher government was that it once again reunited lesbians and gay men, who have never really had much in common except for the experience of bigotry and social exclusion. Around that time, and of course interlinked, was the HIV/Aids crisis.

According to Tatchell, Aids was a 'bolt out of the blue, and the demonisation against gay and bisexual men was pretty much unprecedented. Even in the pre-law reform days it was never as bad as it was in the mid-80s. You know there was just non-stop blaming and scapegoating from politicians, the tabloid press and large sections of the clergy.

'It is interesting that up until the time just before the Aids pandemic, public attitudes had moved quite significantly from the early 70s until the mid-80s in support of and in terms of acceptance of gay people. HIV put that immediately into reverse, so by the mid- to late 80s two-thirds of British people polled said that homosexuality was "always" or "mostly wrong". Faced with HIV, a lot of lesbians who had gay male friends rallied to support, and that was the first coming back together of the male and female parts of the movement. Section 28 exacerbated that; it was the first new anti-gay law for 100 years, and the first one that put us together.'

The response to Section 28 and the wider public reaction to the HIV/Aids crisis saw lesbians joining forces with gay men once more and the movement became homogenised. The phrase 'lesbian and gay' became fashionable and Lesbian Strength marches became merged with Gay Pride. However, many of the battles fought at the time directly benefited gay men rather than women.

From rainbow to blue

From this point – sadly, I would argue – the radical politicisation of gay rights started to come to an end. Instead, the prevailing focus was on assimilation and acceptance. The research and campaign group Stonewall was founded in 1989 as a response to the introduction of Section 28. It was named after the Stonewall Riots, a series of spontaneous demonstrations triggered by a brutal anti-gay police raid on the Stonewall Inn gay bar in the Greenwich Village district of New York on 28 June 1969. The riots have been seen by many to be the start of the lesbian, gay and bisexual (LGB) rights movement. Its founders included Sir Ian McKellen, Lisa Power and Michael Cashman.

These days Stonewall focuses on working with organisations to bring equality to LGB people at home, school and work. It currently has a 'Diversity Champions Good Practice' programme for major employers, and the membership of this scheme stood at 550 in 2013. Organisations now engaged in the programme between them employ over 4 million people, and range from Deloitte and American Express to the Royal Navy, the Royal Air Force, the British Army and MI5.

In 2005 Stonewall launched an 'Education for All' programme, supported by a coalition of over 70 organisations, to tackle anti-gay bigotry in schools. Stonewall's education work also includes the increasingly recognised slogan 'Some people are gay. Get over it!', which has been shown on billboards and public transport across Britain. The charity has also produced research reports in areas such as anti-gay hate crime, lesbian health and anti-gay bigotry in football.

I asked Ruth Hunt, deputy director of Stonewall, if the organisation represents the depoliticisation of the gay movement. She said no, and that Stonewall does not speak for gay people but rather provides 'solutions and insights'.

She continued: 'Legislative change needs less of a consensus in the community. Should there be equal marriage? Yes. Should lesbians and gays be allowed to adopt? Yes. Should gays be allowed to serve in the military? Yes. Now, you may disagree with the military, but you are not going to say gays should be excluded.'

Stonewall's aims are evidently conservative, aiming to ensure gay men and lesbians can join society as it is, but with an absence of bigotry. It does not appear to be interested in dismantling a patriarchal and oppressively capitalist society, but rather merely wants to join in with it.

The fact that it is the Conservative party that now boasts more openly gay MPs than all the others put together is telling of the direction in which the shifts of the 1980s have taken the movement.

Within a few decades in the UK we have gone from a state where male homosexuality was illegal and punishable by prison, and lesbians were sectioned under the Mental Health Act if they were discovered, to one where sanctions are applied to those who discriminate against us on grounds of employment and in other areas. We are now allowed to marry in church, and for several years have had civil partnerships and the right to adopt children as same-sex couples.

Many gay men and lesbians these days have money, social standing and cosy domestic arrangements, and are protected from the worst excesses of anti-gay bigotry. These are naturally the ones whose voices we hear most often. Stonewall snuggles up to the Tories, the House of Lords and any number of corporate sponsors, and when David Cameron announced that he is in favour of gay (equal) marriage 'not in spite of being a Conservative but because I am a Conservative', it spoke volumes. In order to cease to be a threat to heterosexuals, all gays have to do is copy them. And to end the threat of radical politics from homosexuals, just give them the right to marry.

But when has a social movement ever achieved radical, long-term change by asking for handouts? The disability rights activists raged against the cap-in-hand approach that led to a 'help the poor cripples' response. The women's liberation movement grabbed its rights by the throat. But the gay rights movement has not just lost its teeth, it is operating like an elderly claret-soaked Tory making his way to the bedpan in the corner of the room: bloated, smug and plodding.

My beginnings

How things have changed since I came out to a world full of bigotry, hatred, disgust and fear. I was still at school, and coming out was not a free choice, but how glad I am today that I did. My life as a lesbian is so much richer, fulfilled, happy and meaningful than it ever could have been had I taken the path to heterosexuality that had been firmly mapped out for me.

I grew up in a loving working-class family in the north-east of England. The middle child of three, I fought relentlessly with my two brothers, often coming off worst, but my mother always stuck up for me. My dad was largely absent. He worked shifts in a steel factory as a roller and sometimes came in from his shift tired and ill-tempered. The pub was his respite, as it was for most of the men of his generation on the estate. Mum worked in a corner shop and I would help her all I could by cleaning the kitchen and getting tea ready for when Dad came in from work if he was on earlies. The boys did nothing and I would go crazy, shouting at them for leaving their plates and mugs on the floor as well as their stinking socks and shoes. When Mum came home, I would be ready with a list of complaints about how it 'wasn't fair'. Mum knew it wasn't, but had little energy left to challenge it. My paternal grandmother had instilled in my father traditional patriarchal values. She would serve the men in the family bigger portions of food than the women and would say that housework was women's work.

My grandmother died when I was 13, but it wasn't until years later that I discovered that my grandfather used to beat her up and once fractured her jaw. He pawned her wedding ring on several occasions and, when she was dying in agony, of cancer, he would stop off for a pint before bringing back her painkillers.

My local comprehensive, serving the sprawling housing estate on which we lived, was notorious for being rough. Being different in any way was far from cool. I was different, and we were, as my mum kept telling us, 'not raised to be sheep'. I was a bit of a proto-feminist, complaining about girls not being allowed to do woodwork. The prospect of a factory job, marriage to a boy from the estate, children and evenings out at the working men's club or bingo did not appeal. It was never that I thought I was better than my upbringing, more that I knew that the limits of ambition placed upon me by society because of my class and sex would not stop me being everything I was capable of doing and wanted to do.

Nevertheless, until I met lesbian feminists in my late teens, I had no clear view on how my sexual preference had developed. When I was 13, I fell in love with Colin, a beautiful blond-haired boy with a gentle manner who seemed to like me too. Our liaison was short-lived. After a gorgeous snog one Saturday by the river, by which time I had decided he was the one for me, Colin told me he was still in love with his ex-girlfriend and that we would have to finish. That night I sobbed into my pillow to David Bowie's 'Young Americans'.

After Colin was Jeff (not his real name), a cocky, arrogant boy who was a couple of years older than me and from the middle-class side of the tracks in Darlington. Jeff's kisses felt like my lips were being forced open by a wet sponge while being rubbed by a cheese grater. While sitting on a bench in the middle of my housing estate, Jeff tried to feel me up. When I told him to stop, he said: 'You're a lezzer anyway. Everyone knows it.' I swear that his words did not upset me at all, but simply made me curious. While my older brother, Paul, was leading Jeff somewhat roughly off the estate (word had got back to him that I was being felt up by some posh boy on a bench and Paul's strong sense of family honour would not allow that to happen in broad daylight), I began to think about what he had said. Was I a lesbian? Is that why I had wanted to be a boy? Perhaps that explained my crushes on other girls? Maybe it explained my lack of interest in experimenting with sex with boys?

My teenage years progressed with no more boyfriends. My reputation at school was firmly one of 'lezzer', which served to separate me from the 'slags' and the 'nice girls'. No one could risk being my best friend. The 'slags' had enough on their plates without risking the double-taint of also being labelled a 'rug-muncher', and the nice girls hung on to their identity by a thread. When I was 15, in 1977, Alice moved to the area and we became best friends and lovers. Since then I have never been attracted to a man or remotely considered having sex with one.

There was no need to come out at school once it became obvious I was rather more keen on my best friend than the eligible boys in my class, and I told my mother I was a lesbian after she found a letter I had written to a lesbian pen pal in my bedroom.

I left school a year before I was supposed to, still aged 15. I would go in to sign the register, then disappear off to my friend's house a few doors along. Mandy had already left school and was looking for a job, but would let me in to watch TV until it was time to go home. When I officially left school, I had no qualifications whatsoever. As I went to collect my national insurance number the teacher informed me that I had wasted the school's time and resources and that I would 'never amount to anything'. I had done very well at primary school and in the first couple of years at secondary, but as the bullying kicked in, by the teachers as well as the pupils, I gave up and started to imagine a different world to the one I inhabited.

I started to have proper girlfriends and go to gay clubs in 1978, after meeting David, a young man who was to become my first ever gay friend. We had met at my Saturday job in a hair salon, where I swept up and shampooed the customers' hair and where he was training to be a colourist. David took me to Rockshots in Newcastle and Club 54 in Middlesbrough.

The women I met at the disco with David were either so butch they looked like they could donate to a sperm bank or so feminine they appeared to be in drag, and congregated together at the bar while their butch girlfriends played pool together and fought with each other, drunk out of their minds. I now know it was a kind of self-protection – that lesbians experienced so much hatred from others that they internalised most of it and tried to become invisible by aping heterosexual couples.

During this time I was pilloried, threatened with violence and endured constant sexual harassment from men who wanted to 'straighten me out'. There were no positive lesbian role models in the media or elsewhere, and it was easy to get the impression that lesbians were psychotic predators who kickstarted their vibrators and secretly wanted to be men.

That same year I read in *Gay News* of something called the Campaign for Homosexual Equality (CHE). They met every month and 'everyone was welcome'. On my way to the meeting, 25 miles away, I was terrified. What if the women were all like Beryl Reid in *The Killing of Sister George*? And the men like Quentin Crisp? But in reality they were only as odd as I was.

Soon after my 16th birthday I decided to move away from Darlington to broaden my horizons. I moved in with my great-aunt Gwen and my cousins Susan and Diane in Harrogate, North Yorkshire. Around that time I picked up a copy of *Gay News* at the train station and looked in the 'Find a Friend' section. (Today it would be the 'classifieds' or one of the many commercial online dating services.) There were two notices I was interested in – one from an 18-year-old woman in Birmingham and another from someone who described herself as 'an Aries from York'. They both wanted to meet other 'gay girls'. (No one used the word 'lesbian' in those days.) I wrote to both of them and received replies.

I met Marion first, in Birmingham. I took the coach and was extremely nervous. She met me at the bus station, tall, black and sophisticated. We spent the day together but didn't have much in common. Marion kept trying to prove she was better than me and appeared to want to put me down. I returned to Harrogate depressed.

The next day I travelled to York, where I met Andrea. She lived at the back of the university in a posh semi-detached house with her son, Nigel. Andrea, it turned out, was 30 years old. Recently divorced, Andrea was on the look-out for a female partner. She was quite butch and overpowering. I was an unconfident 17-year-old; it was all wrong. While I was there, though, Sandra dropped round. She was 20, beautiful, mixed race and majorly fucked up. At the time she was living with a man more than twice her age. Barry was the father of her former school friend, and Sandra had moved in with him when her adoptive parents had thrown her out of the house after they caught her kissing a girl in the kitchen. In return for company and a roof over her head, Sandra slept with Barry even though she hated sex with men.

Sandra and I hit it off immediately. It was as though we understood how different we both were, and how desperate to find something else in life. Sandra worked for a large, successful hair company and would commute to Leeds every day from York to work for a pittance while being trained to cut the hair of the rich, famous and fashionable. We decided to move to Leeds together and start all over again. Six weeks later Sandra and I found ourselves in a room at the Headingley YWCA with no money, few possessions and big ambitions. I knew exactly what I wanted to do.

Feminism and 'compulsory heterosexuality'

On moving to Leeds, I was lucky enough to meet feminists who were out and proud. They helped me understand that sexuality is a highly political issue, and that to be a lesbian under a system of patriarchy is a serious challenge to the status quo. Gay men, I came to understand from attending CHE meetings, also shook up the system by refusing to conform to masculine gender stereotypes.

Rather than gravitate towards the bars and clubs that working-class lesbians frequented, I became involved with the sort of women who went to meetings in pubs and rolled their own cigarettes. These feminists told me lesbianism was a positive choice, not a medical condition. We defied those who called us 'dirty queers' by kissing each other in the street and wearing badges proclaiming our proud love for women.

The same month I moved to Leeds, I discovered *Spare Rib* magazine in a newsagent's, in which there was an article about feminists organising protests against male violence and pornography in the city. I decided to go looking for these women.

The Corner Bookshop, over the road from Leeds University, had been there for years, run by hippies, lefties and feminists. It was crammed with books by radicals and decorated with leaflets and pamphlets advertising various political rallies and meetings. It took me less than five minutes to find what I was looking for. A handwritten note was pinned to the noticeboard with the words 'Women Against Violence Against Women (WAVAW) meeting, tonight, 7pm' and details of the venue. During the bus journey to the meeting I kept imagining what it would be like to meet such feminists for the first time. I was terrified but excited. Would they like me? Would they think I talked funny? Was I dressed differently to them? Would I fit in?

The revolutionary feminists I met that day were the militant wing of the women's liberation movement. These women – all lesbians – were disappointed with the soft-centred heterosexual-focused approach of those feminists who refused to name men as the enemy and spent their energy supporting them. Their focus was on male sexual violence towards women and children, and heterosexuality was branded as bad for women, while the nuclear family was named the context in which men maintained their superiority.

My heart thumping, I entered a large terrace house, struggled past the bicycles in the hallway and into a kitchen full of women sitting around a table stapling a newsletter together. I had entered the world of lesbian feminism and instantly threw myself in at the deep end.

Later that year, 1980, I started up the first advice line for lesbians by nicking a night off the helpline Gay Switchboard. I had told another (older) lesbian feminist I had met on work experience that I wanted to give support to women who were having difficulties coming out or living as lesbians. Every Tuesday evening between 7pm and 9pm we would sit in a damp university basement by a landline and take call after call from women in crisis.

Sometimes a caller would just want to know where to go to get a date. We would direct her to our fortnightly fundraising disco above the only pub in town that would have us. The Dock Green was an old police station in Harehills; it was as rough as a badger's crotch. The landlord did not need to call time at the end of the evening as the police sirens that followed officers to break up a fight did that for him.

More often than not, though, the calls on the advice line would be from distressed, suicidal, confused women with the most horrific stories to tell. The shame and fear experienced by those who called us further compounded my sense that feminism was crucial for women in order to challenge what Adrienne Rich described as 'compulsory heterosexuality'. When women opted out of a straight existence, men lost power and privilege, and women benefited from that improved autonomy.

At that time there was no legal or civil protection for either lesbians or gay men. We could have our children removed, get sacked from our jobs and be refused entry to clubs, restaurants and hotels without any recourse. There was no legal protection against discrimination.

Since those early days I have been deeply and constantly involved in radical feminist activism, mainly against men's sexual violence and abuse towards women and children. I have seen huge changes in the women's movement and in lesbian and gay culture over the past 30-odd years, but no equality legislation has progressed so quickly as that affecting lesbians and gay men. In fact, as I hope this book will demonstrate, legislation is far ahead of society, possibly for the first time in history.

What is it like to be gay today?

We have undeniably come a long way since I came out as a lesbian and yet, despite the huge and important shifts in attitudes and legislation in both the UK and US in particular, virulent anti-gay bigotry is ever present, bubbling away beneath the surface and regularly on top of it. Indeed, in the same year that Cameron made his gay-friendly remarks in support of equal marriage, he appointed Maria Miller as minister for equality, despite her opposition of gay adoption and giving lesbian couples the right to fertility treatment.

It's not limited to English politics either. When the Scottish government announced plans to introduce legislation that would allow same-sex couples to marry in church, an online petition opposing it attracted around 30,000 signatures. While many homosexuals understandably want equal access to marriage, plenty of people within heterosexual society remain determined to keep us out.

In Northern Ireland, too, former MP Lord Maginnis left his post after being suspended for comparing same-sex relationships to bestiality during the ongoing debate about equal marriage. On the one hand, legislation and the attitudes of many in society make these statements unacceptable, but there is clearly a great number of people who continue to maintain the old prejudices of anti-gay bigotry.

While things may well appear to be tickety-boo for privileged lesbians and gay men, let us remind ourselves of the imperative work that remains. In schools around the UK, young lesbians and gays are being bullied, attacked and, in some cases, driven to suicide. There are still towns and villages in England in which there is not one out gay person. Anti-gay attacks, including punishment rapes of lesbians, are on the increase in some areas, and there are countless individuals who have been rejected by their families and colleagues.

Currently in the UK and the US, the Christian right and other religious fundamentalists and traditionalists are attempting to take us back to the bad old days of criminalisation and isolation. Gay rights – in the main, the debate about equal marriage – were a significant issue in the recent US election. Here in the UK, the debate has been vicious and polarised, bringing the bigots out of the woodwork and opening up old arguments we thought had been won.

The Christian Institute published a poll in September 2012 that claims to have found only 2.6 per cent of people questioned by the Office for National Statistics are lesbian, gay or bisexual. This led the Christian Institute to question whether such a small demographic should be given the right to marry.

But is this statistic true? How many gay people *are* there in the UK?

Previous estimates have ranged from one in five to as few as one in 100, and many people have believed the figure to be one in 10. In fact, in 2005 the government estimated that 6 per cent of the population, or about 3.6 million Britons, are either gay or lesbian, amounting to one in 16.66. Treasury actuaries came up with the estimate when analysing the financial implications of the new Civil Partnership Act, which allowed same-sex partners similar rights to married couples in areas such as tax, pensions and inheritance. In the 30-million-strong workforce in 2005, there were an estimated 1.5 million to 2 million gay men, lesbians and bisexuals, according to the Department of Trade and Industry, as it was known then.[5] Given the UK population is now approximately 64 million, this means that the gay community has between 3 and 4 million members in total.

But however many of us there are, and however large or small a minority we are, the simple fact is that we cannot know how many of us would opt out of heterosexuality if bigotry and prejudice no longer existed.

Rightwing fundamentalist Christians tend to believe that being gay is a sin and that sinners can reform their behaviour. They are even perfectly open about homosexuality being a threat to the patriarchal world order.

From religious zealots to rightwing commentators, there are still significant numbers of individuals and organisations who have fear and loathing for us gay guys. The debates on whether or not gays should have access to full legal and civil rights on a par with heterosexuals within religious institutions both here and the US show how far there is to go.

Contrast that with the lax attitude of those gay people who eschew radicalism and activism, happy to settle for marriage and cosiness and security that extends only as far as the couple they are in. It is my belief that many of those getting married and doing the whole canapés of mini fish and chips, and dancing to 'Make You Feel My Love', are subconsciously or consciously trying to please their parents and wider straight society. It's like saying: 'We're all the same really.'

Marriage is growing in popularity among younger gays in particular, and what could be more conservative than the institution of marriage? Many lesbian and gay long-term couples I know who were perfectly happy before this pro-marriage hysteria kicked off now feel they are looked down on as 'living over the brush' by the marriage-mongers, both gay and straight. Even Labour MP Ben Bradshaw, who used to argue that gay marriage was not a campaigning priority because civil partnerships were perfectly fine to establish legal and social equality, has recently changed his tune and joined the pro-marriage cabal.

Gays who are single, either through choice or circumstance, must feel about as welcome as a pork chop in a synagogue. Given the homosexual monoculture's veneration of marriage, straight folk probably find less disapproval if they choose not to marry than gays do these days.

Gay actor Rupert Everett hit the nail on the head during a recent interview when he admitted that he 'loathes' heterosexual weddings. 'The wedding cake, the party, the champagne, the inevitable divorce two years later is just a waste of time in the heterosexual world, and in the homosexual world I find it personally beyond tragic that we want to ape this institution that is so clearly a disaster.'

Conclusion

The contemporary gay rights movement, epitomised by Stonewall, asks that gays be tolerated. Rights for gays to join the military, marry in church and raise children are the main campaigning issues. But I would argue there are many other areas we should be focusing on. A cross-party parliamentary committee reporting in 2012 found that anti-gay bigotry in football in Britain is currently a bigger problem than racism. Since Justin Fashanu's suicide, there has not been a single out gay professional footballer in the whole of the UK, despite much talk and media criticism about anti-gay bigotry in sport. In an attempt to address this issue, the Football Association formed the Inclusion Advisory Board, aimed at promoting equality in the game, and appointed the former player Michael Johnson to sit on it, regardless of the fact that in 2012 he said on a TV debate that homosexuality was 'detestable'. Johnson has since stepped down in the light of this controversy. This is a clear example of how, despite the introduction of new policy and legislation to tackle anti-gay bigotry, many of those mandated to prevent it often do not have a clue.

The statistics on young gay people at school show how far we have to go before we see an end to anti-gay bigotry: of the 1,600 children interviewed, 55 per cent of LGB young people said that they have experienced bullying in UK schools; 99 per cent hear anti-gay remarks such as 'poof' or 'lezzer' used in school; 53 per cent experience verbal bullying; 23 per cent cyber bullying; 16 per cent physical abuse; and 6 per cent are subjected to death threats.[6]

How is this the case? Now that we have equal marriage, full legal protection and support in fostering, adopting and raising our own biological children in same-sex couples, why are young people apparently even more anti-gay than before?

CHAPTER 2
ALL HET UP: THE BIGOTS

As far as I am concerned, LGBT can only stand for
Leprosy, Gonorrhoea, Bacteria and Tuberculosis,
all of which are detrimental to human existence.
Gambia's president Yahya Jammeh, February 2014

[Clare Balding] is a horse woman [who]
appreciates power between her thighs ... And we all
know, there is no woman that can't be cured.
Radio 5 Live presenter Bob Mills, June 2013

In October 2013 a man was sent to prison for five months for harassing his gay neighbours. In sentencing Reg Brayford, the magistrate said: 'This sort of grossly offensive behaviour cannot be tolerated in today's society.'

Brayford had admitted in court that he harassed the couple for nine months, leaving one of the men feeling 'sick and depressed'. He would shout at his neighbours that gay people had 'no right to be in society' and that they should 'go back to where they belong'. It is not known, given his wish that they 'go back', if he thought that homosexuals all come from the same foreign country.

Six months earlier, on 21 March 2013, Justine McNally, an 18-year-old lesbian, was sentenced to three years in prison for six counts of sexual assault by penetration against her 16-year-old girlfriend. There was full consent to the sexual contact at the time, but when McNally had sex with the complainant, she was doing so while posing as a young man named Scott. The sex amounted to a crime of fraud. The prosecutor commented: 'Because of the abuse of trust, the trauma to the victim and the peculiar circumstances, this is an extraordinary case. She obtained consent to physical intimacy between them by fraud. The case involves a very serious abuse of trust.'

McNally will be on the sex offenders register for life and is banned from contacting the victim or her mother. The judge noted McNally had had trouble coming to terms with her sexuality.

Meanwhile, undercover police officers who targeted women in leftist protest groups in order to gather intelligence on illegal activity had sex with them using real penises. The level of deception and the consequences for their victims were extreme, and yet these men have so far escaped justice.

Anti-gay bigotry is rooted in misogyny. Without one the other would not exist. If gay men were allowed to be non-macho and lesbians were not under pressure to uphold the feminine ideal that makes us distinct from men, neither lesbians nor gay men would be a threat. Women and girls are severely punished for rejecting men sexually, and men are isolated and rejected for denying their role of foot soldier in the war against female emancipation and liberation.

The many faces of bigotry

In 1983, for my 21st birthday, a group of lesbian friends took me out to a pub, the New Penny in Leeds, and then on to a club largely inhabited by gay men. After the drink had been flowing, a group of men associated with the far-right organisation Combat 88 came in to do a bit of queer-bashing. The gay men made themselves scarce, but us lezzers piled in and fought back. We came off worse: I was thrown down some stone stairs and smacked in the face, giving me a broken nose and two black eyes. Others also suffered injuries. The police came and I made a statement. By then the fascists had disappeared, but one of them was later caught and arrested. In court the magistrate threw out the case of actual bodily harm against him because by wearing a T-shirt with 'Lesbian Army' across the front, he believed I had provoked the violence against me.

Over the years I directly experienced a number of anti-lesbian incidents and witnessed hundreds of others. I saw friends of mine in pieces because ex-husbands were taking them to court in an attempt to win custody of their children for no other reason than because they had left them for another woman. Judges would often grant custody to a violent father rather than allow the children to remain with a woman in a lesbian relationship.

Among the tragedy was the comedy. I remember one evening in the early 1980s attending a fundraiser for WAVAW called Mrs Big's Bop at Bradford University. There had been reports in the media of an anonymous group of hardline feminists known as Angry Women attacking sex shops at the time. The authorities just couldn't understand who was in charge. Someone official was heard to say: 'We need to find Mr Big.' There were hundreds of women at the gig, but I was approached by a man in another part of the building who asked me why there were so many women in the hall 'on their own'. I drew to his attention that it was impossible to be 'on your own' with at least 200 other women there and suddenly the penny dropped. 'Fucking lesbians!' he spat. 'Not a cock between you.'

Over the years the way such bigotry is expressed has become less crude and somewhat more successful in disguising itself as something other than pure hatred or prejudice. In October 2013 a rabbi of the Jerusalem-based Hasidic sect Gur banned the students of his yeshiva from consuming soya-based products on the basis that they might increase 'gay sexual activity'. Three years earlier, Bryan Fisher, host of the talkshow *Focal Point* on American Family Radio, broadcast the startling revelation that Hitler was in fact gay. Nazi storm troopers, he went on to explain, were handpicked from the gay population who had 'no limits to the savagery and brutality they were willing to inflict'.

In 2000 I appeared on a radio programme discussing rape. I am known as an expert in the law surrounding sexual violence and have campaigned against it all my adult life. On the programme I was critical of the government's proposal to pay those who have children a 'toddler tax credit'. Carol Sarler was so offended by my suggestion that not all women want children that she devoted her *Daily Express* column the following week to ripping me to shreds under the headline 'Women's issues can't be resolved by man-haters'.

Sarler poured scorn on my concern about date rape by suggesting that because I am a lesbian, I am unlikely ever to be out with a man, ergo will never be raped by one, and then moved on to her disgust of the lesbian dominance of women's issues: 'Lesbian domination of these groups [she was referring to any feminist organisation in the press] kicked off back in the 1970s, when the streets were buzzing with fish riding bicycles and the ultimately admired woman was the woman who didn't need a man at all.'

She continued: 'As it happens, I would have no problem with Bindel and her kind if she called her group Justice for Lesbians and kept her excellently honed campaigning skills for lesbian issues … Bindel's views, Bindel's prejudices and Bindel's voice have no place within the lives of the happy, or even the unhappy, heterosexual female majority.'

The anti-lesbianism here was clear – so long as we are in our place and not upsetting *real women* by encroaching on their turf (children – or, as Sarler put it, 'the sunshine miracle that is motherhood' – rape, domestic violence and men), we can be endured.

Julie Burchill wrote a letter to the *Express* in my defence in which she argued: 'Saying that [Bindel] does not have sex with men and therefore knows nothing about their behaviour seems as silly as saying that a gay man cannot be a gynaecologist, having no experience of female genitalia.'

The Carol Sarler example is from over a decade ago, but I get comments such as hers on a regular basis. Bigots often take offence at lesbians who dare to speak about issues mainly affecting heterosexual women because we are not really viewed as 'regular' women.

Sarler's assumption that I could not be a victim of rape because of my sexuality is one shared by the man who approached me in a bank one morning having just seen me on TV bemoaning the low conviction rate for rape. This charmer told me I was 'too ugly to rape' and wasn't I 'a dyke anyway'?

This attitude highlights an interesting paradox within anti-lesbian bigotry – throughout my life I have been told by men, mainly when I was younger, that I need a good fuck to straighten me out. However, when I, as countless other lesbian feminists do, campaign and advocate on behalf of heterosexual women who are being abused by their intimate male partners, I am told to butt out as it is not my business. If I protest this attitude, I am informed that I am not actually good enough to rape. The reality is that women of all orientations are raped as a punishment for transgressing the patriarchal norm, and in many countries where homosexuality is illegal, lesbians are systematically raped to 'turn them straight'. Just look at the so-called punishment rapes of lesbians in South Africa. In 2008 South African footballer Eudy Simelane, equality rights campaigner and one of the first out lesbians in her hometown, was gang-raped and murdered, having been severely beaten and then stabbed multiple times in the chest, legs and face. She was not the first gay woman to suffer this fate and, sadly, won't be the last.

Erin Pizzey also pitched in to the Sarler debate. Pizzey, who founded the first ever domestic violence refuge for women and their children in 1971, has since turned her attention to the male victims of domestic abuse and has been a patron at the men's rights pressure group Mankind since 2008. Her letter read: 'The radical end of the lesbian movement has long ago invaded the cause of domestic violence. Many of them run refuges, both here and abroad, which enable them to bully and brainwash vulnerable women and children into believing their pernicious rubbish.'

As the Erin Pizzey quote shows, lesbians are not appreciated for supporting heterosexual women against abusive men but resented for interfering on their turf. It is the anti-gay version of 'they come over here and take our jobs'. Maybe this is what Brayford meant when he said of his gay neighbours that they should 'go back to where they belong'. It would appear that out and proud lesbians and gay men have no place in Hetero-land. That's despite the presence of lesbians and gay men who believe they can be 'just like them' by getting married, having kids and having a weekly row in Ikea, and be peacefully assimilated and tolerated.

A note on language

You may have noticed I have been careful to use the term 'anti-gay' rather than 'homophobic' when describing the hate crimes above. This may seem unusual. Apparently coined by New York City psychotherapist George Weinberg in 1960, the term 'homophobia' has at least had some success in transferring stigma from the victims of prejudice to its perpetrators. But what do we really mean when we say 'homophobia', and why do I generally avoid using it in this book aside from when quoting people, or when describing it in its true meaning – an irrational fear of male (homo) sexuality?

Simply put, bigotry is not a mental illness. Nor is it always an irrational fear. As I will explain later in this chapter, the anti-gay agenda is fuelled by the need to keep women in their place – in other words within heterosexual relationships – to ensure that patriarchy survives and is effective.

However, in recent decades 'homophobia' has become the word of choice to describe every negative view of gayness from hatred to ignorance. To ascribe a medical term to a socio-political phenomenon is as inappropriate as it is misleading. In 2012 international news agency Associated Press (AP) warned reporters against using phobic terms in 'political or social contexts'. 'It's ascribing a mental disability to someone and suggests a knowledge that we don't have. It seems inaccurate,' wrote the AP assistant style guide editor. 'Instead, we would use something more neutral: anti-gay, or some such … We want to be precise and accurate and neutral in our phrasing.'

But the gay rights campaigner and journalist Patrick Strudwick disagreed and wrote an article that appeared on the *Guardian*'s 'Comment Is Free' in response: 'Being anti-gay is, without exception, at least partly fuelled by fear. Fear of the unknown, fear of unwanted sexual attention, fear of gender roles being flouted, fear of humanity being wiped out by widespread bumming, fear of a plague of homosexuals dismantling marriage, the family, the church and any other institution held vaguely dear. And, of course, never forget: fear of what lurks repressed and unacknowledged in the homophobe. Irrational fear. It's a phobia, people.'[7]

I use the terms 'anti-gay' and 'anti-lesbian' throughout this book because they cover a range of prejudicial and bigoted behaviour and attitudes. It is my opinion that ascribing a phobia to a person who simply hates lesbians and gay men for supposedly rational reasons (eg because it challenges his masculine power) lets them off the hook and almost renders them irresponsible for their views and actions.

So how widespread is the problem?

Ask any lesbian or gay man and they will be able to come up with anecdotal evidence that anti-gay prejudice is still alive and kicking, despite the signs of changing official attitudes. But what are the statistics? To find out, I turned to the Gay British Crime Survey 2013 on 'Homophobic Hate Crime', which provides a comprehensive overview of the subject.[8] It found that hate crimes and incidents remain a serious issue in Britain, with one in six LGB people experiencing anti-gay hate crime or incident in the three years leading up to the survey.

- One in 10 were physically assaulted.
- Almost one in five victims were threatened with violence or the use of force.
- One in eight victims experienced unwanted sexual contact.
- One in eight victims had their home, vehicle or property vandalised.
- Harassment, insults and intimidation were the most common incidents, reported by more than eight in 10 victims.

A large proportion of perpetrators are young. Half of those who experienced a hate crime or incident said that the perpetrator was a stranger aged under 25. However, three in 10 victims said they knew the perpetrator or one of the perpetrators, whether it was someone living in their area, a colleague or even a friend or family member.

Many victims of hate crimes and incidents do not report them to the police. The research shows that little has changed in the last five years. The reasons for not reporting include anticipation that it will not be taken seriously, the fear of a negative response and a belief that there is little that the police can do.

Many who report anti-gay hate crimes and incidents to the police complain of unsatisfactory results, ranging from the way the crimes or incidents were recorded to the actions taken by police and the support they received personally. The survey found that:

- Fewer than one in 10 victims who reported hate crimes and incidents to the police said it led to a conviction.
- Half of the victims who reported a hate crime or incident to the police said it was recorded with no further action taken.
- Two in five of those reporting a hate crime or incident to the police said it was not recorded as a homophobic incident.

- Half of those reporting a hate crime or incident were not satisfied with the way it was handled.

The fear of hate crimes and incidents leaves many feeling unsafe in their homes and local community. Two-thirds feel they are at a bigger risk of being insulted, intimidated or harassed than heterosexual people. A quarter feel the need to alter their behaviour so they're not perceived as gay to avoid being the victim of crime.

We only have to look at the attitudes of heterosexuals to understand where hate crime is coming from. The 30th edition of the annual government-funded British Social Attitudes Survey (BSAS) found that nearly a quarter of people in the UK still disagree with homosexuality: 22 per cent of respondents thought that 'sexual relations between two adults of the same sex' were 'always wrong'. A further 6 per cent described them as 'mostly wrong'. Fewer than half (47 per cent) thought that same-sex relations were 'not wrong at all', with a further 10 per cent describing them as 'rarely wrong'.[9]

The figures also indicate a marked increase in the acceptance of homosexuality over the last 10 years. When the survey began, in 1983, the number of people who thought it was 'always wrong' stood at 62 per cent, before reaching a peak of 75 per cent in 1987 in the wake of the HIV/Aids crisis. A decade ago the proportion of respondents agreeing that same-sex relations were 'not wrong at all' stood at just 37 per cent, compared to 47 per cent today. This is hardly a huge difference, although according to the report's authors, the figures represent the change in public opinion towards homosexuality as 'perhaps the most dramatic attitude shift of all' over the last 30 years, and they found that each successive generation is more liberal than the one before.

In 1983 only 41 per cent of respondents to the BSAS thought it 'acceptable for a homosexual person to teach in a school', while just 53 per cent felt it was acceptable for a homosexual to 'hold a responsible position in public life'. By 2012 these figures had risen to 83 per cent and 90 per cent respectively.

However, issues such as adoption and same-sex marriage continue to prove divisive: just 48 per cent agreed that 'homosexuals should be able to adopt a baby under the same conditions as other couples', though the figure has dropped markedly from the 87 per cent who opposed it in 1983.

In 2009 a poll appeared in *The Times*, conducted by Populus, which reported that 61 per cent of the public supported gay marriage. Today it has risen to 65 per cent, and support had risen in every age group. The BSAS survey of 2012 also found that on the issue of same-sex marriage, 56 per cent agreed that 'same-sex couples should have the right to marry if they want to' – up from 47 per cent in 2007. In addition, *The Times* survey revealed that 76 per cent believed gay couples should have exactly the same rights as straight couples, up from 68 per cent in 2009.

It would appear, then, that far higher numbers of straight folk support the idea and principle of gay marriage than are fully OK with homosexuality per se than ever before.

The new reality: is it any different?

Given these changing attitudes, then, can we assume that gay-bashing is on the way out these days in our brave new gay-friendly world? Will hate crimes soon become a thing of the past?

Tell that to the thousands of school-aged young people having to hear the word 'gay' used regularly as a pejorative; according to research by Stonewall, 99 per cent of gay young people hear 'You're so gay' and 'That's so gay' as a negative term every day, and over 80 per cent of those who hear it find it damaging and distressing.[10]

In addition, the debate on equal marriage brought the prejudice and hate that still prevails in the UK and elsewhere into the open. I took part in one TV debate in which a Christian activist compared gay people to child abusers and those who have sex with animals. Hansard, the transcript of parliamentary debates, is full of comments from MPs opposing marriage for gays and speaking at length about how same-sex relationships are abnormal.

Jeremy Irons, the man made famous for his portrayal of Evelyn Waugh's definitely entirely straight Charles Ryder, raised the somewhat bizarre concern that the introduction of same-sex marriage may lead to fathers marrying their sons for tax purposes: 'Could a father not marry his son? It's not incest between men; incest is there to protect us from inbreeding, but men don't breed. I don't have a strong feeling either way. Living with another animal, whether it be a husband or a dog, is great. It's lovely to have someone to love.'

Just because gay couples can now walk down the aisle does not mean that bigotry has disappeared. Recently a man was jailed after a court in Gloucester heard how he shouted 'You queers' at a gay couple, before punching and biting them in an unprovoked attack. Both men say they have been profoundly affected by the assault and are no longer confident of challenging anti-gay remarks. Unfortunately, according to experts researching the levels of hate crimes, they are far from alone.[11]

A short while ago I received an email from a 70-year-old woman who had been married for 45 years. When her husband died recently, she called Gay Switchboard to ask how she could meet 'other women like me'. She had never dared to come out and leave her marriage because, in her own words, 'I have never believed I would be safe. We are not very well liked, are we?'

Certainly we cannot rest on our laurels. The latest Stonewall report, 'Gay in Britain' (2013), found that 'significant numbers of gay people fear they would still face discrimination if they sought to play an active part in politics, whether as a potential member of parliament or local councillor. And many of the political parties' own gay supporters believe that gay candidates would face discrimination.'

Then there are the small but significantly persistent examples of media representations making a mockery of being lesbian or gay. An advertisement for Flora margarine, for example, was recently pulled following complaints that it was 'homophobic, vile and an abomination'. The ad compared coming out gay to your father to being shot in the heart by a bullet. Such bigotry has a terrible effect on gay people who have little or no support to counter it.

Many journalists and commentators are still given a platform to voice their prejudices. In 2009 *Daily Mail* columnist Jan Moir upset even a number of *Mail* readers when she suggested that the death of Stephen Gately of Boyzone was somehow the fault of his sexuality. Before the man had even been buried, her poisonous article cast doubt on the official postmortem's report that he had died of natural causes, suggesting instead that his lifestyle was to blame. Her article brought on a wave of outrage, but she was far from alone in her anti-gay views.

In *The Times,* in 2010, journalist AA Gill referred to sports presenter and out lesbian Clare Balding as 'a dyke on a bike' in his review of her TV programme in which she travelled around Britain by bicycle. Balding reported this to the Press Complaints Commission (PCC), saying the word 'dyke' was 'too often used as a pejorative and insulting term'. The PCC upheld the complaint, pointing out: 'Newspapers must avoid prejudicial, pejorative or irrelevant reference to an individual's sexual orientation and the reference to Miss Balding plainly breached its terms.'

Clare Balding was on the end of yet another insult in 2013, when Colin Murray challenged Bob Mills on the all-male panel of BBC Radio 5 Live show *Fighting Talk* to come up with a strategy to turn Balding straight. It reminded me of the times I have been told that any 'proper man' can do conversions from lezzer to 'gagging for a missionary-position shag' with the flash of a hairy chest.

I was surprised at the decision of the PCC in relation to the AA Gill review, bearing in mind how rarely it finds in favour of a complainant. For example, the PCC rejected a record 25,000 complaints about the Jan Moir column on the grounds that 'it was an essential point of principle that papers could print views which might offend readers'.

In 2012 Lib Dem MP Chris Huhne's partner, Carina Trimingham, lost a case against the *Daily Mail* for damages for alleged breach of privacy, and harassment against the *Daily Mail* and *Mail on Sunday.* Trimingham was seeking compensation and an injunction over 65 'highly unpleasant and hurtful' articles in which she was referred to as a 'crop-haired', 'sturdy', 'Doc Marten-wearing' 'lesbian-turned-bisexual'. In his *Daily Mail* column, Richard Littlejohn described her as a 'comedy lesbian from central casting'.

There are also plenty of religious zealots who have provided invaluable insight into the current nature of anti-gay bigotry in the response to the gay marriage debate. That there even *is* a debate on both sides of the pond on whether or not gays should have access to full legal and civil rights on a par with heterosexuals within religious institutions shows how far there is to go.

After all, it was only in 2012, in the wake of hurricane Sandy's devastation, that Rabbi Noson Leiter, of Torah Jews for Decency, triumphantly declared that the storm was sure proof that God was coming for the gays once and for all. Reminding us that 'the Great Flood in the time of Noah was triggered by the recognition of same-gender marriages,' he asserted that God had this time flooded Lower Manhattan because it is 'one of the national centres of homosexuality'. Apparently that means that God also dislikes the neighbours of gay people, and those who live next to the neighbours of gay people, as the storm was not especially accurate in only targeting gay people as its victims.

Like it or not, there are still significant numbers of individuals and organisations that fear and loathe gay people. And let us not forget that in other countries, the situation is even worse: a report commissioned by the Australian Kaleidoscope Human Rights Foundation in November 2013 identified that homosexuality is still illegal in 41 out of the 53 Commonwealth countries.[12]

Asylum-seeking lesbians and gay men, fleeing from such repressive regimes, can also suffer dreadful prejudice by the British authorities. Take the Ugandan lesbian Brenda Namigadde, who, having fled to the UK to escape life-threatening anti-gay bigotry, was escorted by two border control officers on to a plane about to take leave for Uganda. With minutes to spare, Namigadde's lawyers secured an injunction against the decision and she was saved. Namigadde is safe for now, but she and countless other asylum-seeking lesbians in the UK could again face deportation unless the government recognises that sending them back to countries such as Uganda is a death penalty.

This is the reality for asylum-seeking lesbians in the UK. But according to research from Southampton University in 2013, to stay in Britain they are going to have to learn about everything from dildos to Oscar Wilde. The research, based on interviews with 12 lesbians from countries including Pakistan, Saudi Arabia, Uganda and Jamaica, found that the interviewees were disbelieved about being lesbian in the first instance and required to provide all manner of 'evidence' to back their claims. It was found that judges asked the women if they had been on a Pride procession, used sex toys, read gay literature or visited certain gay clubs. Unbelievably, until recently, the Home Office had a policy of rejecting asylum claims from lesbians and gay men on the basis that they could avoid torture and imprisonment in their homeland by being 'discreet'.[13]

So how do the recent legislative changes in the UK affect public attitudes?

I get very upset by gay marriage and its wider context. Not because some bigots are against it, but because it is being held up as a symbol of our liberation and freedom from anti-gay oppression. Now that we can get properly married, a Martian landing on earth would be led to believe that bigotry towards lesbians and gay men is a thing of the past. The fact that gay men (and, to a lesser extent, lesbians) turn up in the Tory party, at English Defence League meetings and as CEOs is one indicator of how we now have the opportunity to be every bit as rotten as the straights; ergo we have arrived. It is an indication that sameness is a goal we have almost achieved.

So perhaps the shift is partly due to (as opposed to in spite of) having a Conservative prime minister advocating gay marriage; now public opinion suggests that widespread acceptance of gay marriage and gay adoption is very much here to stay. But the level of prejudice that affects lesbians and gay men on a day-to-day basis has reduced comparatively little.

In any case, David Cameron's championing of the gay marriage cause has not necessarily filtered down to the rest of the party. The BSAS survey mentioned earlier in this chapter broke down its statistics by political identification, finding that 35 per cent of self-identifying Conservatives thought homosexuality was 'mostly' or 'always' wrong, compared with 29 per cent of Labour supporters and 22 per cent of Liberal Democrats. The Tories are still considered the anti-gay party.

In my own survey of gay men and lesbians, respondents were asked to rank the political parties in order of what they believed was their opposition to equal marriage. The results found that 57 per cent consider the Conservatives to be the mainstream political party most opposed to equal marriage, beaten only by the UK Independence party at 73 per cent. The Liberal Democrats, followed by Labour, then Green, were viewed to be the most in favour of it. Over three-quarters of all respondents (on both the survey aimed at gay men and lesbians, and that answered by heterosexuals) supported gay marriage, with approximately 90 per cent of 'other than heterosexual' respondents supporting it. However, around three-quarters of all respondents on both surveys had come across opposition to gay marriage, with the majority stating that it was from the Christian church, followed by politicians.

Given how much effort has gone into forcing the recent changes in legislation through parliament, it is perhaps depressing that, for some people, it has only fuelled their anti-gay hatred all the more. After I wrote a column for the *Guardian*'s 'Comment Is Free' section, entitled 'Gay Britons still face fear and loathing', I noted some of the responses from readers. Two very telling comments were about how much the readers believe the pendulum has swung in favour of gay rights. The first read as follows: 'While nobody should face "fear and loathing", we have had a situation in which 1. homosexual couples were granted civil partnerships, with virtually identical rights to marriage, and the government promised they would go no further; 2. the present government, egged on by the militant gay lobby, and with no mandate whatsoever and no proper public consultation, has redefined the institution of marriage; 3. we are now having homosexuality shoved in our faces by the media on a daily basis and, if we find the topic in any way objectionable, we are at best called "homophobes" and, at worst, threatened with civil legal action or prosecution. Hardly surprising that is inspiring "fear and loathing", is it?'

The second comment read: 'You cannot alter social attitudes through legislation. This is the essential truth that Cameron et al ignored when, without a shred of a mandate, they pushed "gay marriage" through parliament. The gay community might care to reflect on warnings that were issued at the time – from within the gay community – that the legislation would be counterproductive – quite apart from the fact that it ordained "equal marriage" for some groups but not others – for instance those in consensual incestuous relationships.

'Legislating for "gay marriage" was an act of linguistic rape – in that it forced the word "marriage" to have a meaning it was never intended to have. But now that the deed is done, please don't complain that social attitudes haven't meekly followed suit. Can I also advise that labelling those opposed to "gay marriage" as "homophobic" is objectively incorrect? People have a right to their beliefs, and to articulate them, without fear of base insult just because others – in this case the gay community – find these beliefs offensive.'

It seems, then, that for some people the recent legislation has only made their prejudices worse.

What is behind anti-gay bigotry?

Anti-gay prejudice, then, remains alive and well in the modern world. But why is it so? Is it because we are a threat to the patriarchal world order? Is it fear of difference? Insecurity? A belief that we recruit? Envy?

On one level, people are obviously afraid that lesbians will steal their girlfriends and wives, and that perhaps gay men will steal their boyfriends and husbands; something the 'born that way' theory that has become so dominant in how we think about sexuality attempts to appease – reassuring the heterosexuals that there is no danger that our threatening behaviour will rub off. But I think it is an indication of a prejudicial attitude to say that we need to figure out why gay people are the way they are; that we should understand them as a fluke of evolution, who, because of their inability to reproduce are essentially worthless to the species. On countless occasions I have heard straight women say of a good-looking gay man 'What a waste', because he is not available to her or other heterosexual females. Similarly, prior to the normalisation of gay parenting, I have encountered attitudes about the 'waste' of good potential parenting skills – for example, 'What a shame they are lesbian/gay. They would make such a lovely parent.'

The rise of the gay anti-gay – as we might call those devotees of normality – and the gay assimilation of other heterosexual pursuits is a response to the unrelenting dominance of conservatism in society, where lesbians and gay men fighting for their rights were given the choice to either continue to struggle as stigmatised separatists or join the majority in the name of equality rather than difference. Many have chosen the latter.

The use of stereotypes by the media is a telling symptom of our society's reluctance to relinquish the old models of heterosexual life. Gay men's sexuality is often trivialised as 'camp'. Gay men on TV or in adverts are portrayed as every woman's ideal best friend – very fashion-focused, a hair stylist or something similarly woman-friendly – a way for the patriarchy to make 'manly' men feel less threatened by gay men; because they are effeminate, they therefore pose no threat to masculine guys. Straight women collude, often unknowingly, by making these men 'honorary women'. We have all heard 'fag-hag'-type comments, such as 'I need a gay man to come shopping with me/advise me on my hair/help me decorate'. This reduces gay men to an accessory.

Obviously this is linked to sexist attitudes. Gay men are often mocked and ridiculed on TV, or represented as drag artists. Gay men who present as traditionally 'masculine' also face barriers. They are accepted by groups of men (say on a football team) so long as they don't 'act gay'. If the individual does 'act gay', there are often violent repercussions against him by his former friends. 'Beating it out' is often used against gay men to make them straight – could this be a violent backlash against anything that's willing to associate with femaleness?

Lesbians are fetishised and loathed at the same time. Despite the fact that lesbian visibility is increasing, with the likes of Sue Perkins, Clare Balding and Mary Portas popping up on our TV screens, there are few, if any, who actually talk about their sexual identity and openly celebrate it.

Could this be because female sexuality is feared in our society, and has been since Socrates? 'Girly' lesbians are fetishised by simply becoming the straight male's sex fantasy. (Mainstream) lesbian pornography is never about an intimate relationship, and often involves a man on whom the sex act centres. Even in lesbian dramas like *The L World* or *Lip Service*, almost all the gay couples are 'femme + butch' (and it's the same with male gay relationships), and the only seemingly 'femme + femme' is fetishised.

The patriarchal society we live in turns lesbians into sex objects solely for male viewing pleasure – real lesbians don't matter. Femme lesbians are accepted in society because they still 'conform' to what patriarchy demands. I'm sure many lesbians will tell you about some guy asking her for a threesome. One respondent to my survey of non-heterosexuals described such an example of misogynistic bigotry: 'As a stereotypically "pretty" lesbian, I've been told I "just need a good raping" – more than once (I remember being harassed at Pride by a group of "men" who reckoned I needed to be "made back into a real woman with a good dicking") – and this isn't in Africa, where you hear about "corrective rape"; this is here in the UK. So don't tell me the threat of rape for lesbians only happens in other, less progressive countries.'

Butch lesbians are also penalised, and society tries to hide them in the media. The media says they don't conform to beauty standards and so aren't worthy of our time. 'Manly' lesbians are treated with sexual hatred – possibly because society sees them as free.

A history of hatred

Historically, of course, the weaponry employed against gay people has been far more than just cultural. Research by Peter Tatchell and David Smith, then the editor of *Gay Times*, identified that between 1986 and 1991 at least 50 gay men were murdered in circumstances that very strongly point to an anti-gay motive. There were hundreds, if not thousands, of other gay-bashing attacks that the police were doing almost nothing to investigate and bring the perpetrator to justice.

Tatchell told me that in 1989 the number of gay and bisexual men convicted of the consenting victimless offence of gross indecency was over 2,000, almost as high as in 1954 and 1955, when homosexuality was completely illegal and the country was gripped by a hysterical anti-gay witch hunt. In addition, many gay and bisexual men were charged under other laws – for example, under the indecency clauses of the Town and Police Causes Act 1847, 'plus the common-law offence of outraging public decency, [and] the law against "soliciting for an amoral purpose"'. Under that law men were arrested and convicted for 'persistently smiling and winking at other men in the street', says Tatchell.

Police also used the Public Order Act 1986, introduced to combat football hooliganism, on the grounds that a same-sex couple kissing or holding hands in the street was behaviour likely to 'cause alarm, harassment or distress'.

For lesbians, fears of losing their children or ending up in a psychiatric unit were well founded. The acclaimed author Maureen Duffy, now 80, was the first lesbian in the UK to come out pre-1967 and speak against anti-gay discrimination. I asked her why she thought lesbians and gay men still experience bigotry today.

'[Heterosexuals] are scared of an alternative. They like us to be comfortably fitted into society and that may be a cultural society or a religious society, and we can, potentially, force them out of their comfort zone. Religion and culture have become comfort zones for people. It's basically an animal instinct. It's a form of territorialism, tribalism.'

The assumption, says Duffy, is that lesbians have historically not suffered as much direct prejudice as gay men because the criminal law, until Section 28, targeted only men. I asked Peter Tatchell if this is a common assumption among gay men.

'I think it is true to say that in terms of the criminal law, gay and bisexual men bore the brunt of social victimisation. In terms of child custody, it was overwhelmingly lesbians that suffered discrimination, mostly in terms of being denied custody of their own children on the grounds that they were, quote, "unfit mothers". In the 1970s the cases were shocking. Lesbians suffered, but mostly silently and invisibly.'

Despite a number of changes in the law, today discrimination and downright hatred are still evident in the UK. For example, in January 2013 a press conference was organised by the Society for the Protection of Unborn Children (SPUC), an anti-abortion and pro-traditional family organisation, to launch its campaign against same-sex marriage, targeting teachers. Dr Lisa Nolland, a social historian who is described by SPUC as a child protection expert, argued that 'homosexual activists' were spreading 'shockingly explicit material' in schools and that 'in places where same-sex marriage has been enshrined, it is becoming socially unacceptable to object to the negative influence of homosexual material on young people.'[14]

The Archbishop of York, John Sentamu, said in 2013 of same-sex marriage: 'In Christian understanding, the meaning of human sexual difference is in the good gift of God in creation. The maleness and femaleness of the human race are given to us.'[15]

Prominent anti-gays such as Cardinal Keith O'Brien, who slated same-sex relationships as 'harmful to the physical, mental and spiritual wellbeing'; Archbishop Philip Tartaglia, who said the late David Cairns MP may have died because he was gay; Alan Craig, the Christian People's Alliance leader who compared gay equality advocates to the invading forces of Nazi Germany; and the journalists Melanie Phillips and Richard Littlejohn all add to the anti-gay sentiment of the wider public.[16]

Furthermore, according to a report in the *Independent* in August 2013, 44 British schools still have the statement 'governors will not support the promotion of homosexuality' in their sex and relationships policies, with some still containing anti-gay language from Section 28, which banned the 'promotion of homosexuality'.[17]

How anti-gay bigotry affects individuals

It is unsurprising, therefore, that in my survey aimed at heterosexuals, just over 50 per cent of respondents had witnessed some form of anti-gay prejudice, with the vast majority of this being verbal. Approximately 60 per cent of respondents challenged such behaviour; others did not for some of the following reasons:

- 'I would have been killed' – male heterosexual
- 'We should all be able to take good-natured teasing about who and what we are' – male heterosexual
- 'Nothing to be gained' – female heterosexual
- 'It was the 1980s. I'd have been hugely outnumbered (and a "killjoy" with no sense of humour)' – male heterosexual

I also asked heterosexuals in my survey: 'Why *don't* you consider yourself an ally of gay people?' Their replies might go some way to explain why some straight people do not challenge anti-gay behaviour. Some respondents said they did not know how to be one. One religious respondent, for example, explained: 'I would be if I could! I'm not sure how, though. But as I've been reading the news about the situation for LGBT people in Russia, especially LGBT teenagers, it makes me really want to be able to stand with them in some way. Because I know Jesus loves them. And I want the church to find the truth, to be able to talk sensibly and sort out their ideas on this issue, but I'm not sure how that would happen either.'

Others were not politically engaged generally and so not willing to engage specifically for gay rights: 'Well, I'd stick up for someone if they were being abused, but then I'd say that whether or not they were gay. Would I actively campaign for gay rights, etc? Probably not, but then I'm politically disengaged anyway. If my friends asked me to help them, then yes, I would.'

And others were simply bigots:

- 'I will not actively discriminate against gay people, but nor do I believe in equal rights for them' – male heterosexual
- 'I believe the gay agenda is too strong' – male heterosexual
- 'I have nothing against non-heterosexuals, but I am also against the promotion of homosexuality' – male heterosexual

Some people ignored the relevance of being homosexual in a political sense, seeing it as a private matter and having no importance within wider society:

- 'It implies I am an enemy of others. I don't like the term "ally". I am indifferent to people's sexuality' – male heterosexual
- 'To claim to be an "ally" would be to give some significance to people's sexual orientation. I don't boast about my own heterosexuality' – male heterosexual
- 'I consider being gay perfectly normal and mundane, same as male/female and therefore not needing me as an "ally"' – female heterosexual
- 'Straight or gay, I treat the same. I try not to create divisions when there are so many already' – male heterosexual

Yet sexuality cannot exist in a vacuum and, like it or not, the onus is still on lesbians and gay men to make the decision whether or not to come out to their family and friends or stay in the closet. In the survey targeted at lesbian and gay respondents, I asked if they were out, and if so, to whom, with 64 per cent of respondents replying they are out to friends/family/colleagues (of those, 40 per cent are only 'partially out'). Some 12 per cent of these were outed against their will. Reasons given for not being 'fully out' included:

- 'I do not want to jeopardise my career potential and believe that coming out would limit my career' – lesbian
- 'A lot of people I know are very homophobic because of their religion' – female bisexual
- 'Fear of losing job, stigma, potential for abuse' – gay male
- 'A sense of privacy' – gay male

Survey respondents provided invaluable views and information about the effects and prevalence of anti-gay bigotry. Some three-quarters of those who answered the 'other than heterosexual' survey stated that they had experienced anti-gay prejudice at some point in their life, the majority of this being verbal, followed by psychological. Over a quarter (27 per cent) suffered physical violence. Fewer than half (47 per cent) challenged the perpetrators at the time. Most felt the best way to combat such attitudes and behaviour as a community was through education of the general public, and in particular young people, followed by political change, then better enforcement of current laws and education of law enforcement.

It is upsetting and disturbing to read the extreme examples of violence and hatred described in the responses:

- 'Religious maniacs screaming about how gay people [are] a stain upon humanity' – lesbian
- 'At school, seeing kids who were thought to be gay and lesbian being called poofs and lezzers, freaks, unnatural, etc. Sometimes I challenged it. Sometimes, to my continuing shame, I didn't' – lesbian
- 'A client refused to work with a gay colleague because he said he was "perverted" and a "paedo"' – lesbian
- 'A colleague advocated not offering a job to the most qualified candidate because he was a "gender-bender"' – lesbian

- 'Spat at and shouted at in the street. Hotel tried to make us book separate rooms. Cab driver refused our money and banned "our sort" from using his company' – lesbian
- 'A guy threatened to kill me' – gay male
- 'At school, a group of boys would take turns to stand outside my lessons and shout "fudge-packer" through the window throughout the lessons. This went on daily for three years' – gay male
- 'Being attacked in the school changing rooms aged 14 for being "queer", being stripped and beaten and having a metal ruler forcefully inserted into my anus' – gay male

These anecdotes support the extent of discrimination that still goes on in Britain and abroad. It might seem that the quest for equality has only worked in legislation and some attitudes of society – plenty of people are still victims of violence and hatred.

The role of religion

So where does the religious right stand in all this? Some survey respondents gave further examples of bigotry directed at individuals, seemingly sanctioned by the church. One gay man replied: 'A church group had a stand on Market Street in Manchester, and on the stand they had signs denouncing homosexuality as an abomination.' Another responded: 'My priest told me in confession I was going to hell.'

Religious bigotry is seen as being particularly pernicious as it is perhaps the last bastion of officially sanctioned persecution in the UK. As one respondent put it: 'Being gay is a lot better than it used to be and society has changed. Generally, the only homophobia I now encounter comes from religious people. The homophobia endorsed by the Church of England is particularly repugnant because they have a place in the centre of establishment and an unelected voice in our legislature. They have persecuted gay people for centuries, using the same book that used to justify slavery.'

I discussed this issue with Giles Fraser, *Guardian* columnist and currently the parish priest at St Mary's church in Newington, London. Fraser is a regular contributor on *Thought for the Day* and a panellist on

The Moral Maze. He is openly critical of anti-gay bigotry in the church, and a vocal advocate of gay rights.

'The church's historic homophobia has provided an alibi for bigots the world over. And it continues to do so,' says Fraser. 'Only a full acknowledgment that homosexuality is no sort of sin whatsoever would be a start in helping to put right what the church has got so very badly wrong.'

What is so hypocritical, he says, is that the church has been run by and filled with lesbian and gay people from the very start, and that without them, it would not be able to function. 'But instead of openness and honesty, the church has specialised in double-speak – talking the language of love but not recognising and celebrating its existence beyond the heteronormative.'

The time for the church to put this one right is way overdue, believes Fraser. 'Those who trot out bumper-sticker theology about the Bible being about Adam and Eve, not Adam and Steve, need to read more closely. There are alternative narratives. What about David and Jonathan? What about the constant biblical call for greater inclusivity?'

The irony is, as church attendance declines, the negative attitude of most religious institutions has only served to make them even more irrelevant to gay people. Many of us now feel that we don't want their approval even if they were to give it.

I asked on social media: 'How important do you think the C of E decision to allow priests to bless same-sex unions and why?'

One person responded: 'If I was religious (which I'm not), I think I'd struggle with the crumbs offered by the church. If they wouldn't marry me in church, I wouldn't want their blessing.'

Another said: 'The problem is that this is a sop, after years of reluctance to accept and acknowledge people in their midst. So, this blessing would not be liturgical, were it to happen.'

'Curing' with conversion therapy

There is no better example of the church's continued bigotry towards lesbians and gay men than the existence of gay conversion therapy in the UK and elsewhere.

In 2009 Patrick Strudwick embarked on an undercover investigation into the unethical practice of conversion therapy, in which a counsellor attempts to turn gay people straight. Strudwick's investigation was sparked by the research of Professor Michael King from University College London, which found that one in six therapists and psychiatrists in Britain have either attempted to cure someone or lessen their gay tendencies. Strudwick then noticed publicity for a conference taking place in London for therapists to learn how to convert gays, so went along. He spent the next two-and-a-half years fighting to get unethical therapists struck off.

Despite Patrick Strudwick's excellent undercover exposé of Christian conversion therapists operating in the UK, which was published in the *Independent* in 2010,[18] they are still going strong. One such example is the Core Issues Trust, a small but growing organisation that helps gay and lesbians 'seek change in sexual preference and expression', and which began in 2007 as an outgrowth of the founder Michael Davidson's experience of his 'journey away from homosexuality'.

In 2012 the Core Issues Trust ran a poster campaign on London buses reading: 'Not gay! Ex-gay, post-gay and proud. Get over it!', in response to the much-talked-about campaign run by Stonewall to highlight sexual diversity in which it ran the slogan, also on London buses, reading: 'Some people are gay. Get over it!' Following a number of complaints, London mayor Boris Johnson pulled the Core Issues Trust campaign.

Michael Davidson agrees to meet me at the Christian Legal Centre in London, the organisation that funds legal cases, such as that of Lesley Pilkington, a counsellor who was secretly recorded by Patrick Strudwick during a counselling session in which she claimed that she would be able to 'cure' him of his homosexual feelings. Pilkington was struck off by the General Medical Council in 2012, but has been supported throughout her case by the CLC.

I ask Davidson, who appears very measured and gentle, and, I have to admit, camp, if he believes that I am mentally disordered.

'I think folks in the gay community are more vulnerable to an awful lot and to be, you know … We're always getting told that … gay men are committing suicide at such an alarming rate. My reading of the research is that a lot of that comes from the dysfunction within the relationships,' says Davidson. 'I think [dysfunctional relationships] are more common among women than among men, but I can't substantiate that.'

Davidson seems to be a troubled soul and I find his unswerving loyalty and devotion to a religion that tells him his gay tendencies are a sin distasteful and confusing. But he does not appear to be a bigot, and we both agree that sexuality is not innate.

At the time of the ban on the bus campaign, Davidson appeared on a national news programme with Andy Wasley from Stonewall. Wasley said he was an advocate of freedom of speech, but that the notion that one could be 'cured' of feelings of same-sex attraction was 'unscientific'. The high court ruled that the advertisement could cause 'grave offence'. There is clearly a problem in the way that the spokespeople for the 'gay community' handle religious anti-gay sentiments. In order to achieve the moral high ground and score points over the likes of the Core Issues Trust, the notion that sexuality is innate and a fixed state is peddled out. The science, however, does not back this up, something discussed in more detail in the next chapter. There is a strong argument to be made against conversion therapy of any sort, which has nothing to do with whether one can 'help it' or not.

I noted that the majority of organisations offering gay conversion therapy focus on men. There were none I could find in the UK that mentioned working with lesbians specifically, and I could find only one in the US, Janelle Hallman & Associates (JH&A), in a small town near Denver, Colorado. My interest piqued, I spoke to a 'survivor' of the 'ex-gay movement' by Skype.

Christine Bakke-O'Neill runs a campaign called Beyond Ex-Gay[19] and describes herself as 'ex-ex-gay'. She grew up in a fundamentalist Christian family and was unable to accept her attraction to women. When Bakke-O'Neill graduated and left college to attend university, she came out as a lesbian. Her family were upset and unsupportive, and her Christian peers rejected her.

In 1998, indoctrinated by the ex-gay movement's slogan 'Change is possible!', Bakke-O'Neill moved to Denver to take part in an ex-gay ministry, 'one far more extreme even than JH&A', as she described it.

But after five years of exorcisms, reparative therapy and many hours at the altar, she accepted she was not going to change; having met other survivors of the ex-gay movement, she came out of the closet once again.

'When you go to these sessions, or one of their big conferences, maybe 10 per cent are women,' says Bakke-O'Neill. 'These people are far more focused on changing men. They probably think our sexuality is not real anyway.'

I decided to go undercover and book myself some therapy with JH&A. Calling myself Joanna, my cover story was that I was visiting a Christian friend in Colorado and she, knowing how being openly lesbian had led to my estrangement with my family and church, advised me to see if I could be helped to 'become whole' (straight) again. My story was that I (Joanna) had always been filled with self-hatred due to the anti-gay bigotry I had experienced since coming out at 16. Any professional therapist hearing Joanna's story should refer her to a counsellor to help her with self-esteem issues and to feel good about her sexuality. This was not going to happen in Denver. Armed with a discreet voice recorder and a copy of the Bible, I set off for the US to meet Kelley Klassen, my therapist.

At the counselling centre, Klassen looked for evidence that I was sexually abused in childhood. When she failed to find any, she asked if my mother had neglected me. She drew a baby and asked me why I thought it might cry, stating that babies need three things, 'food, movement and touch', and 'if Mom doesn't meet baby's needs, all is not well with the world'.

Despite my insistence that my mother was never neglectful, Klassen maintained that she could detect in me 'a deep sense of shame'. Part of me wanted to break my cover and point out that this shame gay people struggle with is nothing but a product of bigots like her.

I told her that I had only ever felt romantic love and sexual attraction for women and had never considered an intimate relationship with a man.

Klassen told me my lesbianism was simply a habit I had adopted. 'If you have been touched and aroused by someone of the same sex, then you say: "That's my arousal pattern," wherever the tracks have been laid.'

In another session, she handed me some papers written by Janelle Hallman, outlining her theories about why some women end up like me. What I read was deeply offensive. Hallman asserted that lesbianism itself – through 'symbolic behaviours, such as nestling into each other's arms, suckling on breasts, dressing alike, daily multiple phone calls or contacts' – is simply a collection of symptoms of emotional dependency.

'Can I change?' I asked Klassen.

'It's a lot of work – I just want to let you know,' she said. 'When a woman is truly in her own identity and can work through some of these wounds, she can get to the point where she doesn't need another woman to nurture her.'

Prior to travelling to Denver, I had been required by JH&A to fill out a number of forms and return them to Klassen. Some were about my family background, and others were clearly designed to assess me for risk of suicide and paranoid schizophrenia.

It is stated on the organisation's website: 'Intensive therapy ... is not recommended for any folks who have no local support.' Yet I made it clear to Klassen during therapy that if Joanna's gay friends were to discover she had undergone conversion therapy, they would cut her off without hesitation. I told her that Joanna was part of a house church, but that she had no one-to-one friendships with any of its members. Dr Georgina Smith, a trauma specialist who I had asked to help me look over the JH&A literature, had expressed concern at their willingness to take Joanna on, since she 'is obviously vulnerable, and away from any support from family or friends'.

In the final session, I began asking Klassen a number of questions about whether I should access the type of therapy back home that would make me feel better about being a lesbian, rather than pursue a route that would end with me losing my identity and support network. At no time did she suggest I should access counselling that would make me feel better about being gay, or refer me to one of the UK's many gay-friendly churches.

On my return to the UK, I emailed Klassen and told her who I really am and what I was doing in Denver. She admitted she was shocked at my revelations, but politely responded to my accusations about gay conversion therapy being 'unethical' and 'damaging'.

'To refer Joanna to a "gay-affirming therapist" would have been unconscionable and unethical since Joanna explicitly stated that she desired change. To ignore that desire would be to violate the fundamental principle of mental health counselling and to impose my viewpoint and ideology on Joanna.'

I also received an email from Janelle Hallman, who sought to explain her work: 'The conflict between a person's faith and sexual orientation can be considerable and, in and of itself, often creates serious psychological distress.'

This sort of therapy is becoming less popular in the UK because it has been exposed for what it is, but is growing in popularity in Africa, South America and Asia – worryingly, the countries and regions where being gay is massively stigmatised. During my counselling in Denver – despite the fact that I was in character and I am normally confident in my sexual identity – I had become depressed and anxious. We would begin each session with a relaxation exercise; I was told to clear my mind. 'What would it look like if your body, your soul and your heart were healed?' Klassen would ask.

Several hours of being told I need fixing, despite there being nothing damaged, took its toll. I began to question whether there *was* something 'broken' in me that had caused me to go 'off the rails' and into lesbianism. I left Denver with a heavy heart, weeping for all of those innocent men and women who find themselves embroiled in the conversion racket. This is anti-gay bigotry presented as 'support' for unhappy lesbians and gay men. My concern about gay conversion therapy is that in order to 'heal' someone, you have to believe they are broken and damaged in the first place. We are not.

As the Department of Health commented in response to Patrick Strudwick's findings, 'Homosexuality is not an illness, disease or mental health disorder. It does not need treatment.' It is not necessary to argue that sexual orientation is innate and therefore cannot be changed in order to argue that gay conversion therapy is dangerous and damaging. We simply need to name it as anti-gay bigotry.

Conclusion

Social attitudes are currently lagging behind legislation. While equality may be making inroads into our courts, its progress has been much slower in our hearts and minds.

Stonewall's deputy director Ruth Hunt admits that, in 2013, despite all the legislative changes, hate crime did not decrease and people's confidence did not increase in terms of reporting it. 'People's perceptions are not changing as to what constitutes hate crime. There is something not working.'

Certainly Tatchell, ever the optimist and change-maker, believes that anti-gay bigotry is still a serious problem in the UK: 'The issue is that there is still that hardcore minority. This is not surprising when the BSAS found that over a quarter of British people still believe that homosexuality is "always wrong" or "mostly wrong".'

He does, however, see some signs of change: 'There was a survey a few years ago around the time just before the pope's visit to Britain which found that only 11 per cent of British Catholics support churches' stances against homosexuality.'

But until such day as anti-gay bigotry is completely eradicated, there will always be some lesbians and gay men remaining in the closet, or avoiding certain careers. There are still hardly any prominent sports people who are openly lesbian or gay and, as we have seen, not one of Britain's 5,000 professional footballers is out. Business finds itself in a similar position, or at least at the top end, with very few CEOs of major companies openly gay. The City is still, for the most part, an aggressively macho, anti-gay environment. There are no significant religious leaders who are openly gay and not many who actually support gay rights.

For Peter Tatchell, there are a variety of reasons for people to be anti-gay: 'The huge backlash against same-sex marriage from a small minority: some of it is politically, religiously and ideologically motivated; some of it is about a fear of the unknown or what is different; some of it is like a queasiness about sex between people, like what people of the same sex do in bed; and some of it defies rational explanation.'

So does the introduction of same-sex marriage signal lesbian and gay liberation? Not at all. In fact, it is a useful smokescreen to mask the true extent of bigotry in the UK and elsewhere. It also divides us up between 'good gays' and 'bad gays'. As I will explore at length later, the fact that 'assimilation' has overtaken liberation as a goal suits the status quo down to the ground. So long as we are in faux-straight family set-ups, with a civil partnership and children to prove it, we are harmless and good. This means there has to be a baddie. 'Bad gays' are still carrying on being different and totally distinguishable from heterosexuals. Liberals are far more likely to invite you to dinner or ask you to babysit if you appear to be just like them. At least you will have something to discuss over the Jamie Oliver roast salmon if your children go to the same primary school. I can't imagine a dinner party with one couple discussing a recent trip to Ikea and the other advising on where to buy the best poppers in Vauxhall. Liberals, in reality, still think we are weird. They can't understand why we are like we are, and often wonder what horrible things we get up to in bed.

Liberal straight men are not keen on lesbians as a rule, unless they are watching parodies of us in a porn movie to toss off to. Many of them would be horrified at being accused of bigotry, but often their ingrained, reflexive sexism bleeds into their view of lesbians. One example that really brought this home to me loud and clear was the column written by Will Self, the liberal, anti-establishment writer and darling of the left. In 2005 I organised a memorial service for my late friend Andrea Dworkin, the infamous radical feminist writer and campaigner. Dworkin was an out and proud lesbian and often her work was dismissed on the basis that she was a 'man-hater' (read 'dyke'). I invited Self to attend as they had met in New York when he had interviewed her for a UK broadsheet. The memorial was moving and uplifting. We heard extracts from Dworkin's writing on pornography, sexual violence and misogyny, and those who knew her paid tribute to her warmth, generosity and commitment to women's liberation.

Later that week, in his column in the *Evening Standard*, Self wrote: 'The vast majority of the 200-odd present were … mostly radical lesbian separatists who eschewed so-called "feminine" fripperies and furbelows. Speakers poured as much scorn on "liberal feminists" as they did on the hated "patriarchs". How curious it was, therefore, to observe that these women in their neutral trousers and jackets, sporting short haircuts and only the most discreet jewellery, looked so much like, well, like men.'[20]

With liberals like Self, who needs bigots?

Whenever I ask the question of reformists 'What needs to be done to rid the world of anti-gay bigotry?' someone raises the issue of role models. But today we are awash with role models, often cited as such because they are famous and known to be gay or bisexual. Now a celebrity is likely to be on the *Independent on Sunday*'s Pink List simply for being gay – they don't have to have done anything. People described as role models for lesbians are merely people who have come out and don't appear to have done anything famously awful. That's not a role model; that's just someone who isn't a monster.

Today we are in the midst of a crisis. In the UK we have reached a stage where little more, if anything can be done to improve our legal rights, but religious leaders refuse to acknowledge same-sex relationships as valid. There are organisations such as the Core Issues Trust that believe it possible and desirable to pray away the gay.

Many young people in the UK are, despite legislative equality, still suffering social exclusion and abandonment. In September 2013 the Albert Kennedy Trust opened the UK's first safe house for young people at risk from or abandoned by their families. As gay men and lesbians are more likely to be homeless than straight people, there is obviously still more work to be done against discrimination.

In Russia, discrimination abounds, as highlighted by the painful but brilliant Channel 4 documentary *Hunted*. Broadcast on the eve of the 2014 Winter Olympics in Sochi, the film portrayed horrific violence and abuse being perpetrated by individuals and organised gangs against the LGBT community. Britain sent a team to Sochi, and none of the presenters or athletes took part in any protest during their time in Russia.

In the meantime, more than 80 countries around the world have legislated against same-sex encounters. The past year has seen gay rights be reversed in perverse policy and legislative decisions. In February 2014 Germany's highest court ruled against giving same-sex couples in civil partnerships the right to adopt children. The case was introduced by a gay couple who want to adopt their two former foster children, who are now adults. The decision followed a landmark ruling just one year earlier in which couples in civil partnerships were given the same legal rights as married couples when it came to adopting the biological children of one of the partners.

In December 2013 India reinstated a law passed under British rule 153 years previously that 'carnal intercourse' between consenting adults of the same sex be once more defined as 'unnatural' and punishable by up to 10 years in jail.

In the US in February 2014 the conservative southern state of Arizona passed a law allowing businesses to refuse to serve gay people if it goes against the owner's religious beliefs.

Our work is not yet done.

CHAPTER 3
IS IT SOMETHING IN THE GENES?

*It doesn't matter if you love him or capital H-I-M / Just put
your paws up / 'Cause you were born this way, baby.*
Lady Gaga, 2011

I've been straight and I've been gay, and gay is better.
Cynthia Nixon, 2012

In the 1970s being lesbian or gay was still seen as an illness, a genetic
deformity or deviance. Despite the decriminalisation of homosexuality
in 1967, and after almost a decade of the gay liberation movement in
the US and UK, 'gay pride' was thin on the ground.

When I took calls from distressed women on Lesbian Line (at the
Gay Switchboard), there was a recurrent question those worried by being
attracted to other women would ask: 'What made me this way?' Indeed,
it was the first thing my mother pondered when I came out to her. She
wondered if she had done anything 'wrong' to give birth to a daughter
who was destined to favour Suzi Quatro over David Essex and never give
her any grandchildren. She asked me if being lesbian was to blame for
my pathological hatred of clothes shopping, makeup and other feminine
fripperies. I told her I doubted it, because all of those pursuits were
rubbish and I obviously had better taste than other young women.

I got used to the questions from friends and strangers alike as to
why I was different from them. Being straight was normal – it was
how the population reproduced and how the world kept turning. By
default that meant that I was abnormal and not much use. The feelings
of isolation and fear that pretty much all of us felt in those days literally
sent many of us mad, which, of course, added strength and legitimacy
to the argument that there was something not quite right about us. The
gay liberation movement had a hard job on its hands. Not only did we

have to convince the heterosexuals that we were perfectly normal, we also had to convince ourselves. Some of us, as I did, responded with a fuck-you attitude and went out of our way to appear different and proud of it, whereas others went to great lengths to assimilate, either by remaining in the closet or attempting to replicate the lifestyle and values of the straight majority.

Neither tactic was particularly effective.

Things have changed for the better since my days on Lesbian Line, but one thing remains the same. We still live in a world where folk commonly look to scientific expertise for the truth about their own sexuality and the sexuality of others, hoping to find some evidence to back up their entrenched opinions. But just because an argument is politically savvy does not make it true.

Why is the notion of choosing, with pride, to be lesbian or gay treated with far more hostility by the majority of lesbians and gay men than it was in the early days of the gay liberation movement? Have we gone backwards?

Nature or nurture?

The 'nature versus nurture' question has been bothering scientists, religious fundamentalists, parents and gay people themselves for over 100 years, with the first scientific study into the issue being published by the experimental psychologist Evelyn Hooker in 1956,[21] and it was indeed her pioneering work that helped to establish the fact that homosexuality is not a mental disorder.

It is still a hotly debated subject. In July 2007 the *New Statesman* ran two articles on the topic in its 'Gay Special'. One was by a gay man who had converted himself back to heterosexuality, and the other by a gay man who had spent two decades trying and failing to do the same, both with the 'help' of the anti-gay Christian conversion movement. The former argued strongly that being gay is a choice, the latter equally strongly that he was 'born that way'.

For anyone vaguely liberal, it is persuasive to think that gay people are 'born that way', appealing to basic principles of tolerance, while reassuring the majority that support for minority rights will not impinge on their own prerogatives – that is, the need and desire to uphold the status quo. It reassures people more won't choose to jump ship from traditional society. It is also about believing that gay people cannot help the way we are and therefore should not be on the receiving end of prejudice.

The positive side of the nature, or essentialist, argument is it allows some gay people surviving in a hostile environment not to have to feel responsible for their actions and desires; it can mean that heterosexuals having difficulty coming to terms with a loved one or colleague who is gay can rest assured that it is not catching; and for those who make the laws, policies and rules, thinking that 'gayness' is an inherent condition means that any sanctions against it are pointless.

The flip side of this is that those young men and women growing up in a hostile environment who do not wish to pursue a straight life and feel dissatisfied with their lot are being fed the line that some people are born gay and some straight, and that biology is most certainly destiny when it comes to sexual orientation. The nature line also gives the impression to bigots and sceptics that no one would actually choose such a lifestyle, and that everyone who is gay just can't help it, otherwise they would be straight.

Obviously, the argument that being lesbian or gay is a choice gives the bigots an opportunity to argue that we should be made to live a straight life. After all, goes the logic, if one can choose to be gay, then one can choose to be heterosexual. However, it's unlikely that any bigots will be reassured by the fact that some of us insist we are happily and proudly choosing being gay or lesbian over heterosexuality, even if it does mean more potential candidates for conversion therapy for them. Anyway, since when did a proud liberation movement allow its enemies to define the terms of the debate?

I have always believed that pushing nature over nurture plays straight into the hands of anti-gay bigots. By arguing that we are born this way, gay men and lesbians do not represent a challenge to the status quo. A gay gene is, by implication, something that is not really supposed to be present, and so to adopt this theory means that we are accepting that heterosexuality and straight folk are normal and we are outside of that, looking in.

When I argue that, for me, being a lesbian is a positive choice rather than something imposed upon me by a quirk of nature, I am roundly criticised and viewed with suspicion. I have been accused of being a fake lesbian, a cold fish and of appropriating the term 'lesbian' to further my man-hating, anti-heterosexual agenda.

I made a conscious and happy choice to be a lesbian and reckon that when we have less anti-gay bigotry, more people will be free to do so. But when I use the word 'choice', I don't mean in the same manner that you choose your cereal. Rather, I am suggesting that if we were not under such extreme pressure to be straight, and if we did not fear the inevitable prejudice and bigotry, we might be more open to falling for someone of the same sex.

In November 2012 I gave a speech on this very topic at the Free Thinking Festival in Gateshead, Newcastle, which was later broadcast on Radio 3. It was entitled 'Not Born That Way', and I argued that sexuality was a choice and not inherent, and that much of the science claiming to have discovered a gay gene was weak and had proved nothing. Following my speech, which was in front of a live audience, several heterosexual women and men approached me and told me that I had significantly challenged their beliefs – all had, prior to the event, assumed that sexuality was innate and therefore fixed and static. They all said that my arguments made sense to them, and that they had only ever heard anti-gay bigots suggest that gay people 'choose' their sexuality.

I abhor the bigoted view that promotes the notion of a cure for being lesbian or gay. My position is that if something is not a sickness or disease, there is no need to find a cure. I came away from the event feeling pleased that I had opened up some people's minds to the possibility that being gay is such a positive alternative to heterosexuality that it is good enough for some of us to choose it.

Yet clearly not everyone thinks this way. Why has so much time and effort been invested in discovering a cause for being gay or lesbian? So parents can decide whether to abort? Or is it because the majority of people cannot get to grips with the fact that bigotry and prejudice are the problems that need solving, and we do not need a cure. All the comments us lezzers have endured over the years – such as 'You don't you know what you're missing' – come from the mistaken belief that batting for the other side is a disadvantage. Actually, a lot of us know precisely what we are missing. That is the point.

In researching for this book, I went for a drink with the staunch cynic Brendan O'Neill, editor of Spiked, the online current affairs magazine. We are not natural soul mates: O'Neill has a habit of describing most of the issues I campaign against, such as child sexual abuse, trafficking of women and sexism, as moral panics. But on one thing at least we agree: O'Neill thinks that the arguments supporting the existence of a gay gene are nonsense.

'Science is never in a vacuum,' he says when I ask him why he is adamant that there is no biological basis for sexual orientation. 'Nazis saw being gay as a weird pathology, which is why they began looking for a gay gene. We are now seeing a revival of that in politically correct terms.'

One particular bugbear of O'Neill's is the way that the existence of so-called 'gay animals' has been used to bolster claims of a gay gene. This includes research into the genetic basis of behaviour involving fruit flies. The study showed that by manipulating an individual gene, male fruit flies can be made to initiate homosexual courtship. It is interesting to note that the male fruit flies that had not been genetically modified nevertheless also engaged in courtship and sexual behaviour with the 'homosexual' fruit flies. The study was written up as a paper entitled 'Queer Creatures' and published in the *New Scientist* in 1999.

'Looking for moral guidance from the animal kingdom is pretty low,' says O'Neill, before launching into an impassioned rant against the current state of the lesbian and gay movement in the UK.

'The gay movement is pretty fucked,' he says. 'It started in the 1980s with Aids and Section 28. We saw the collapse of the politics of autonomy and the emergence of identity politics. This led to a very conservative view of "[homosexuality] is natural", which is the argument that has been used against women, black people, etc. It says that certain people are born to do certain things.'

There is, he argues, a tendency towards attempting to prove that everything, including political views, can be explained by a gene.

'Gays cannot countenance any criticism of the idea that they were born that way, because it prevents the bigots from looking for any other excuse. And the irony is that most religious and rightwing people don't say gays are born that way. They patronise them, but really they just want gays to behave.'

What about the argument that subscribing to the 'born that way' theory protects us from the bigots?

O'Neill is having none of it: 'The "we can convert you" argument has more humanity than the "we will tolerate you" one,' he says. 'Gays used to not care what wider society said about them, but now they do, which is where science and marriage come in. They need constant validation and recognition.

'Some gays might feel that finding a gay gene might diminish prevalent homophobia. This is also a naive view. Racism has not diminished because we know that blackness or whiteness is genetic. Sexism exists even though we know that sex is genetic.'

After all, neither scientists nor the regular heterosexual population ever have to consider whether there is a straight gene that predisposes them to sexual attraction towards the opposite sex. If we argue that some of us are simply born different, then all lesbians and gay men are the ones forced to explain and question who we are, leaving straight people feeling that heterosexuality is natural and homosexuality is a genetic mistake.

Either way, the world appears to be divided between those who believe there is a biological and/or genetic basis to sexual orientation and preference, and those who believe it is purely, or at least largely, down to social and environmental factors. There are few folk who do not have an opinion either way, and views tend to be polarised. My view, prior to researching this chapter, was clear: there is no gay gene; ergo sexual orientation is not innate. I have grown up, at least since coming out, always believing that sexual preference is partly choice, with a healthy dose of environment and circumstance/opportunity thrown into the mix. I have spoken at various conferences, seminars and other public and media platforms on this issue.

Unfortunately, the current debate tends to be split along the lines of: 'I was born gay. I have always known I was different. Because we can't do anything to change who/what we are, we deserve equal rights'; and 'Gay people are immoral and promiscuous. They are making a lifestyle choice and are selfish and shortsighted. With a little help and guidance, they could be living a normal life.'

Why is it that the majority of the gay rights lobby appears so nervous and offended when some of us speak of being gay as a positive alternative to heterosexuality? Is our sexuality really something genetically imposed on us that we have no control over? Why is so much effort put into locating a gay gene? Do we have so little pride in who we are that we wish to abdicate all responsibility for who we fancy?

The popular consensus of the gay liberation movement today is that between 5 and 10 per cent of us are born gay. According to popular doctrine, some of us only realise we are gay later in life, which explains the so-called 'late bloomers' and those who are indeed gay but choose to live in the closet through fear or shame. The rest of us grow up feeling and appearing different from straight people, with gay men being a bit camp and liking Madonna and lesbians favouring kd lang and power drills. Because we are hard-wired to be gay, goes the theory, it is pointless for anyone to attempt to convert us to being straight. But surely we can be against anti-gay aversion therapy and still argue against a gay gene?

How beliefs about sexuality have changed over time

Despite the domination of the 'born that way' theory these days, it is interesting to note that it is a relatively recent phenomenon and has only become prevalent in the last couple of decades. In her 1999 book *Genderations of Women Choosing to Become Lesbian: Questioning the Essentialist Link*, Australian academic Lorene Gottschalk interviewed three different generations of lesbians on whether they believed in biology. Gottschalk found that those who became lesbians in the 1970s believed they chose their sexuality, but those who became lesbians in the 1990s thought it was biology. More evidence that what we're talking about is a set of fashionable ideas, rather than something that has a scientific basis.

Certainly, starting in the 1950s to the 1960s and 1970s, social constructionism was fashionable among scientists and academics generally. In 1968, for example, the late British sociologist Mary McIntosh wrote a wonderful piece entitled 'The Homosexual Role', which argued that the idea of the homosexual was constructed to keep the rest of the hetero-patriarchy safe: as long as they separated it out and said it was biological, everybody else was OK.[22]

It seems, therefore, that gay sociologists were questioning the notion of innate sexuality as far back as the 1960s and 1970s. And before this time it was fashionable to believe that turning out lesbian or gay was all down to the parents: for men, an emotionally distant father or stifling mother; for women, an underemotional mother and father, who took her to the pub often due to the absence of a son.

But by the 1980s this began to change and the idea of the gay gene (or, as anti-gays refer to it, 'gay germ' – homosexuality transmitted as some sort of infection) was born. Work began in earnest the following decade to try to track down the elusive gene. Such research was often perceived as pro-gay because it presented homosexuality as something that could not be freely chosen. However, biological accounts continued to describe gays and lesbians as somehow ill, deficient or imbalanced, and to suggest that heterosexuality was the norm.

The GLF, as evidenced in its 1971 manifesto, spurned the idea of a gay gene. But today we have an almost 180-degree shift in thinking. I asked Peter Tatchell, who was a member of the GLF, his views on the debate.

'My argument at the time [of the GLF] was: "Let's not play fast and loose with the truth. Let's stick to the principle that the right to be different is a fundamental human right. We don't have to be the same to get equal respect; we shouldn't have to be the same to get equal respect and equal rights." In this period there was very little evidence that gave any biological credibility to the coordination of homosexuality. A much more plausible explanation was the Freudian one that everyone is born with bisexual potential and that homosexuality is part of the natural spectrum of human sexuality. My view at the time was: "What causes homosexuality or heterosexuality is irrelevant; we are human beings and we deserve human rights."'

In recent years, however, Tatchell's views have shifted towards believing in a genetic or biological basis of sexual orientation, as he argues that the science is now more advanced. He believes that there is a 'genetic component to sexual orientation' and that there is 'some significant influence from hormones in the womb'. He continues: 'I say that as someone in the past who in the absence of this research was very sceptical about the biological factors having anything other than a small marginal influence, but I think over time the evidence has grown. However, I don't believe it is the whole story, only part of it.'

Indeed, he retains an essential clarity as to the reason why so many people wish to argue in favour of the 'innate' argument: 'I think there was really this kind of desperate sense to make whatever appeal might work. It was all about sympathy and appealing to people's conscience regardless of the facts or the truth.'

The idea of being born gay has always seemed bonkers to me. I don't know about you but I was born a baby, not a lesbian. At least, I don't remember fancying the midwife. But perhaps my holding such strong and contrary views on this topic is partly because of the fact that I was exposed, while still in my teens, to the radical but commonsense position of some feminists on sexual preference – ie that it, like gender, is a social construction.

These feminists, living in the West Yorkshire city of Leeds, subscribed to the theory of political lesbianism that came from the early US feminists such as Jill Johnson and Adrienne Rich. In 1981 a small group of them had written the infamous booklet *Love Your Enemy? The Debate Between Heterosexual Feminism and Political Lesbianism*. It reads: 'All feminists can and should be lesbians. Our definition of a political lesbian is a woman-identified woman who does not fuck men. It does not mean compulsory sexual activity with women.'

Appealing to their heterosexual sisters to get rid of men 'from your beds and your heads', the authors of *Love Your Enemy?* called for all feminists to embrace lesbianism. 'We think serious feminists have no choice but to abandon heterosexuality,' the manifesto reads. 'Only in the system of oppression that is male supremacy does the oppressor actually invade and colonise the interior of the body of the oppressed.'

The message of *Love Your Enemy?* immediately provoked a strong and often negative reaction. While some radical feminists agreed with the group's arguments, many went wild at being told they were 'counter-revolutionaries', undermining the fight for women's liberation by sleeping with men.

The publication of *Love Your Enemy?* was one of the first times that the notion of sexuality as a choice had been publicly raised in the UK women's movement. Many feminists considered sexuality purely a matter of personal desire, and the idea that lesbianism could be a political decision was perceived as 'cold-blooded'. Heterosexual women tended to believe that one did not choose sexual orientation or feelings, but was overcome by them.

I learned from the feminists that, to them, lesbianism was a choice that women could make, not a condition we are born with. 'All women can be lesbians' was the mantra. I loved the sense that I had chosen my sexuality. Rather than being ashamed or apologetic about it, as many women were, I could be proud and see it as a privilege.

The revolutionary 1980s feminists in Leeds may have pioneered the way for the idea of political lesbianism, but the cause has also been taken up by some postmodern academics. In her 1995 book *Queer by Choice: Lesbians, Gay Men, and the Politics of Identity*, Vera Whisman disputes what she understands to be the fixed nature of sexual definition and desire: 'That a characteristic is innate does not mean it cannot be altered or prevented if the will exists to do so, and in the control of that will it is not scientific research but political struggle that will protect gay men, lesbians and bisexuals.'[23]

Whisman also supports the notion of a radical feminist interpretation of sexuality as a positive choice when she argues: 'If heterosexuality is forced on everyone, not merely on those whose homosexual orientation makes it impossible to achieve, then to choose to be gay is to resist coercion, an assertion shared by lesbian-feminist and early gay liberation theory.

'Woman-identified lesbianism is, then, more than a sexual preference, it is a political choice. It is political because relationships between men and women are essentially political, they involve power and dominance. Since the lesbian actively rejects that relationship and chooses women, she defies the established political system.'[24]

The science bit

Despite these voices, though, it is clear that the tide has turned towards the essentialist view of sexuality in recent years. Given this swing in popular opinion, we need to take a look at the latest scientific research to see where the search for the gay gene has led us.

It is first important to note that such scientific studies span 100 years. The history of these experiments is not a proud one. The Nazis specialised in them, with a view to eradicating homosexuality. Since then there have been countless attempts to identify a gay gene or some simple, biological basis for being attracted to the same sex.

More recently, one of the most controversial studies was conducted by gay neuroscientist Simon LeVay, who studies brain structures and sexual orientation, and is often cited as a supporter of the gay gene theory. In 1991 LeVay published 'A Difference in Hypothalamic Structure between Heterosexual and Homosexual Men' in *Science*, in which he argued that a particular component of the brain, known as the INAH3, was the same size in gay men as it is in women. However, after much criticism of his methodology, sample size and ethical approach, he cautioned against misinterpreting his findings in a 1994 interview: 'It's important to stress what I didn't find. I did not prove that homosexuality is genetic, or find a genetic cause for being gay. I didn't show that gay men are born that way, the most common mistake people make in interpreting my work. Nor did I locate a gay centre in the brain.'

However, LeVay appeared to admit that he was pleased if his research helped to counter the bigots, despite the lack of evidence of a gay gene. 'In a practical sense it does influence people: lots of opposition is rooted in the idea that homosexuality is sin. Knowing that it has a deeper basis does seem to make people more accepting of gay people.'

Gays seemed to accept LeVay's finding despite the sexism inherent in the thesis, namely that gay men are more 'womanly' than other men (and conversely, that women are similar to 'cissy' men).

As recently as 2012, a study by Andrea Camperio Ciani and her colleagues from Padova University in Italy concluded something quite extraordinary: mothers (and their sisters) who give birth to boys with the gay gene tend to have significantly more children than the female relatives of straight men.[25]

Calling this phenomenon the 'balancing selection hypothesis', the authors conclude that a gene that leads to homosexuality also leads to high reproduction among the female relatives, so that while the gay gene may not get passed down directly, it will survive through the generations via the family. The gene makes the women more attractive to men and leads to women who are more fertile, who display fewer gynaecological disorders and less complications during pregnancy, as well as being more extrovert, happier and more relaxed.

This theory has been around for a while. In 1994 Dr Dean Hamer published a book called *The Science of Desire: The Search for the Gay Gene and the Biology of Behavior*, in which he wrote: 'The gene may do the same thing in men and women, so if you're a man, you'll be gay, but in a woman she'll be attracted to men – perhaps more so than usual – and she'll have enough children to make up for those that gay men won't have.'

Another study relates male homosexuality to older male siblings. According to Ray Blanchard of Toronto University, an older brother will increase a man's chances of being gay by 33 per cent. Apparently the mother's womb is key. After giving birth to a boy, her immune system might create antibodies to foreign, male proteins in her bloodstream. Subsequent sons in the womb could be exposed to these 'anti-boy' antibodies, which might affect sexual development in the brain.

On the other hand, in 2014 neuroscientist Dick Swaab claimed to have discovered that the lifestyle of women while pregnant can help determine the sexuality of the baby. Swaab, professor of neurobiology at Amsterdam University, claims his research found that smoking, drinking and living a stressful life can increase the likelihood of having a child who turns out to be lesbian or gay.[26]

Then there is the 'gay finger-length' theory. This so-called scientific finding is based on a study in California in 2000 of 750 women and men that suggests that lesbians have a greater difference in length between their ring finger and index finger than straight women do. The same pattern was also found for homosexual men – but only when the researchers looked at those males who had several older brothers (the 'big brother' theory again). Another theory, which claims that gays have distinctive fingerprint ridge patterns, is largely discredited.

According to similar scientific 'findings', lesbians are almost three times more likely than heterosexual women to suffer from a hormonal disorder that causes infertility and excessive hair growth. Other theories include the foetus development being affected by a mother's illness, such as stress, and a female foetus developing soon after the mother has given birth to a boy being affected by the excess testosterone. There is also the theory that left-handed or more ambidextrous people are gay.

My favourite, however, is one conducted on a beach popular with gay men. Entitled 'Excess of Counterclockwise Scalp Hair-Whorl Rotation in Homosexual Men', it appeared in a 2004 issue of *The Journal of Genetics*. JS Amar 'discovered' that anticlockwise hair-whorl rotation is found in more gay men than straight. One of the many problems with the study in terms of its lack of scientific rigour is that Amar did not ask the men whose hair was being included in the study whether they were gay or straight, and nor did he examine any of the scalps up close.

The idea that human behaviour and character are determined by our genes has been used to justify all kinds of ills, from racism and slavery to eugenics and patriarchal social structures. The word 'natural' carries negative connotations for women, gays and black people, because it has been used to justify dehumanising and unequal treatment towards those groups.

No serious academic believes that all human thought and behaviour is programmed by our genes. And to date, none of the science adds up to any actual proof. Yet, somehow, the gay gene theory has become widely accepted.

Confused as to why so few people seem to be critical of the theory, I asked doctor, science writer and *Bad Science* author Ben Goldacre his views on the experiments. I was surprised to find that he did not discount the theories at all; rather, he was critical of laypeople for expecting to see physical evidence of brain difference between gays and heterosexuals.

'There's a very odd idea around, which I guess journalists and the public seem to find very seductive, that things have to be seen in a physical change in the brain before they can be accepted as valid,' wrote Goldacre during an email exchange on the topic. 'There's probably something driving this, like people wanting some kind of higher adjudicating authority for the human experience. They're wrong to think they've found it in brain scans.'

Not everyone agrees. Qazi Rahman is one of the leadings scholars in the science of sexual orientation. He is adamant that there is physical evidence of sexual orientation in the brain. I called Rahman and asked if I could hang out with him for a while in order to try to get my head around the science. A warm and affable chap, Rahman said yes, and the next day I found myself in his office in the department of psychology at Guy's hospital.

The room was not, as I might have expected, decorated with x-rays of brain scans or skull casts. Sitting at his almost paperless desk, Rahman, a small-framed, good-looking man with infectious energy and verve, couldn't wait to tell me why my brain is different from that of a heterosexual woman.

Rahman is a senior lecturer at the Institute of Psychiatry, King's College London. He studies the biological basis of sexual orientation using methods from genetics, neuroscience and experimental psychology. He also studies LGB mental health and works on the public understanding of the science in this topical field. Rahman's mission is to find concrete scientific evidence that would establish an innate factor in sexual orientation.

'Your brain will definitely look quite a bit different from a straight woman's, yes,' he told me.

My supposedly differently shaped brain began to hurt as I recalled all those times I had, as a prepubescent girl, wished I had been born a boy and developed intense crushes on school friends. As I sat chatting to Rahman about nurture versus nature, I gripped my notebook, keen to hold on to my political identity as an out and proud lesbian who has made a positive choice to reject heterosexuality.

I asked Rahman if the changes he says occur in lesbians and gay men would have begun in childhood and whether my brain would have known I was a lesbian before I did.

'Being gay or straight is strongly predicted by whether you were gender nonconformist as a child. We can measure it from very early on … Gay men tend to be more like girls – cissy boys – whereas lesbian women are more tomboyish, that kind of thing. It's a really strong predictor,' he replied.

Mariana Kishida, a PhD student supervised by Rahman, is studying the 'big brother effect', as pioneered by Ray Blanchard. Has Kishida ever been criticised for looking at the cause of same-sex attraction?

'Yes, that has been put to me before, people saying: "Are you examining us like animals in a lab?"'

But Rahman is obviously genuine in his belief that the discovery of a genetic basis for sexual orientation can and will be used for positive rather than negative effect, as is Kishida.

'I am interested in things that feel elusive,' said Kishida, 'such as sexual attraction – to see if it can be correlated with a particular biological component. I know this type of study can be a double-edged sword, but it is good to be used against the reparative therapy lot.'

Looking for some feminist-influenced science, I met with Gia Milinovich, feminist, TV presenter and self-identified 'science groupie', and her friend Dr Adam Rutherford, geneticist, broadcaster and editor for the scientific journal *Nature*. I asked Rutherford if he believes in the gay gene.

'I feel I can give you an unequivocal answer to that question, which also applies to the biology of almost any complex trait, which is, there isn't a gay gene.'

Milinovich told me she had concerns about the way in which the so-called evidence of a gay gene is heavily reliant on sexist stereotypes and gender essentialism. 'I don't understand how gayness could be passed down and there being an evolutionary advantage to it,' said Milinovich – in other words, a characteristic that means you reproduce more is more likely to be passed on genetically, so there is no evolutionary reason for gayness to be passed down. 'I was just reading about the Fa'afafine in Samoa [born male-bodied but raised as girls in large families with no daughters]. There are evolutionary psychologists saying there's an advantage to being a part of this particular family because these boys are feminine so they stick close to the family and help with nieces, nephews and so on.'

I take Milinovich's point. Although the Fa'afafine are often hailed as an example of how innate sexuality is identified, they are, in fact, raised and socialised as female in order to fulfil the role of subservient female. This contradicts the 'born that way' theory because these boys are chosen by their parents to fulfil a traditional gay role. Few scientists, however, seem to understand the impact that sexism has on the viewpoint of scientists studying sexual orientation.

Qazi Rahman believes the Fa'afafine highlight the fact that gayness is inherent because these 'feminine' boys are attracted to men. But could it not be argued that this 'femininity' is imposed on them and constructed? Perhaps they are chosen for this role because they are physically smaller and have softer facial features?

Not as far as Rahman is concerned. 'They are not gay, they don't call themselves gay, they don't identify as gay,' he replied, 'but they *are* androphilic: they are attracted to men entirely. They show the same kinds of childhood factors that we know predict sexual orientation.'

The feminist voice is often missing from the scientific debate on sexuality. There is, however, a recent emergence of feminist science that is beginning to challenge the essentialist view of gender and sexuality. Take Cordelia Fine, for example. In her excellent and necessary book *Delusions of Gender* she takes down the notion of hard-wired sex differences in the brain. Fine explains in the book that gender differences in sexuality are not immutable and are certainly affected by the social environment. While hundreds of gender differences were found, almost all were marginal – only a handful could be described as tangible or significant. Such differences diminish as societies become more gender equal. She explains how sexist attitudes have permeated neuroscience, challenging the idea that scientists are neutral and drawing attention to the fact that science in general is moving more towards the conservative end when it comes to studies of gender and sexuality.

Another staunch critic of the quest for the gay gene is Sheila Jeffreys, professor of political science at Melbourne University, Australia. I spoke to the veteran lesbian feminist campaigner during her visit to London.

In *Love Your Enemy?* the argument 'We think serious feminists have no choice but to abandon heterosexuality' was the line that stirred up the most controversy. The idea that one could 'choose' lesbianism was seen as not only controversial but downright crazy, even by other radical feminists.

I asked Jeffreys why she thinks so many gay men and lesbians cling to the gay gene theory despite evidence to the contrary. She explained it as a firm belief in gender being innate as opposed to a social construction.

'I think these things have not been critiqued by the liberal left because they are founded upon patriarchy and gender in the same way as patriarchy in general,' she said. 'Gender is the very foundation of male supremacist society and it is the thing that cannot be questioned.'

Jeffreys believes that the notion of sexuality as a choice is different for men and women. 'For women, lesbianism is liberatory. It's a feminist liberation – them being allowed to come out of all the terrible restrictions of heterosexual femininity and reach freedom. For gay men, it's not about freedom. They lose the power over women. They've already got the freedom of being the top dog and ruling the country. So for them it's very, very different. Women can say "I choose" because they're actually choosing to come out of oppression, and for gay men, it's a totally different matter.'

Back in Rahman's office, I was invited to sit in on a supervision session with William Jolly, one of his PhD students. Jolly is heterosexual. I was surprised by this, as Rahman had told me that the majority of the 30-plus scientists studying sexual orientation are gay men.

Jolly told me about his research. He is looking at how people make judgments as to sexual orientation and preference by looking at the face. 'I want to see how these judgments might be based on gendered behaviour from movement and faces using experimental techniques, such as tracking eye movements.

'For example, we know that gay and straight people are not actually very good at so-called "gaydar",' explained Jolly, 'and lots of gay people get labelled straight, while lots of straight people get labelled gay.'

I left Jolly wondering what particular benefit his research findings might have, although he told me that he is attaining knowledge as to how and why straight people make assumptions about who is gay and who is not. I am still at a loss. Perhaps it is simply research for its own sake.

Assumptions based on sexist stereotypes of gender play an important role in this research. Take the project led by Michael Bailey, an American psychologist best known for his work on the aetiology, or cause, of sexual orientation in 2005 on men in Chicago.

The Molecular Genetic Study of Sexual Orientation appeared to be aimed at proving one of Bailey's old theories about gay men, namely that they all are 'feminine' as young boys.

'I think the controversy has mostly been due to misunderstanding of the article,' Bailey said, referring to his paper on genetic selection. 'Nothing we wrote has any negative implications for gay people.' Stating that he doesn't believe 'homosexuality is morally inferior', Bailey said: 'My argument here is in no way anti-homosexual but rather pro-parental liberty.'

Bailey went on to argue that if it becomes possible to use genetic selection technology to make it more likely for parents to bear heterosexual offspring, such choices would be 'morally neutral'.

'To avoid having homosexual children does no harm to anyone,' he said. 'It is quite hard to see how being heterosexual causes any harm to the child.'

Rahman favourably quoted Bailey and told me he is 'misunderstood' and a 'lovely guy', neither of which I doubt. But Bailey clearly subscribes to the gender essentialist notion that 'masculine' and 'feminine' characteristics are innate. And is it really 'morally neutral' to talk about selecting children on the basis of their sexuality?

Today we seem to rely more on science than basic morality or politics. Despite the majority view that peddling this argument protects us from the bigots, the gay gene theory lets those off the hook who argue that being gay is unnatural and harmful. For example, Lord Jakobovits, former chief rabbi, said in 1993: 'Homosexuality is a disability, and if people wish to have it eliminated before they have children – because they wish to have grandchildren or for other reasons – I do not see any moral objection for using genetic engineering to limit this particular trend. It would be like correcting many other conditions such as infertility or multiple sclerosis.'

In February 2014 the (heterosexual) journalist Nick Cohen wrote a passionately argued column entitled 'Gay people are not genetic aberrations. If you welcome research that says being gay results from genetic inheritance, don't be surprised when they start offering a "cure".'

Dismissing the recent attempts of Michael Bailey to convince his peers of a gay gene at the American Association for the Advancement of Science in Chicago, where he argued that genetics is responsible for determining between 30 to 40 per cent of a population's variation in sexual preference, Cohen pointed out: 'The idea that they could find a reductionist explanation for a phenomenon as complicated as human sexuality was, well, optimistic. All you could say was genetic inheritance probably influenced it. But then you could say the same about anything.'

The following week the LGBT news service Pink News ran a story about earwax. George Preti, an organic chemist at Monell, had authored a report on how earwax may be able to provide information about all and sundry: 'Our previous research has shown that underarm odours can convey a great deal of information about an individual, including personal identity, gender, sexual orientation, and health status. We think it possible that earwax may contain similar information.'

What next? So far I have been informed that it is possible to determine my sexuality by my finger length, earwax and whether I was 'gender variant' as a child. Oh, and whether my mother ever took Valium while pregnant with me. If anyone needs to know, they could simply ask me.

Nature versus choice: personal views

I wrote about political lesbianism for the *Guardian* in 2009. Some of the comments below the piece clearly indicate how many gay people feel the need to maintain the 'born that way' explanation as a way to fend off the bigots bent on converting us to heterosexuality. For example, one gay man responded: 'I thought one of the arguments for tolerance of homosexuality is that it *isn't* a choice? Isn't that why religious reactionaries persecute gays, because they see it as a choice, a sinful choice?' A second gay man made the comment: 'To accept the thesis that sexual orientation is purely a matter of choice is to accept the agenda of the deeply deluded and damaging "ex-gay" movement, whose patently absurd arguments follow on from the same core assumption.'

Further to those responses, many of the people I interviewed about this topic had firm views either side of the fence, but believe that it should not matter in terms of arguing for equal rights under the law whether we were born or became gay. But it does matter, for a number of reasons. Not least because to argue that sexuality is innate, we are depriving scores of young people of the opportunity to dare to think outside of the heterosexual box.

Numerous survey respondents also expressed discomfort with such gay gene research. Over three-quarters of all respondents completing my surveys were aware of scientific experiments to establish a gay gene, and the overwhelming majority on both surveys were aware of the views of some rightwing and religious people that there is a 'cure' for homosexuality.

In response to the questions 'Are you aware of the scientific experiments to establish the existence of a "gay gene"?' and 'What are your views on these experiments?' some respondents – on both surveys – expressed concern, interestingly whether or not they viewed sexuality as innate or socially constructed:

- 'Waste of time and expense – like it is going to change anything. Might lead to abortions, however, if they did' – lesbian
- 'Dangerous nonsense. I don't fancy eugenically minded autocrats having their hands on such research. *No, scrap that* – let's find the gene and use it to make everyone gay' – gay male
- 'Possibly dangerous, and I do not believe sexuality is always fixed' – lesbian
- 'Bad. I think this is pathologising what is innate – ie sexuality' – mostly lesbian (occasional bisexual)
- 'I am highly concerned about how any research findings would be used, especially being only one generation removed from the second world war. It is naive in the extreme to imagine that the discovery of the gay gene, in a world which is still profoundly homophobic, would not be a threat to the safety of gay people – for instance, in Russia, China, Africa …' – lesbian

- 'I think that the discovery of a "gay gene" would be extremely dangerous as it would then open up the issues of the "designer baby" argument, as theoretically there could be a choice to abort a baby with a "gay gene"'– gay male
- 'I hope they don't succeed, because if there is a definite, simple explanation, some people will inevitably try to "fix" us' – male bisexual
- 'Trying to find out why people are homosexual or heterosexual is valid, and the lack of [a] clear answer is probably part of the problem for gay people. [However], trying to establish that there is a "gay gene" is bad science and sounds like something that is driven by sectional interests on both sides' – female heterosexual
- 'Idiotic. Understandable, but no one investigates a "straight" gene; it's just taken for granted' – lesbian
- 'If a "gay gene" is discovered, I would hate to think that some people would abuse it to choose their child's sexuality' – female heterosexual
- 'Trying to find the gay gene is shocking and wrong' – female heterosexual

Not everyone agreed, however. One lesbian responded: 'I think anything that could possibly help to explain to/educate people who can't identify/understand/accept LGBTs is a good thing,' while a gay man answered: 'There is possibly a genetic component, so I would like to see research continue.'

Survey results show that 60 per cent of lesbians and gay men believe that they are 'born that way', and 45 per cent of respondents to the survey aimed at those who do not identify as lesbian or gay agree that sexuality is innate.

Comments ranged from one male bisexual who said: 'I come from an incredibly bigoted area and family; why on earth would anyone in my situation or worse choose to be hated?' to another gay male who declared: 'I feel strongly that gay people are born, not made.'

Interestingly, just over 17 per cent more men than women believed in the 'born that way' theory. Almost 8 per cent more women thought we are *not* born gay, and over 10 per cent more women than men were 'unsure'.

In the survey aimed at those who identify as lesbian or gay, 2,656 lesbians responded to the question 'Would you say people are born gay?' Just over half (51 per cent) answered 'yes', 16 per cent answered 'no', and one third (33 per cent) 'not sure'. Of the 2,776 male respondents to the same question, 69 per cent answered 'yes', 8 per cent answered 'no', and 23 per cent 'not sure'.

A significant majority of both male and female heterosexuals who responded to my second survey believe we *are* 'born that way', with a slightly higher number of straight men than women saying that they do *not* think we are born gay.

The selection of comments below highlights the range of views held about this issue:

- 'It's as simple as someone knowing when you're hungry or tired. I don't choose to be tired or hungry; I just am. I don't choose who to fall in love with; it just happens' – lesbian
- 'I believe homosexuality is a lifestyle choice' – female heterosexual
- 'I never choose to be gay. It's not a lifestyle choice like getting fitter. I always knew from an early age that I was different. Then later as a teenager I realised that difference was being born gay' – lesbian
- 'Sexuality, like other human behaviour, is learned. Hence [the] differences between sexuality practices in different societies and ages' – female other than heterosexual
- 'I have known from a very early age that I was gay. I don't believe this was in any way due to my upbringing' – gay male
- 'Life experiences have much more impact on sexuality, which can change throughout the course of a person's life' – female heterosexual

For a number of gay men and lesbians, the idea that there is any choice over sexual preference/orientation holds no sway. A typical comment was: 'If I could choose, I'd probably be straight. It'd make my life a lot easier.'

A number of respondents directly tackled the connection between the belief in a gay gene with the issue of anti-gay bigotry. One gay man replied: 'I don't know for sure, but it feels innate. Whether I was born "fully gay" or born with just a "tendency" that was triggered by environmental factors in my childhood, I can't say. I don't think it really matters. If the science one day points to sexuality being determined more by nurture than nature, I wouldn't like this to serve as ammunition to those religious nutters who would try to change gay people's sexuality.'

Another gay man responded: 'I don't think, in the face of so much hatred in some countries, and prejudiced opinions, that many people would *choose* to be gay. The opposition, the confusion, the ostracism, the risk.'

For others, the belief in a gay gene helps to deal with self-hatred or doubt. One gay man wrote: 'When I was less secure in my sexuality, I needed the "reassurance" that it wasn't my "fault", or my mother's "fault". Now that I've been out as long as I have been, I don't deny the possibility that there may have been some "nurture" as well as some "nature".'

Some respondents who believe in the gay gene saw it as analogous with medical conditions. For example: 'I didn't wake up and choose to be epileptic. I didn't wake up and choose to be gay. I am what I am.'

Others made sense of the debate by arguing along equality lines: 'Because sexuality is as intrinsic as the colour of our eyes ... we should not separate out people based on these qualities. Equality means all have the same access and rights to the same things.'

Playing into the enemy's hands?

For a number of lesbian respondents, the notion of choice was a more positive approach to explaining sexual preference. One woman responded: 'I lived my life straight until my thirties. I chose to leave a marriage, and I chose to become a lesbian.'

For many gay people, this is still seen as a contentious comment. Those who share my view on sexual orientation are accused, by other gays, of playing into the hands of the enemy. When the actor Cynthia Nixon said to a journalist at the *New York Times Magazine* that she 'chose' to be a lesbian following a perfectly happy heterosexual past, she was vilified and bullied into apologising. A few weeks later she withdrew her comment and said she must have been born with 'bisexual potential'.

Hostility to the notion of choice comes from the fear that we will lose sympathy and be made to feel responsible for a lifestyle choice. It also, say the critics, gives credibility to those who advocate conversion therapy for gays.

It was the Cynthia Nixon kerfuffle that opened my eyes to how essentialist and cowardly many gays have become in recent years. Perhaps, I have been thinking, it is how we won the battle for equal marriage. By placating the bigots with the 'we can't help it' mantra, and by bending over backwards to appear to be just like them, we have effectively convinced our enemies that we are no threat. We are not contagious, and nor do we recruit. Lesbians and gay men exist because of dodgy wiring.

In the UK, the Nixon story was broken in 2012 by gay journalist Patrick Strudwick in the *Independent*. He accused her of playing 'straight into the hands of the homophobes' in her interview with the *New York Times* when she disclosed that she had chosen to be gay. In response, Strudwick claimed: 'You do not choose to be straight or gay; it chooses you.' His hostility and anger towards Nixon was obvious. Why?

Perhaps it has something to do with Strudwick's own earlier experiences, over the course of his undercover investigation into conversion therapy, which was detailed in the previous chapter.

'What kept me going throughout both the investigation and the two-and-a-half years I spent fighting to get those therapists struck off was seeing for myself just how ugly the abuse is and the effect it has on the people who undertake it, wanting to say to the world, I suppose, that you don't choose your sexual orientation. You cannot. You don't choose to be gay, and therefore you can't choose by means of prayer or therapy to be straight.'

But many people, in particular lesbian feminists, are clear that they *have* in fact chosen to be in relationships with women and not with men. Is Strudwick wedded to this point of view because it disables bigotry rather than because he is necessarily convinced by it? Despite the fact that I had been openly critical of Strudwick's take on the Cynthia Nixon affair, he agreed to meet to discuss this thorny topic.

'I've had some gay people say to me: "But it shouldn't matter why you're gay or how you came to be gay, or whether or not you can choose it, the fact is you are gay and you therefore deserve human rights," and I agree with that,' says Strudwick. 'However … one of the components of homophobic rhetoric is the notion that you can choose not to be gay and that there are things you can do to stop it, and [this theory] is used as a justification for all kinds of homophobic oppression. So even though, in an ideal world, it really shouldn't matter why we're gay, whether it's a choice, whether it isn't a choice, the fact is we're a long way from there yet. And I felt that if I can do just one thing to debunk the notion that it is a choice, and it can be cured, then that is what I will do.'

But should we not be brave and challenge the bigots with pride as opposed to dodgy science? I ask Strudwick. After all, feminists do not attempt to counter sexism by explaining that there are irrefutable differences between women and men. Even in countries ruled by extreme misogynists, such as Saudi Arabia and Pakistan, there are feminists who refuse to argue the 'different but equal' line.

Strudwick was unconvinced by my analogy. He tells me how worried he is by the argument per se because it plays into the hands of those who wish to eliminate us: 'The "you can choose not to be gay" message is becoming more prominent as conversion therapies spread to more developing countries such as Malaysia, Uganda and Kenya. Mixed in with evangelical Christianity, the notion that you can choose not to be gay, that it is a perversion that can be treated, is actually becoming more prevalent. I just wanted to do something that said: "Actually, in Britain, we don't believe this is true; we don't believe this is right. It is an abuse of people, and it is based on no scientific evidence whatsoever."'

What about the issue of women, such as Cynthia Nixon, who come out in later life?

Strudwick believes they must be bisexuals. 'I can only assume [Cynthia Nixon] chose to be gay out of a choice between men and women by virtue of the fact that she feels able to have sex with and fall in love with people of both sexes … I suspect that there is potential for greater fluidity in women. I think that basically comes down to not anecdotal evidence but a study that I saw not long ago where women and men of all orientations were shown a range of different erotic images and women showed physical sexual arousal regardless of what the images were.'

I ask Strudwick if he thinks it possible to be against conversion therapy and still say that we can make a positive choice to be gay.

'If a woman chooses to be with a woman as a way of just getting the fuck away from men, cool. But I can only assume that that is possible because that option is made available to her, by virtue of the fact that she is inherently able to respond sexually to other women. I don't believe that your environment can have any impact on your tastes as far as gender is concerned. The gender or genders that you respond to sexually is, I think, innate. What I mean by innate I don't know yet, because no one knows. I'm not a biologist or a geneticist, and neither side knows. It might transpire that that innateness is born in the first few days of conception or during childbirth, I have no idea, but innateness is good enough for me.'

I worry, I tell Strudwick, that the bigots have set the tune and that is what we are dancing to.

'Of course they have set the tune, and of course we have to respond.'

But what about responding by saying this is a perfectly decent choice that we've made, this is something that we're proud of, this is a positive alternative to heterosexuality? This is what we want to be and therefore we're afforded the same rights regardless of whether or not we can be 'fixed'?

'There's nothing wrong with saying that, but good luck to you: it's not going to work. It hasn't worked; it's never really worked. The fact is, we are still at the foothills of equality with regard to sexual orientation and we've only got that far by using and alluding to the civil rights movement and the feminist movement – ie we are how we are and that is immutable, just as race is immutable, therefore give us some rights.

'I don't think it has an air of "Poor me – I've got this disease, this affliction I can't do anything about. Please help me." I think it's more like "Deal with it. This is who I am. This is just the same as having a racial difference. There's no difference."

'Large parts of the world are still tied up in the narrative of pathology and deviant criminal, evil behaviour, as something no different to someone committing a murder or stealing or committing adultery. It's all a deviant choice. And so one of the first things you have to do is say: "Well, a) it's not a choice, and b) it's OK – it doesn't harm anyone."'

Does he think he was unkind about Cynthia Nixon? Would he write the same again?

'I would write the same again; the reason is that she chose not to explain herself fully. Clearly it is the case that she is able to respond sexually and romantically to both sexes, by virtue of the fact that she had a good marriage to a man, had children and a perfectly functional marriage, and that she also fell in love with a woman. For her to say that she chose to be gay is not explaining fully what she means by that. And if she really thought about it, I bet that she would admit that she chose to be with a woman, not that she chose to be gay. She chose to be with a woman because she fell in love with a woman, because she could fall in love with a woman.'

I ask him again about women who come out as lesbian in later life and are proud to call themselves lesbian.

'I have certainly found that women who have fallen in love with women after being with men have realised that, regardless of whatever might be happening in bed, they really value being with a woman for a host of other reasons: kinship, a mutual understanding, better oral sex. I'm joking, but I completely understand why someone with that history would self-identify as a lesbian, because they don't want to go back to being with men. It might be the case that they just feel more emotionally rewarded and stimulated by being with another woman.

'But what I would say is that I still don't accept that they have chosen to be a lesbian. They have fallen in love with a woman because they are able to fall in love with a woman; they choose not to be with men, that's fine, but that isn't really choosing to be a lesbian – that is choosing not to be with men, which they could be if they wanted to.'

Strudwick's views are persuasive, but I remain unconvinced. Just because a person has always felt attracted to the opposite sex (or the same sex) does not mean that there is any genetic or otherwise innate explanation for their sexual orientation. And the theory, posited by some of the men I interviewed for this chapter, including Patrick Strudwick, Adam Rutherford and Qazi Rahman, that female sexuality is more fluid and that we pretty much get turned on by anything (unlike men, who are fixed and static) is downright sexist.

In June 2013, the Core Issues Trust held a conference at the Christian Legal Centre offering sessions on gay-to-straight therapy. David Pickup, who runs therapy sessions to turn gay men into heterosexuals, was speaking at the event. He told a national newspaper in 2012 that if a gay gene was discovered, he would acknowledge the harm he had caused. Surely this proves that the 'tactical' approach to insisting we are born this way is counterproductive?

Conclusion

A liberal response to the 'gay question' is not to wonder openly why a loved one is lesbian or gay but merely to accept. We have been taught to tolerate difference rather than delve too deep in order to understand it. A liberal view of sexuality is to accept that someone cannot help being that way, rather than attempting to look for causes, as this would imply that someone or something is to blame. We leave that to the scientists. However, this approach results in an assumption that sexual preference is innate rather than positively chosen.

Liberals, like reactionaries, believe in gender. The enlightened among them will say: 'We don't believe in gender stereotypes.' But that means they subscribe to the idea of gender being a tangible phenomenon. Surely this is contradictory. There is no gender that is not derived from gender stereotypes.

At a time when the mainstream political parties are paying attention to the gay rights movement, we have an opportunity to present ourselves as truly proud, rather than apologetic. We can be horrified by the idea that fundamentalist Christian therapists think they can 'pray away the gay' and turn us straight and yet still argue that there is no evidence of a gay gene that determines to whom we are sexually attracted.

All these claims serve the notion that there is something wrong with those of us who shun heterosexuality. Many lesbians and gays want to believe we were born that way to provoke sympathy and understanding. In the mid-80s, during the kerfuffle around Section 28,

I dared to write in a gay publication that being lesbian or gay was a positive choice. I was inundated with letters telling me what trouble I had caused, because if heteros thought we were choosing to be deviant, that means *we* are responsible, not our genes. Some said: 'I have known I was gay since I was three months old. How can it be a choice?' Obviously she was exaggerating. It is rare to remember anything before two years old, by which time we are significantly socialised. You just have to look at the cries for Barbie dolls and Action Men from toddlers to see how masculine and feminine traits are taught to children almost from the womb.

Paul Burston, author and former editor of the gay and lesbian section of *Time Out*, is a friend and colleague with whom I have had impassioned disagreements about this issue. Burston has been out as gay since the 1980s and is a lifelong campaigner against bigotry and the oppression of lesbians and gay men. He firmly believes he was born gay and tells me that some of his earliest memories are of crushes on other boys.

'When I reached puberty and these crushes evolved into sexual fantasies, I was terrified. Being gay was the last thing I wanted to be. Like many gay teenagers, I tried to repress my feelings. I lied to myself and to my family. Coming to terms with my homosexuality took time. It was something I learned to accept. It wasn't something I chose.'

But what about those feminists for whom lesbianism is a positive alternative to heterosexuality?

'I've met lesbians who say that their sexuality is a choice – a political rejection of heterosexual norms. I've yet to meet a gay man who put his politics before his penis. For them, gay desire came first.'

Burston's main concern about the 'choice' theory is how it is appropriated by the anti-gay bigots. 'I don't think we choose our sexual desires, but we can choose whether or not to act on them. What concerns me is that, all too often, people who claim that homosexuality is a choice are the same people who stand in the way of lesbian and gay equality. If it's a choice, they argue, then we only have ourselves to blame.'

While it is understandable, as a response to horrific anti-gay bigotry that still prevails in all cultures and societies, that some gay folk wish to pass the buck for their choice of sexual identity to a rogue gene, it plays into the hands of reactionary geneticists, whose agenda is terrifying. They are seeking to prove that those outside of the white, able-bodied heterosexual norm are inferior. Why do we, once a proud, unapologetic people, collude?

The more we break down the taboos of same-sex relationships, the more people will recognise that we have a choice in our sexual desires and orientation and whether we act upon them or not, especially in later life, as Cynthia Nixon did.

So when people say: 'If being gay was a choice, then why would we choose to live a life where oppression, violence and discrimination are inevitabilities?' I say to them: 'But this is just the same as being a feminist in countries where sexism exists. Yet feminists do still exist and persevere in these circumstances.' We only have to think about Pakistani activist Malala Yousafzai to realise that we stick to our guns because we want to be part of creating a better world.

There is a biological basis to sex differences between women and men, but this fact is not used as an argument to challenge men's sexism – indeed, it is used against women.

Many gay people want to believe we were 'born that way' to provoke sympathy and understanding. We should instead say we like being gay, and campaign not to get married in church but for gay conversion therapy to be illegal. Then we will have nothing to fear, and the bigots will have nothing to prove.

Being gay or lesbian is obviously not a choice like which sauce to have with your pasta, but more a mix of opportunity, luck, chance and, quite frankly, bravery. It is a positive choice, and we do not need anyone with a test tube telling us otherwise. Besides, who wants to be told that the way we are today is the way we have no choice but to remain? But the notion that there is a gay gene has become so mainstream that even Lady Gaga was able to have a hit with a song entitled 'Born This Way'. Macklemore's 'Same Love' runs along similar lines: *The rightwing conservatives think it's a decision / And you can be cured with some treatment and religion: / Man-made rewiring of a predisposition. / And I can't change / Even if I tried, / Even if I wanted to.*

But people change sexual preferences all the time: look at Tom Robinson, Jackie Clune, Jake Arnott and others. The genetic and hormonal theory presupposes that sexual orientation is a biological given and that the combination of genes and hormones predetermines what your sexual orientation will be. However, it doesn't explain bisexuality, and it doesn't explain people who change their sexual orientation midlife after being happy with one orientation and then become equally happy with another.

As Nixon said in an interview following the fall-out from her declaration: 'Why can't it be a choice? Why is that any less legitimate? It seems we're just ceding this point to bigots who are demanding it, and I don't think that they should define the terms of the debate.'

The last word goes to a straight man, because it is so rare that they get involved in this debate. As Nick Cohen so eloquently argues: 'Gay people are not entitled to human rights because of a gene but because they are human.'

CHAPTER 4
'WHERE ARE ALL THE LESBIANS?':[27]
AN EQUAL UNION?

*Simply, gay men and lesbians feel isolated from one
another because we are two completely different
animals who are forced to share the same cage.*

Tyler Curry, *Huffington Post*, 30 January 2014

*The notion that queer politics could represent the
interests of lesbians as well as gay men arises from a
mistaken idea that lesbians and gay men can form one
unified constituency with common interests.*[28]

Sheila Jeffreys, *Unpacking Queer Politics*, 2003

What do lesbians and gay men have in common? Being on the
receiving end of prejudice and bigotry? Social exclusion? I struggle to
think of anything else. I see gay men at 'community' events and count
a handful as friends and colleagues, but ultimately we are chalk and
cheese, pushed together by those who wish us harm.

Over the years we have been a bit like Elizabeth Taylor and Richard
Burton. We can't live together, but find living apart impossible.

That there is a gulf between the experience and reality of men and
women is in no doubt, so of course this also applies, to an extent,
between lesbians and gay men. How is it, then, that some of us
are convinced that gay men and lesbians share the same needs and
experiences simply because we gravitate towards same-sex liaisons?

It is often assumed that gay men can't be misogynistic and that
they somehow relinquish male power and privilege over women
because of their sexuality, but male privilege is seldom not on show.
Acts of hostility and downright disrespect can be misinterpreted as

'appreciation' for women's bodies, when those bodies are treated as accessories or something to be objectified bitchily with just as much venom as a straight man might use. Gay male fashion designers, such as the late Alexander McQueen and Versace, either make women look like teenage boys or parodies of women. Many will design clothing and accessories that, when worn, cause pain, discomfort and, in some cases, disfigurement. Many will design clothes that will not even fit the vast majority of adult women.

Gay men are seen to be less sexist than straight men, presumably because they are not interested in women sexually and because they apparently do not conform to masculine gender stereotypes. But gay men still benefit from patriarchy, or in other respects are less disadvantaged by it than lesbians and straight women.

It is assumed that lesbians and gay men come together under a common struggle against hostile forces and that both groups are seeking similar change – for example, the right to marry, adopt children and join the armed forces. The term 'gay' is regularly used to include lesbians, including by campaigning organisations that seek to represent both men and women, such as Stonewall. However, our histories and present needs are often as radically different as our separate communities.

The animosity sometimes glimpsed between the two camps is thought to stem from feelings that each has had a harder struggle to gain acceptance. While gay men have been criminalised by the law and the 'spread-of-Aids' issue, lesbians have also had to deal with the sexism that has plagued women for centuries, coming directly from the male community. While lesbians joined the fight against the prejudice of Aids, gay men still indulged in sexism and misogyny. There are shared goals, but with plenty of points on which to disagree, and for reasons of self-interest, we are often set against one another. As Peter Lloyd of *Gay Times* summed up: 'We're all working towards the same goals, but because of the gender divide, it can be easy for people to slip into an insular mindset.'

With the fusing of lesbian and gay to 'lesbianandgay' in the 1980s, the adoption of the all-embracing 'queer' in the 1990s, and the fairly recent extension to 'lesbian, gay, bisexual and transgendered' (LGBT), which currently stands at LGBTQQI (to include 'queer, questioning and intersex'), it is hard to find many who are not included. The list includes heterosexuals, but not (yet) the type who engage in missionary-position sex with another human being in a semi-detached in Essex.

The problem with 'queer' is that a lesbian will probably identify as lesbian first and queer somewhere down the list, in the same way that a Yorkshireman identifies with his county long before he registers an interest in being English. And the problem with 'LGBTQQI' is that lesbian is one of seven groups. It is not that the other six do not face struggles, but that if lesbians and therefore lesbian feminists are marginalised, women as a whole will struggle to be heard and to effect positive change. If patriarchy is not challenged, then the status quo, damaging for women and, to an extent, gay men, will remain steadfast.

When I came out, there were so few lesbians and gay men that we tended to stick together. Gay men dominated in numbers – and in other ways. As I mentioned in chapter 1, I was friends with a gay man, David, when I worked as a Saturday girl in a hair salon and it was he who took me to my first gay club, the notorious Rockshots in Newcastle. I also made friends with a young gay man during my first meeting of Campaign for Homosexual Equality because the only other out lesbian in the room (and, as it later transpired, the whole of Tyneside) was, at 30, much older than me and seemed terribly serious. But shortly afterwards, in 1980, a group of gay men spat the worst misogyny I had ever heard at my lesbian friends when we complained about the anti-woman depiction by the drag act in a mixed club. It would not be the last time I heard similar sentiments from gay men.

In those clubs I frequently heard gay men refer to women as 'fish' (how they claim women's genitals smell), refer to each other as 'she', and adopt female names for those they considered 'cissy'.

The radical feminist critique of men as a social class, developed in the early 1970s, was applied to gay men equally. The late 1970s was the heyday of the women's liberation movement and those of us who were lesbian feminists considered the two identities indivisible. Why give your life to fighting against patriarchy and then allow a patriarch (translated to mean any man whatsoever) in your bed and your head? Why even let him sit at the same table in a pub?

The Leeds revolutionary feminist booklet *Love Your Enemy?* had outlined clearly the contradiction between heterosexuality and the struggle against male supremacy. It also became clear to those of us who rejected men as lovers that we also would not be able to have friendships with them. Gay men were no exception to the rule, then. A man was a man. As we fought our way through the early 1980s, one of the divisions between radical and liberal/socialist feminists was the practice of separatism – cutting ourselves off from all men, wherever possible. Lesbians who were friends with gay men were viewed with almost as much suspicion as those in sexual relationships with the straight variety.

Many liberals feel uncomfortable with the notion that we are not one monolithic community united against the bigots. The bigots would argue that because we are not 'normal', then we must all be queer – but not all of us want to identify as queer, either as our first label or as any of our labels. Queer is a label that goes some way to erasing lesbian identity.

Moreover, policymakers and politicians would surely be irritated at the idea that separate and different provision may be required for our differing needs, and service providers – such as housing support, advice lines and the leisure industry – might be flummoxed as to how to do justice to the two distinct groups. They'd certainly resent having to spend more money.

Nevertheless, many lesbians do feel unhappy about being lumped together with every other minority group whether they like it or not. As one lesbian respondent to the survey said: 'I feel very uncomfortable with the new grouping: LGBT. Suddenly I feel I'm grouped with gay men, bisexuals and transsexuals without my agreement having been sought! My affiliation is much more with other women. There are issues of patriarchal power that permeate this artificial grouping, and being lumped together in this way separates lesbianism from other women's struggles (say around misogyny on Twitter, Page 3, etc). LGBT feels part of the conforming agenda.'

So who has it worse?

When asked: 'Has the situation improved, got worse or stayed the same for lesbians and gay men in the UK in the last 10 years?' it was noticeable that all respondents believed things had got much better for gay men than it had for lesbians.

The first survey, directed at lesbians and gay men, found that 61 per cent believe that things are the same for gay men and lesbians. A third (33 per cent) believed that things had improved more for gay men, with only 6 per cent believing that things had improved more for lesbians.

The responses to the same question of the second survey, aimed at heterosexual men and women, were fairly close to those of the first, with 68 per cent, 27 per cent and 5 per cent respectively.

However, the survey results also reflect the general view that most seem to think that gay men experience more violent attacks and that lesbians are better accepted. There is a view among many gay men and heterosexuals that lesbians are less of a threat to mainstream society and therefore are rarely subject to violent assault and murder. This misconception is down to the definition of a 'homophobic assault'.

Activist and writer Paul Burston commented: 'Gay men have every reason to be political about our sexuality. Historically, laws prohibiting homosexuality tend to focus on men. Most queer-bashers and their victims are male. Women, it seems, are far less hung up about same-sex desire than men. Female friends who identify as heterosexual often confide in me about sexual experiences with other women. Far fewer straight male friends share similar stories.'

As one gay man put it: 'For many people, gay men are more physically abused (attacked, violence, etc), and will be outright challenged. Homophobia against lesbians is typically more verbal, and a lot of men think lesbians are "sexy" and don't find them as threatening.'

Indeed, one young gay man believes that pornography has 'helped' the acceptance of lesbians in mainstream culture: 'We live in a patriarchal society which will always favour men over women, so from that standpoint, things are easier for gays than lesbians. Culturally, however, there is more acceptance of lesbianism because the patriarchy is titillated by the idea of women together (porn has helped that along).'

He continues: 'Some countries and cultures refuse to believe lesbianism exists, such is the flabbergast that people can survive without penis. People are concerned, apparently, about procreation and how not being straight hinders the chances of having children. Here, lesbians may have it better – opprobrium against gay adoption surely hits men worse than women. On the whole, if I had to pick who has had it better, I would say gay men – there is more visibility, and this is a man's world (let's hope that soon changes).'

But a number of lesbians were clear that they face the dual oppression of sexism and anti-gay bigotry. One commented: 'Lesbians haven't really seen much of an improvement in their economic situation. Also, society hasn't really improved much for women in general, so lesbians face those challenges as well.' Another said: 'I believe that, as usual, patriarchal society is pushing forward more for male equality rather than equality for all homosexuals.' And a third stated: 'Medically speaking, gay men have it easier. Most doctors, including those who work in sexual health, know nothing of lesbian sex. Plus lesbians are women! Still seen as second best in this patriarchal society. I can't (because I don't fancy men) marry a man and get that "protection". We are second class.'

However, one woman, although she felt that things have improved more for gay men, did feel that there used to be more violence aimed at gay men than lesbians: 'In my experience it has always seemed easier to be a lesbian; there has been more violence aimed against gay men. Things seem easier for many of them now.'

I also asked: 'Is more public violence aimed at gay men and more private/overall violence aimed at lesbians?' The responses seem to suggest that people do perceive differences between the two groups:

- 'Both gay men and lesbians are tolerated in public life: civil partnership/marriage. I still think men are more at risk from aggressive homophobia' – gay male
- 'The risk of violence seems more acute for gay men. The last time I tried a relationship, no one cared if I held hands or kissed the other woman in public. I suspect a gay male couple would have been physically threatened' – lesbian
- 'Homophobia experienced by men and women is very different. Met *so* many misogynistic gay men!' – lesbian

But one gay man believes: 'Gay men face far worse discrimination than lesbian women. The problem in society is the middle-aged [straight] men who think it's "gross/wrong/whatever" and oppose our equal rights. However, these men find lesbian acts arousing, so it's less abhorrent to them than the acts of a gay man. I do not doubt that lesbian women have a terrible time, but [they] do not live with the fear or violence as a gay man does.'

I would strongly dispute this. The notion that if a straight man has sexual fantasies about lesbians having sex together, then he is not prejudiced towards us is off the wall, particularly bearing in mind the prevalence of sexual violence towards lesbians. There may be an odd theoretical logic to the idea, but it is simply not borne out by the facts.

Moreover, I have never heard gay men argue that they would rather ally themselves politically with lesbians than with other gay men because lesbians face additional discrimination because we are women. However, I hear the opposite from lesbians all the time, particularly those women who do get involved with gay-male politics. Take Lisa Power from the Terrence Higgins Trust, for example, who says, when asked why she has mainly been involved in human rights campaigns that encompass gay-male issues: 'When they put us up against the wall, they are not going to care if we have vaginas or dicks; we are all going to be up against the wall together. I was involved in gay politics rather than feminism, but it was a very pro-feminist gay politics. I spent a lot of time working on gay men's misogyny, particularly those men who thought they couldn't be sexist because they were gay.'

If gay men are openly misogynistic, then it should be questioned whether we really would be up against the wall together. This thinking seems to buy into a patriarchal organisation that hopes to be tolerated, rather than openly challenging male dominance of any kind.

The GLF and 1970s revolutionary politics

As we saw briefly in chapter 1, the political and social alliance between lesbians and gay men dates back to the days of the GLF. Formed in 1970, its manifesto argued that lesbians and gay men needed to embrace and ally with feminism: 'As we cannot carry out this revolutionary change alone … we will work to form a strategic alliance with the women's liberation movement … In order to build this alliance, the brothers in gay liberation will have to be prepared to sacrifice that degree of male chauvinism and male privilege that they still all possess.'[29]

Throughout the early 1970s its members engaged in a broad critique of the capitalist forces, exemplified by the gay sex industry and owners of gay clubs, which drove the exploitation of gay men. They argued: 'GLF hopes to provide a desperately needed escape for people who are tired of the alienated and exploitative "gay" world, furtive sex in public loos, and dangerous excursions to Hampstead Heath. We want to provide a better scene for gay people.'[30]

There was also an important recognition of the importance of lesbian and female oppression and their need to be represented and to have positions of influence. The women in the movement seized their opportunity. Lisa Power recalled: 'Once on Gay Switchboard, we had an all-female shift and one of the guys came in asking: "Have you taken over?" Sort of as a joke, but not. We all turned round and said: "Yes. Fuck off."'

At first, then, there was a sense that we were all in it together, fighting a common cause, as the GLF manifesto made explicit. As Peter Tatchell recalls, 'We saw, in those days, the word "homophobia" had not been invented and we used the term "sexism", which meant, to us, both the oppression of women and of LGBT people. We saw straight male machismo as the common enemy of women and LGBT people; therefore we had a common interest with women in fighting against that straight male machismo.'

But despite its apparent commitment to feminism, on paper and in principle, much criticism has been levelled at the gay men in the GLF. The tensions eventually resulted in most of the women walking out on their gay brothers.

I asked Peter Tatchell why the split occurred.

'I think there was a combination of factors. A lot of the women in the GLF saw the women's liberation movement as energised and focusing on women's issues, which they thought quite rightly were important to them,' says Tatchell. 'There was also some kickback against some degree of sexism among some gay men within the GLF.'

Women in the GLF were a minority – somewhere between a fifth and a third, although, according to both Tatchell and Power, many of the key movers within the GLF were women.

'People like Angela Mason, then Angela Weir, and her partner, Elizabeth Wilson, and Mary McIntosh. These are all big names in the GLF. I don't think it's wrong to say that all the GLF men were sexist and male chauvinists. I think there was an element of that, and there were disagreements about that.'

According to Lisa Power, the split within the GLF came in 'dribs and drabs'. 'Several times women walked out of separate meetings from the beginning. For example, in autumn 1971 there was a big ruck over separatism and over the inclusion of preoperative trans women in the group. There were certainly some occasions where the women stood up and said: "Right, sod you."'

Another issue that created tension between lesbians and gay men in the GLF was the adoption of drag by some of the men. 'It pissed some of the women off because it was seen as parodying the women for some sort of sexist fun,' says Power.

Sheila Jeffreys was not involved in the GLF, as she did not identify as a lesbian until 1977, but her understanding of the split is that the lesbians involved got fed up very quickly with complete male domination: 'The men would wear dresses and sit in meetings knitting, and they thought this was a way of identifying with femininity and women. Well, of course, none of the lesbians wore dresses and they didn't knit. They were horrified by what they saw as an ostentatious mocking of women and femininity. So that was just one example of how the lesbians did not feel comfortable. And so what happened in the early 70s is a lot of the lesbians left gay liberation and they came into lesbian feminism.'

The rise of the clones

By the late 1970s the 'butch shift', as described by gay writers such as Michael A Messner, took place. It was, according to feminists such as Sheila Jeffreys, a celebration of masculinity and, by default, an excoriation of femininity. It was the oppression of women, symbolically and in reality.

This was a change. Effeminacy was something that was very much a part of being gay before the 1970s, and then, as we saw through parodies such as that displayed by the Village People, an imitation of aggressive masculinity. I recall being in gay clubs in the late 1970s and commenting on the sea of 'clones', as they were known on the scene – gay men with cropped hair, moustaches, checked lumberjack shirts, workman boots and Levi's. They wore bunches of keys on heavy chains hanging from thick leather belts, and often sported a handkerchief from a back pocket denoting which sadomasochistic sexual practice they preferred. Meanwhile, straight men were growing their hair and experimenting with a more androgynous or even traditionally feminine look, as evidenced by Glam Rock stars such as David Bowie and Marc Bolan. Ironically, a few years later, in the 1980s, the shift towards gym culture resulted in an even more enhanced masculine aesthetic for gay men.

While gay men were off flexing their masculinity, lesbians, many of whom identified as feminist at the time, were challenging polarised gender roles and the violence towards women that came out of, we argued, the notion that men have an innate masculine and powerful role over women. The gay men asserting their maleness were concerned, it appeared, with their rights as men and *to be* men, rather than adopting a politic – such as did the GLF members – that liberated them *from* the tyranny of the masculine role and the requirement that they present as *real men*. Feminists such as myself were striving towards the elimination of gender, whereas the clones simply wanted a slice of the masculine cake for themselves, and were focused more on individual sexual liberation than the liberation of a sex class.

Lesbian feminists versus 'pro-sex' lesbians

The merging of lesbian and gay culture and politics led to a growing anti-feminism and the lesbian sex wars of the late 1980s. Gay men had long argued that the production and consumption of pornography was liberatory, whereas radical feminists viewed it as sexual violence. Non-feminist or liberal feminists, however, began to believe gay male culture was more exciting than what was then available within lesbian culture and – as we will explore in the following chapter – there was money to be made from lesbian and gay sex.

Towards the end of the decade, the UK saw the launch of the first lesbian sex-toy business and the publication of the first lesbian erotic fiction and pornographic magazine. Lisa Power started a lesbian sex-toy business called Thrilling Bits. 'We named our smallest and most inoffensive vibrator "the Sheila" after Sheila Jeffreys,' she said. (The black dildo was named 'the Whitney': political correctness had not yet touched on the lesbian sex-toy market.) Other lesbians tried to join the party by donning black leather and chains, producing and consuming pornography, practising extreme body modification, donning drag and adopting the gender-neutral 'queer' label.

At that time, the priorities for gay men, if they were politically active, were Aids and Section 28. Many lesbians, such as Lisa Power, supported men in countering bigotry and gaining access to healthcare, and by the time Section 28 was introduced into the Local Government bill by Dame Jill Knight in 1987 and enacted in May 1988 – the first legislation to target both lesbians and gay men together – the two groups had come together as one.

Following on from this fairly logical and almost unimpeachable response from lesbian feminists in response to Aids and Section 28, things got murkier. In the early 1990s a growing number of lesbians became involved in what had previously been seen as traditionally gay male issues, such as anti-censorship, pro-pornography and campaigns to repeal laws against sex in public, or 'cottaging'. It can be argued that some or all of these actions would result in harm against women, particularly pornography.

To put this in context, in 1990 16 gay men were given prison sentences of up to four-and-a-half years or fined for engaging in consensual sadomasochistic activity following a police investigation named Operation Spanner. The convictions have since been upheld by both the court of appeal and the law lords in the UK and the European court of human rights in Strasbourg. The campaign in protest of the police investigation and subsequent convictions was led by gay men, but also supported by a number of so-called 'pro-sex' lesbians.

The arguments put forward by the group were that it was perfectly acceptable to *consent* to assault occasioning actual bodily harm and that the police, in picking on a group of gay male SM-ers (sado-masochists), were motivated by homophobia.

The problem that feminists such as myself had with this argument was that abusive men in domestic and sexually violent relationships with women often coerce their victims to say they 'consent' to the injuries inflicted, and that it is not unlikely that a woman (or gay man for that matter) living in fear of her abuser could be coerced into protecting him. The lines of defence were reminiscent of those used to justify or cover up violence against women.

The lesbians supporting their gay brothers on Spanner, however, accused those of us who were critical of being 'allied with the right wing' and 'anti-sex moralists'. But information from the Metropolitan police's Obscene Publications Squad suggests that some of the videos seized during Operation Spanner contained records of abuse of a 16-year-old boy, and some of the defendants were in possession of images of child abuse.

There was a background to this split that wasn't just linked to this case. Cherry Smyth, author of the book *Lesbians Talk Queer Notions*, explains: 'Over the past couple of years, many lesbians have become disillusioned with the women's movement, particularly its response to Aids and perverse sexuality. Dykes have found they identify more common goals with gay men around these things. We're in touch with what gay men are saying about safer sex, survival on the streets and issues of eroticisation – like our right to cruise and wear fetish gear.'[31]

Aids, Section 28 and the politics of equality

So, in the 1980s there were splits between gays and lesbians, and also between lesbian feminists and the nominally pro-sex lesbians. But that was not the end of the damage done to the radical politics of homosexuality.

The 1980s saw the resurgence of the right wing, in terms of economic and social politics. Sheila Jeffreys remembers: 'What happened in the 80s under Reagan and Thatcher was [that] the left was hugely challenged and pretty much wiped out, including feminism and gay liberation.

'At the same time as all the jolly consumerism [was taking off], an enormous amount of sex in the back rooms of clubs was going on. I think the gay men who came out of that scene ... then became quite conservative and they wanted to get babies from surrogate mothers in India, get married, join in all of the institutions like surrogacy and marriage that are enormously oppressive to women and very anti-feminist in order to become "white picket fence" basically.

'[This was] a kind of reaction to the stuff that was going on in the 80s that was so destructive of their lives and communities. And through all of that no radical politics has survived; there's absolutely nothing out there.'

Through factionalism, sexism and capitalism, lesbian feminist politics had been weakened and isolated. But although Section 28 was something for gay men and lesbians to rally behind together, it came about because of HIV/Aids, and it was this virus that was also one of the reasons for the splits in the movement.

In the 2013 documentary film *How to Survive a Plague,* an account of how activists took on the US government during the HIV/Aids crisis, there was a poignant quote on the abuse of gay men and lesbians: 'It's like being in the trenches.' During an interview with The Gay UK online magazine, filmmakers David France and Peter Staley described the time of the crisis: 'We were isolated. We were living in these geographical ghettos. We were hated – officially and culturally and rejected by everybody across the board including our families.'[32] The government turned its face away from the crisis; later even Clinton was poor on Aids, because however liberal a president is, the gay slur is a vote-loser.

The prejudice faced by gay men during the crisis spilled over on to us lesbians. In one scene in the film, two lesbians were beaten up and came into the hospital at Greenwich Village and were told to 'get the fuck out of here' by the security guards. This prejudice occurred in the UK too. I was once confronted by male bigots and told: 'I hope you get Aids.' Aids had made gay men and lesbians part of the same demographic whether they wanted to be or not.

Many gay men became politicised through Aids; it was their moment. It led to direct oppression and an increase in oppression.

It was understandable and right that this tragedy would lead to an increase in political engagement about their rights.

'There was very much a sense that gay [male] politics was running the show,' says academic and writer Sasha Roseneil. 'I could not ever see that [Section 28] was as bad as everybody else said it was. It always seemed a bit hysterical. I had a social constructionist world view, so when they were going on about "pretended families", I was thinking: "Well, aren't all families pretended?"

'I thought that what they were defending was an essential gay identity – you know, the "we can't help it" idea,' says Roseneil. 'Looking back, it was a huge moment because it was when equality politics took centre stage, and it was the moment when historically everything changed.'

Gay men had been unified by the spectre of HIV. Lesbians had not. Lesbians were not at the same risk of HIV, or anywhere close to the same risk. But lesbians, and other women, were not always feminists. Beyond sexism, an age-old and unglamorous affliction that did not inspire political engagement, there was no single issue to unify us. Perhaps because of this, many lesbians joined in with gay men politically and culturally, because there was an obvious point to build a movement around.

Power refers to what then happened next as 'Munchausen's HIV'. Some lesbians began to use dental dams and talk about how to avoid HIV transmission, despite the almost nil risk to them of contracting the virus. In 1994 a group called Positive Strength was set up by a lesbian in Manchester to give support to other lesbians with HIV. The group advertised in the gay press and reportedly received 400 responses from HIV-positive lesbians. However, it soon became clear that the founder of the group was lying about herself being HIV positive and had only received two responses from other dykes – one who was an intravenous drug user and another who had become infected after heterosexual sex. When it was discovered that the whole episode was a sham, many gay men reacted angrily, accusing lesbians of jumping on the Aids bandwagon.[33]

That same year tensions between the two camps increased as Gay Pride approached, with arguments between the organisers about whether to provide a women-only tent. Personally, I had stopped going after the parade became dominated with roller-skating nuns and SM leather queens.

An article in *MX*, a scene freesheet available in gay clubs and bars, ran an article on 9 September 1994 entitled 'Dicks & Dykes Divided?' It opened with a complaint about the women-only tent at the 1994 Pride march. 'How on earth,' asked *MX*'s editor, Tony Claffey, 'can they [lesbians] feel threatened by men who fancy other men? Do they really think we want to mess with them?' Claffey then went on to march where angels fear to tread. 'If dykes desire women so much, why don't they want to look like women? Bull dykes eat as much as possible, wear no makeup and try to grow moustaches.' He pointed out: 'If you go to a pub frequented by militant dykes, there's bound to be a fight at some stage in order for them to decide who's the toughest. At one pub in London, it's such a regular occurrence that the management are thinking of having a Fight of the Week.'

OutRage! and the Lesbian Avengers

The battle lines had been drawn. It seemed there was a growing gulf between lesbians and gay men. This was reflected in the difference in the aims of two gay rights groups: OutRage!, run and formed by gay men, and Lesbian Avengers, which was a women-only direct action group.

OutRage! was formed in 1990 after the murder of gay actor Michael Boothe the previous year. The first OutRage! action was on 7 June 1990 at Hyde Park public toilets to protest against the Metropolitan police's entrapment of gay men cruising. Peter Tatchell was one of the founder members.

'One of our key demands from the police was protection, not persecution,' says Tatchell. 'It was about asserting our right to engage in consensual sex without being bullied by the state.'

Lesbian Avengers was founded in 1994 and had a somewhat different agenda to OutRage! Describing itself in its mission statement as a 'non-violent direct action group committed to raising lesbian visibility and fighting for our survival and our lives', one of its campaigning aims was to 'combat lesbian chic'. It was also concerned with equal immigration rights for gay partners, education, healthcare for lesbians, and parenting and fostering rights. It's not very chic having your children taken away or losing your job.

The women of Lesbian Avengers raided gay bars and destroyed thousands of copies of *MX* in response to its anti-lesbian article.

'We fucking hated OutRage! and their demands for easier ways to have sex in public and access to younger boys to do it with,' says 'Sally', who asked to remain anonymous as she now works for a governmental department. 'The Avengers was set up to assert the rights of lesbians to challenge gay male domination of the entire so-called queer movement.'

Novelist Stephanie Theobold told the *Guardian* in 2009: '[I was] with the recently founded London chapter of the Lesbian Avengers. Clad in our Lesbian Avenger T-shirts [slogan: 'We recruit'], 30 of us ran out to the statue of Queen Victoria in front of Buckingham Palace and unfurled a banner that bore the message "The Lesbian Avengers are not amused".'

So where are we now?

Two decades on, then, with the depoliticisation of lesbianism and the entrenchment of essentialist theories of sexuality, lesbians have, in a way, ended up back in the 1970s and are accepting a return to a monolithic movement. So-called lesbian 'elders' or role models are more likely to define themselves as 'gay women' than lesbians. The lesbian movement is still fractured; there is no single issue on the horizon to provide a rallying point.

Now, as then, there are areas of feminist politics that overlap with gay identity and rights, and there is sometimes a clash between the opinions and desires of gay men and lesbians. This is likely because many gay men, like many straight men, are taught to believe that feminist struggles are not necessarily relevant to their lives. Therefore, when they promote institutions like marriage and the military in the name of promoting gay rights, there can be a backlash from lesbian activists who see these institutions as anti-feminist.

Often, gay men and lesbians simply have separate agendas. There are advantages in taking on the shared struggles together, but a joint movement is not possible until feminism and women are regarded as equal partners. The main tendency of gay men has been not to notice that lesbians have a different struggle altogether, or indeed that women have been seriously oppressed. Gay men have pursued their interests: upholding masculinity and their own sexual pleasures, and so on. So they have very different things to fight for.

There are noticeable failures of many gay men to join in the fight against lesbian issues that are plainly a matter of morality. Punishment rapes are clearly utterly unacceptable and yet there is no conspicuous gay male support.

There are still things that bond us. Facing prejudice and rejecting traditional sexual orientation are shared experiences. But where we once both challenged traditional gender stereotypes, many have stopped doing so, as we became increasingly tolerated and as the heterosexual world was generally less polarised. Hetero- and homosexual people alike have become ever more conservative, thus the definition of 'normal' has been extended to anything that isn't radical.

Because lesbians face the double oppression of sexism and anti-lesbianism, is the only way for lesbians to achieve liberation to become active feminists and leave gay liberation to the boys? Gay rights don't do us any good. Women have a lot to gain by challenging patriarchy, but do gay men? And what of the young lesbians with rights handed to them on a plate with a sense of entitlement? What is in it for them to challenge patriarchy? And what of gay men? It used to be a positive thing for gay men to challenge machismo, but not when they live within that structure.

I ask Jane Czyzselska, editor of *Diva*, the only national magazine in the UK for lesbians, what she thinks lesbians and gay men have in common.

'I think that some gay men and lesbians share in common experiences of discrimination based on their sexuality and transgressive gender expression, but this is mediated by other factors such as class, race, age, disability, etc,' says Czyzselska. 'But I do think that we can make connections with gay men along other less conventionally "political" lines, such as a shared ethical/spiritual value systems and so on.'

Czyzselska prefers the term 'lesbophobia' to describe anti-lesbian bigotry, saying that it is the 'double whammy of sexism and homophobia, experienced by women who are punished for transgressing heteronormative gender behaviours and expectations'. Lesbophobia, says Czyzselska, can lead to a variety of psychological responses, including self-harm, mental health issues, substance misuse and eating disorders.

Stonewall's Prescription for Change survey of lesbian and bisexual women's health, published in 2008, highlights how lesbians are more likely to develop anger issues, depression, anxiety and suicidal ideation than their straight counterparts, particularly those who are isolated, with no or limited family support, and those who live in areas where LB resources are minimal or non-existent.[34] They are also more at risk of potential sexual exploitation.

However, it is also evident, says Czyzselska, that some young activists are more resilient and politically engaged because of the greater visibility and legal protections afforded to them today.

Czyzselska acknowledges that some 'politically engaged' gay men are aware that lesbians face additional prejudice, but 'there are some, however, who tend to misogyny, who are themselves sexist and who seem to be blind to the ways in which all women are positioned as subordinate to men. Generally, there is a surprising level of misogyny among men, regardless of their sexuality, and I suspect that some of it is unconscious.'

Lesbians are seen, in some ways, as less offensive to mainstream society. 'When people see two men in love, they only think of them having sex. They don't treat lesbians seriously because they don't understand how women can have sex without a man, without a penis.'

One significant difference that has been identified between lesbians and gay men is that of the visibility of the ageing population.

Jane Traies conducted a research project about older lesbians, 'The Lives of British Lesbians Over Sixty', based at Sussex University. The first ever comprehensive picture of older lesbian life in the UK, Traies argues that older lesbians are under-represented not only in popular culture and the media, but also in academic research, hidden from view by a particular conjunction of prejudices that renders them unrepresentable. 'When deep-rooted sexist and heterosexist attitudes combine with ageism, a cultural "black hole" develops into which old women who are also lesbians disappear completely.'

A study of LGBT people over 50 in 2002, despite the intentions of the researchers to have an equal gender balance, ended up with twice as many men as women. They suggest several possible reasons why older lesbians were difficult to access – for example, 'older lesbians may have particular concerns about "going public" about their sexuality, and experience greater pressures to conceal their sexual identities.'[35]

The implication here is that older lesbians are not only made invisible by cultural discourse but are hiding by choice. The authors of the study conclude: 'Further research on experiences of old age by lesbians is an urgent priority.'

TV writer and *Bad Girls* creator Maureen Chadwick agrees. Blaming prejudice and ignorance towards her subject matter, she says she has been shocked by some of the attitudes towards her play *The Speed Twins* about older lesbians in a revived Gateways, the famous lesbian club. 'One art director said that, had *The Speed Twins* been about older male homosexuals, it would have been OK, but that lesbians are very hard to find an audience for. There's also a deep prejudice about older women, as if their lives and experiences are irrelevant. So I have the double whammy of lesbianism and age to contend with.'

According to Chadwick and a number of other interviewees, getting lesbian issues aired in the arts is far more difficult than gay male ones, not because of straight male bigotry but because gay men rule the arts.

Certainly, representation of gay men in popular and high culture is far more advanced than that of lesbians. The sitcom *Vicious*, starring Sir Ian McKellen and Sir Derek Jacobi, broadcast in early 2013, was notable for being the first time a gay couple had been cast at the fore of an ITV comedy. But what makes the show even more unusual is its incidental portrayal of the characters' sexuality. They are not presented as funny because they are gay. They are apparently funny because they are old.

Conclusion

So, have we entered an era of no sexual politics? Why are the majority of feminists today heterosexual and seemingly keen to get men directly involved in a movement that derives its strength from autonomy? In the lesbian and gay liberation movement, such as it remains today, is it possible for both camps to work together despite the decades of acrimony, suspicion, betrayal and, crucially, the apparent lack of concern on the part of gay men about the misogyny that hinders the lives of every single lesbian, despite the victories of late? As feminism filters through all strands of society, it is obvious that gay men are influenced by it as much and as little as other men. But gay culture remains, essentially, hostile to women.

A number of survey respondents believe that lesbians and gay men experience prejudice differently, with many explaining the reason why as inequality between men and women and the therefore institutionalised power that gay men have in relation to lesbians.

- 'I think the idea of the flamboyant, creative gay man is much more accepted than the stereotypical view of lesbians. Hetero women tend to be more acceptant towards gay men, but not as much of lesbian women. Again, I think both are a challenge for hetero men' – gay male
- 'Male gays endure more physical violence and threats of violence than females because violent young straight men may be insecure in their own sexuality. Gay women are less of a threat – more of a pornographic curiosity – to such young men' – gay male
- 'I think lesbians are often perceived as less threatening and more titillating and their sexuality denied or derided by some heterosexual men (and women); I also think they are less likely to be physically threatened compared to gay men, who face more violent prejudice and a greater likelihood of physical attack' – lesbian
- 'Gay men have it easier. They are more visible in the media, more common (I think – maybe I'm wrong), and male sexuality is more accepted (ie men are studs; women are sluts)' – lesbian
- 'Homophobia against lesbians is exacerbated by sexism. Lesbians are stereotyped on a misogynist basis' – lesbian
- 'From a man's point of view, I could always accept lesbianism. It's a male fantasy for many of us. Two men together, though, all hot and sweaty, etc, is a sexual turn-off for me. I feel no threat or

revulsion, just not my cuppa. I also feel no guilt about speaking the truth for myself' – straight male

Perhaps as we move towards full legal and social emancipation, there will no longer be a need for the two groups to be as one and we will drift back into our distinct and separate camps. However, I very much doubt it. Meanwhile, things have not improved much in terms of lesbian-specific rights. For that to happen, we would have to see an end to sexism and the liberation of all women. Gay men do not need anything like as dramatic a shift to ensure their equal rights under patriarchy to other men. So now we see lesbians rally round gay men, blending into their world and playing second fiddle to their needs. In doing so, they legitimise the celebrated aspects of gay male culture – such as pornography, BDSM, prostitution and a tendency towards eroticising the vulnerability of youth – all of which are problematic for the feminist project. In the same way that heterosexual women collude with their own oppression by defending and putting up with the bad behaviour of the men around them, so do lesbians with gay men.

Radical feminists were forced to come to the difficult and controversial conclusion, back in the 1970s, that in order to achieve true liberation, we had to untie the apron strings, withdraw from domestic duties that supported men and organise separately. Women departed from leftist groups, dropped marriages and formed collective housing to create autonomous political groups in which to plot the revolution.

Lesbians need to accept that so long as we remain a 'lesbianandgay' community, gay men will be coming out on top as usual. The specific needs of lesbians will be ignored, and lesbians will be encouraged further away from feminism. But feminism is the key to the liberation of both gay men and lesbians because it will, if successful, result in the end of both patriarchy and fixed gender roles. This will mean a loss of power for gay men, but ultimately, the end of the tyranny of masculinity.

Clearly, there still exists rampant bigotry towards lesbians and gay men. But my view is that all women suffer as a result of anti-lesbianism because such bigotry is fuelled by misogyny. Many gay men are misogynistic, and that misogyny affects lesbians, even if not directly targeted at us. Gay men still have male power, and lesbians often revert to our socialised 'type' and run around after our gay brothers, despite the fact that this behaviour is about us always putting ourselves second as women.

Until gay men recognise that they have power over women, despite suffering from bigotry because they are not judged as 'real men' by the straight patriarchs, they will not and cannot be our allies. Until gay men recognise that lesbians suffer the double bind of sexism and anti-lesbianism, and that the two operate together like a pernicious form of social control, we cannot effectively work together in a way that will benefit both groups equally. If the power imbalance between gay men and lesbians continues to be ignored and denied, we really may as well just resign ourselves to making the tea.

CHAPTER 5
MOCKING THE CRADLE?

*Gay Lib does not plead for the right of homosexuals
to marry. Gay Lib questions marriage.*
Jill Tweedie, 1971[36]

I think gay marriage should be between a man and a woman.
Arnold Schwarzenegger, 2003

*You have given me equality where there was sometimes
prejudice. My life will be better today than yesterday.*
Lord Alli, 2013

As a feminist, it is not surprising that I am critical of the institution of marriage. The argument is fairly straightforward: it is a patriarchal institution based on patriarchal notions of ownership and inequality. But surely the institution has shifted and evolved? Is it still reasonable to be so against something that has changed so much, or is it the same but dressed up to look more progressive?

The current preoccupation by much of lesbian and gay society perpetuates the notion that we should all strive to be one half of a cosy, long-term couple and leaves those excluded by that model out in the cold. But does it in fact also lead to the polarised view of 'good gays' and 'bad gays' in which straight folk are encouraged to view only those living together as married couples to be respectable and decent?

The money spent on the campaign for equal marriage and its subsequent implementation could perhaps have been better spent on supporting lesbian and gay people experiencing bullying and discrimination in education and the workplace, or for creating services for the homeless, ill and otherwise disadvantaged. I would argue that, as we reach the point where, for the first time ever, we have an out ageing lesbian and gay population, money and effort would have been better spent ensuring that there are facilities for older people (in particular those without a partner) to have access to residential care suited to their needs, as well as a legal recognition of close friendships and other 'non-marriage-like' relationships.

But isn't gay marriage different? I hear you ask. How can you be against equality?

Well, I am also critical, for similar reasons, of breeding, calling myself 'child-free' rather than 'childless'. I mourn those feminists and other radical activists who, once they sprogged, gave up on trying to change the world and seemed to see little else but their own family unit. As a subversive, I strongly object to the idea that living in a family unit is in any way more natural or superior to less conventional arrangements such as friendship groups or living alone.

The domestication of lesbians and gay men has crept up on us in recent years. We are now represented in sitcoms, TV advertisements, in home makeover programmes, soap operas like *Coronation Street* and fly-on-the-wall documentaries such as *Wedding Stories*. As we have seen in previous chapters, it wasn't always this way. When the Thatcher government introduced Section 28 of the Local Government Act 1988 – the first time that legislation equally targeted gay men and lesbians – the notion of 'pretend families' was conceived. We already had 'rubbish' families, which included single mothers, people on benefits and those with 'problem' children.

But the word 'pretend' suggested that lesbians and gay men were masquerading as families, rather than merely falling short of the standards set by the traditionalists. For many heterosexuals reading the pro-Section 28 propaganda, we were deluded and living in a fantasy land if we honestly believed that what we had, with our coupledom, kids, godparents and pets, could be called a family.

As we touched on in chapter 1, it was a book about gay fatherhood that provided fuel for Section 28. *Jenny Lives with Eric and Martin* describes a few days in the life of Jenny, her father, Eric, and his boyfriend, Martin, who lives with them. In those days it was very hard to be accepted as same-sex parents, even within the gay community.

It was partly because the traditional family was in decline at the time that Section 28 became law; in retrospect, it can be seen as a desperate attempt to boost support for it. Thatcher's 'Family Values' campaign was in response to the perceived erosion of heterosexual family values as they existed circa 1950. Divorce was on the increase, women were – shock, horror – working, kids were being fed convenience food, fathers were increasingly absent, and the extended family was no longer around to do the childcare. The alternative lifestyles promoted by gays and lesbians must have seemed the final nail in the coffin.

How things have changed. Now, you can't move at the school gates these days for lesbian and gay parents dropping off their offspring. Laws and policy on gay adoption and fostering have changed for the better, and reproduction in general has become commercialised and normalised for a group that would have previously felt excluded from the status quo, and may, in some ways, have relished the fact.

Section 28 didn't change anything. People still identified as gay, whether the authorities liked it or not. But as time went on, the tactics changed. Perhaps the way to save the traditional institutions of the family and marriage was to invite lesbians and gay men to join the party, rather than to exclude them. Meanwhile, the notion that sexuality is innate – based, as we saw in chapter 3, on no scientific proof whatsoever – appeased the traditionalists into no longer worrying that we would recruit our own children into the gay cesspit.

Maybe it was because our home life was attacked that we then made it our mission to convince the world that we lived in real families and subsequently realised that we needed the legal protection to do so.

In the 1970s lesbian mothers were demonised as the root of all evil. Their 'unnatural acts' meant that if they entered a custody battle with an ex-partner, even if it were established that he was violent, they would rarely be awarded custody of their children.

It was very unusual for lesbians to procreate in those days, although the turkey baster was occasionally dragged out of hibernation from a kitchen drawer and used for self-insemination purposes. Buying sperm from a clinic or private source was unheard of, whereas today gay publications and websites are awash with advertisements for them, and there are several annual alternative parenting-type events plugging commercial reproduction.

Back in the day, lesbians would more often than not call upon the services of gay male friends to make a donation to help create a lesbian family. The father rarely asked even for visiting rights.

I recall one hilarious car journey up the motorway with a friend who was trying to get pregnant. She had arranged to meet the donor in a service station, and when he appeared from the loo with a sterilised pill bottle, she ran to the ladies', where she sat for 10 minutes in a cubicle with her legs in the air while desperate travellers knocked on the door.

Fortunately, nowadays there are other options available to lesbian and gay would-be parents. Though some of these are not without controversy.

The price of pregnancy

Children's homes are full to bursting with the abused, neglected and unwanted cast-offs of heterosexuality, and yet increasing numbers of lesbians and gay men are making their own – often spending huge amounts of money to do so. These days surrogacy is fast becoming the parenting method of choice for gay men. Since the very public use of a surrogate by British gay couple Barrie and Tony Drewitt-Barlow in 1999, the association between homosexuality and surrogacy has been cemented. Further, the decision by this couple to open the British Surrogacy Centre with a very public emphasis on gay and lesbian surrogacy shows the strength of the relationship between homosexuality and surrogacy, and highlights what was also apparent in the rise of homosexual sex toys: the gay community is willing to invest in the businesses that further their global freedoms and cause, and this is why these areas of western culture are increasingly becoming gay-dominated.

When the Drewitt-Barlows returned from the US with their first set of surrogate twins, Saffron and Aspen, they were 'inundated with requests' from other gay people wishing to have children via such methods. The couple referred those requests to the US-based British Surrogacy Centre and began to work with the organisation as advisers. Following on from their work with the US-based clinic, the Drewitt-Barlows opened the UK branch of the British Surrogacy Centre in 2011 to 'provide assistance' to lesbian and gay couples. They claim that 'couples in this country are being ripped off by greedy lawyers charging up to £50,000' to have both names on a birth certificate.

Barrie Drewitt-Barlow, CEO of the British Surrogacy Centre, told me that because he and his partner, Tony, were turned down for fostering children in the early 1990s, they decided to take the surrogacy route and have never looked back. 'I now think, "To hell with them – if they don't want me, then I don't want to help them."'

The aim of the British Surrogacy Centre, according to Barrie Drewitt-Barlow, is to 'give the opportunity to all couples and singles to become parents regardless of their sexuality, race, age or religious belief'. It is cleverly phrased like a mission statement from a human rights organisation.

It has been estimated that the number of children nationwide living with at least one gay parent in the US ranges from 6 to 14 million.[37] The American Academy of Pediatrics released a statement that there are more similarities than differences in the way homosexuals and heterosexuals raise their children, and that children are just as well adjusted in families of gay parents as they are when brought up in heterosexual families.

'We helped our first gay couple become parents in 1999, when most agencies around the world would not even consider working with a gay couple. From the period 1999 to 2012 the team behind the British Surrogacy Centre have helped countless gay couples and single gay men become parents through surrogacy. The British Surrogacy Centre believe that the desire to become a parent is the same for all couples, regardless of sexual orientation.'[38]

There is no law to prevent surrogacy in the UK, but it is illegal for surrogates to advertise as they do in the US. Surrogacy agreements are currently permitted but are not legally binding. Family judges will make decisions based solely on the best interests of the child. For instance, in 2011 a surrogate mother won the right to retain custody of her daughter after backing out from a surrogacy agreement with a wealthy couple. The surrogate mother claimed that, during the pregnancy, the woman planning to adopt her child had confessed that her husband was controlling and violent. Justice Jonathan Baker ruled that it was in the best interests of the child to remain with her biological mother.

In the US surrogacy falls under the legal jurisdiction of individual states. While some states prohibit surrogacy agreements, such as Michigan, which imposes a maximum penalty of a $50,000 (£30,000) fine and up to five years in jail for forming such contracts, in other states – most notably California – pre-birth commercial surrogacy agreements are fully legally enforceable and regularly upheld by the courts.

As the British Surrogacy Centre is quick to point out, there has never been a case in which the UK has refused entry to a child born abroad through a surrogacy agreement.

The 'gayby' revolution is booming. Although surrogacy and related fertility services are still accessed mainly by heterosexual couples, gay men are increasingly demanding equity. Known by some critics as 'reproductive trafficking', surrogacy is an ethical minefield. Heterosexuals will use their own eggs and sperm, but will rent a womb for the gestation, whereas gay men will need to use in vitro fertilisation (IVF) and the eggs from a donor in order to impregnate the surrogate.

IVF was developed as a response to infertility in the 1970s, with the first so-called 'test tube baby' being born in 1978. None of the major religions had, in 1978, an official policy on artificial insemination, but the Roman Catholic church raised the strongest objections at the time.

The Human Fertilisation and Embryology Authority, which regulates infertility and IVF clinics in the UK, says that any offer of treatment using a surrogate mother and IVF would be governed by strict guidelines. Nevertheless, for many, choosing an egg donor with the type of looks, character traits and abilities you would like your child to have is seen as a built-in perk of the IVF process.

Class and racial divisions between surrogates, egg donors and the intended parents are stark. Surrogates tend to be working class and to have already had their own children, whereas the egg donor will likely be a college student from an upper-class background who is considered bright and attractive. They generally earn significantly more than the surrogates, who are often poor women from India or the Ukraine who might receive as little as £3,000 for renting out their womb for nine months. Even in the UK, as Drewitt-Barlow says: 'Surrogacy is regulated by law and the maximum expense to [the surrogate mother] is £15,000.'.

In 2007 the Fertility Institute in Los Angeles announced that, due to popular demand, it would be running a programme aimed at providing surrogacy services to gay men. It immediately began to receive numerous inquiries from male couples in Britain who were thinking of having surrogate children. The programme is the first specialist surrogacy scheme dedicated to two-father families.

Many of the gay men who are opting to use surrogacy as a means of reproducing have had bad experiences of the fostering and adoption process. No one can deny that prejudice towards lesbian and gay applicants for adoption still exists, despite changes in the law, but the growing acceptance and popularity of the rent-a-womb industry has resulted in exploitation, mainly because of the large sums of money involved in surrogacy.

Making babies the lesbian way has also become increasingly commercialised, even though lesbians used to say that two advantages of not being heterosexual were never having to worry about unplanned pregnancy and not having the expectation of motherhood hanging over our heads. Consequently, a number of commercial options for lesbians who wish to procreate have popped up in recent years. There are clinics offering IVF, anonymous and known sperm donor services for single lesbians and couples, egg donor, egg swap (for lesbian couples who wish to carry a partner's biological baby) and surrogacy services.

There are of course ethical issues to consider with the purchasing of such services. Until recently India was the destination of choice for gay couples looking to land themselves a surrogate – offering a far cheaper alternative to the US – which amounted to shocking exploitation.[39] The British Surrogacy Centre commissioned a study in 2009 in India, where there were almost 400 clinics providing surrogacy services to couples from the UK and elsewhere, to look at the exploitative practices used by a number of establishments. It found that in the poorer, rural areas of India, families who have multiple daughters and are struggling to find them husbands are selling their elder daughters to trafficking gangs and pimps. They are then taken to the cities to become surrogates, enabling them to earn the money required by the family for dowries for younger siblings.

Nowadays, however, recent legislation passed in India stipulates that prospective parents looking to engage a surrogate must be 'man and woman [who] are duly married and the marriage should be sustained at least two years'.

Other ethical issues exist – for example, egg transplantation can be painful and cause health problems for the donor, and many of the women recruited to be gestational surrogates are pressurised into doing so by abusive partners or, as we have seen, exploited by criminal gangs for commercial gain.[40] In addition, gestational surrogates are required to take Lupron, oestrogen and progesterone medication to help achieve the pregnancy, all of which can carry serious side effects.

Hannah Latham, publisher and editor of the magazine *We Are Family*, which offers help and advice for LGBT families, ensures that she promotes adoption and fostering as well as IVF, sperm donor services and surrogacy in the magazine. Latham is shocked when I tell her about the appalling attitudes of some of the gay men I have interviewed about their choice to use cheap surrogacy services, such as suggesting that surrogates should be 'grateful' for the opportunity to earn 'substantial amounts of money' despite living in developing countries (in the case of two separate interviewees who accessed surrogates from India); or believing, as one British gay man said, that it would be good for the surrogate to know her baby would be raised in a rich household; or insisting, as one couple informed me, that their babies be born via C-section so that they did not have to come into contact with a vagina.

One of the biggest commercial outlets providing reproductive services is the London Women's Clinic. Its website reads: 'Fertility treatment will be considered for any patient, irrespective of social status or sexual orientation, provided applicants meet the stated medical criteria of the clinic. Thus, heterosexual couples, lesbians, gay couples, single women and women with transsexual partners will be considered equally for treatment.'[41]

Could we be forgiven for mistaking this commercial service for a liberation campaign blurb?

Pretend families?

Perhaps it is understandable that so many lesbian and gays are opting for IVF and surrogacy rather than adoption and fostering. There is still prejudice towards lesbian and gay parents today, despite the change in the law that came into force in 2003.

Some gay men have told me that the reaction from even good liberal folk to the notion of their having children is one of suspicion and a lack of understanding. There are those who will assume that dark, ulterior motives are involved in the decision. Barrie Drewitt-Barlow had a similar experience, saying: 'Ten years ago everyone thought we were a pair of paedophiles. They could not get their heads around a gay couple wanting to be parents.'

My eyes were opened to just how much of a threat lesbianism was to the patriarchal order back in the early 1980s when I attended a meeting to support lesbian mothers in danger of losing children in custody battles. One lesbian mother I knew at the time, who lost her four-year-old son to her former husband, tells me that 30 years later she still recalls the exact look on the judge's face as he awarded sole care of her child to a man who had never been an involved father. 'That judge had asked me what I did in bed, and whether [her son] had ever been in the room when I was having sex with my lover,' she remembers.

Fast-forward to the present day and how attitudes have changed – officially, at least: as ever, legislation is ahead of much of society. In September 2013 a vicar refused to baptise the baby of a lesbian couple when they both asked to be registered as mothers.[42] So there is still a way to go.

But never mind others' attitudes – what does this revolution in gay parenting mean for us?

We do know the consequences of children being brought up by loving and stable lesbian and gay parents, because there are enough examples around for us to judge. Many of my lesbian friends have children, and some have chosen gay men to be the co-parent. Without exception these children appear to be well balanced and happy. However, the fact remains that these days I regularly feel more judged and pitied for not having children than I do for being a lesbian. Several child-free friends say they feel the same. Will the fact that so many of us are tied down by nappies and childcare mean that we will forget to be activists and retreat further into our own selfish world, or will creating more children brought up in alternative families result in a better world for all? There is a possibility that children brought up by same-sex parents will result in an attitude shift in a lot of society, but consider, too, that there will be a reduction in the radical activism that reduces prejudice and bigotry.

The passing in 2004 of the Civil Partnership Act brought some lesbians and gay men institutionally much closer to the traditional heterosexual lifestyle and marked a significant shift in public understandings of the notion of a conjugal couple.

Have we now reached a stage where being a 'sexual outlaw' and maintaining the 'only gay in the village' mentality has no place in a society that has granted (almost) full legal and civil protection and acceptance of same-sex relationships? Did we always want to be part of the landscape rather than a thorn in the side of normality?

The contemporary gay rights movement, epitomised by Stonewall, no longer sees a gay lifestyle as a countercultural challenge to heterosexuality, but rather asks that gays be merely tolerated. Rights for gays to join the military, marry in church and raise children are the main campaigning issues. Challenging the accepted family practices of the previously solely straight world is barely mentioned, and the movement, the gay community and the straight community are weaker for the absence of criticism. It is not that radical politics is necessarily right about everything, but that intelligent discussion of family life, work-life balance and capitalist exploitation serves us all.

The campaign for equal marriage was unlike any other in recent history in that it did not involve public displays of anger, such as placard-waving and shouting slogans through megaphones. There were no marches through cities or abseiling into the parliament debating chamber. There was no need for protest. Even of the bigots, all we were asking for was to be like them, and to be given legal assistance to curtail our dangerous ways. Imitation is flattery, after all.

Data on the new family

So just how common are civil partnerships and same-sex parenting? The number of civil partnerships in the UK peaked in the first quarter of 2006 at 4,869. This was because many same-sex couples in longstanding relationships took advantage of the opportunity to formalise their relationship as soon as the legislation was implemented, the previous December. The number of civil partnership formations has since decreased, fluctuating between 6,200 and 7,200 per year since 2008. Initially the numbers of males forming civil partnerships were much higher than females, but the numbers of male and female civil partnerships converged in 2009 and 2010.

The latest Office for National Statistics figures show that civil partnerships in the UK reached an all-time high (with the exception of 2006) in 2012, seven years after the Civil Partnership Act came into effect. In 2012 there were 7,037 civil partnerships, an increase of 3.6 per cent on 2011.

The average age to form a civil partnership has been decreasing year on year, as older couples who had been waiting for the legislation took the opportunity to form a civil partnership early on. The most common age group for men and women to form a civil partnership in 2012 was 30 to 34. There were more female civil partners in the younger age groups (under 40) and more male civil partners in the older age groups (40 and over).

London has consistently proved to be the most popular area to form a civil partnership, with 25 per cent of all civil partnerships in 2012 registered there, while the Brighton and Hove unitary authority has also been popular.

Unsurprisingly, the number of gay and lesbian couples bringing up children has risen by 8 per cent since 2012. In 2012 there were 12,000 same-sex couples bringing up children, and one year later there were 13,000. This new normalcy is considered to be wholly positive by the majority of the lesbian and gay population, it would seem. Certainly I have barely ever seen or heard any critique of lesbians and gay men opting into the heterosexual model of the family unit.

A new form of family life?

The *Telegraph* is not noted for its love of the alternative family. On 31 October 2013, under the headline 'Sharp Rise in Number of Cohabiting gay couples', it wrote: 'The number of same-sex couples living together outside of a civil partnership has increased by almost a third since last year, according to figures published by the Office for National Statistics.' This rightwing publication was a little bit 'tut, tut' about our living over the brush. Civil partnerships had become not just accepted but respectable. The article's accompanying photograph, posed by models, was as sickly and off-putting as any picket-fence vision of idealised heterosexual family life – a couple (for these purposes, lesbian) having breakfast together while the stay-at-home housewife (depicted by her apron) poured coffee for her partner in their sunny kitchen. The gender roles had been preserved in the ideal; the genitalia was simply matching. It's progress, but only of a sort.

Sasha Roseneil came out as a lesbian in her teens and is today one of the leading academics on the evolution of family structures and friendship. In a talk given at the British Library in December 2012 and entitled 'Queering Home and Family in the 1980s: The Greenham Common Women's Peace Camp', Roseneil argued that the women living at Greenham Common in the 1980s subverted the traditional family and it is important that, in the light of the recent move by lesbians and gays towards the 'family', we keep them in our thoughts.[43]

Roseneil's research has found that friendship groups can be more supportive than biological family members and has closely examined the move away from the 'traditional' family set up by heterosexuals. I ask her what she thinks, in the light of her argument that straight people are becoming more alternative than gays, about whether she feels a sense of loss towards the dwindling radical edge of the movement since the gay migration towards respectable family life.

'Every movement of social transformation needs its radical edge and its not-so-radical edge. So it needed the crazy lesbians and GLF boys and girls [as well as] its more reformist movement,' says Roseneil, remaining upbeat about the changes.

While acknowledging that there is a persuasive critique of normalisation that sees it as a complete sellout, Roseneil argues that such a shift is positive progress that has improved the everyday lives of many lesbians and gay men. 'Most people can't live their lives as political activists. While gay marriage has never been my thing, it is a good thing,' she says.

Nevertheless, Roseneil agrees that there are losses associated with normalisation: 'Such as the secret world I inhabited, which isn't there any more because lesbians and gay men won't be facing exclusion and marginalisation.'

Some feminists have argued that allowing same-sex couples to marry diminishes its patriarchal power.[44] Roseneil agrees, and adds that the meaning of marriage has diminished as fewer people embark on it, at least in the straight world.

'The latest projection is that the majority of children will soon be born out of wedlock, aside from those with lesbian parents,' she adds, laughing. 'There is no one meaning of marriage any more, but it still is the gold standard in relationships and has that cachet; it still feels like permanence for people, though.'

Does Roseneil, a lifelong radical and lesbian rights activist, think that extending marriage to gay people is true progress?

'It is not my idea of a pinnacle of gay rights. I said in 1999 that gay marriage was an inevitability. Those people who were coming into power [Labour] were not homophobic. The world was changing. I had heard stories of Peter Mandelson dancing at Heaven in his spangly shorts.'

Paula Ettelbrick, who died in 2011, was a US-based lesbian feminist activist and human rights lawyer. Ettelbrick had long argued that the LGBT community should be pressing for social and legal changes to support alternative family structures. 'Marriage is a great institution – if you like living in institutions,' she wrote in 1993, in her paper 'Since When is Marriage a Path to Liberation?', a feminist critique of how the institution of marriage had historically constrained the freedom and rights of women.[45]

Similarly, for Roseneil, one thing that has got lost in the shift from 'queer' to 'respectable' is a radical analysis of gender roles. 'There has been a diminution of the worst aspects of patriarchy and of heteronormativity, but not with gender equality. The changes in what has happened around sexuality are much more evident.'

Sheila Jeffreys is equally dismayed at the move by gay men and lesbians into married respectability. 'I'm puzzled because even women I know who were lesbian feminists of the last generation are getting married,' she says. 'I'm completely puzzled by it because I've been with the same woman for 27 years and we have absolutely no intention of getting married, and it would be horrifying to think of that. But eventually there will be serious financial penalties if we do not.

'In Australia, in order to promote civil partnership-type legislation and the fact that lesbians and gays were now going to be seen as equal to heterosexuals, they had an advertisement from the state [with a photograph] of a toothglass on a sink with two toothbrushes in it. It said: "Remember that if you have, up until now, received benefits or a pension as a single person but if you live with a person of the same sex, you must register at your benefits or pensions office and tell them." It doesn't say – the small print – "And your money will be lowered." That's it, folks! It's a huge benefit. And they did it with this nice little toothglass and toothbrushes. It's supposed to be equal rights, but it's equal rights to have less money and not to be treated as independent human beings because that is who we are. So no, I have never gone for marriage.'

Legal changes

In 2008 Ailbe Egan gave a speech at a LINC (Lesbians in Cork) 'Same-Sex Marriage' seminar in Cork, which was published as an edited speech in the *Belfast Telegraph*.[46] She described the problems that came with only one parent having rights over the child, as she was raised by two women. One mother could be registered as a parent and had legal rights, and the other did not. This caused fundamental problems: 'If Fiona, my biological mam, goes away for a few days, my other mother can't sign my permission slips for school or consent forms should I need medical treatment.'

In 2009, following a campaign by Stonewall, the law was changed to allow women in same-sex relationships to register both their names on the birth certificate of a child born from fertility treatment. From April 2010, with the introduction of the Equality Act, it became a legal requirement that same-sex couples are treated on an equal basis to opposite-sex couples.

As a result of the new legislation, same-sex couples, including civil partners, are legally recognised as parents of children conceived during their relationship from the moment of conception. Previously, same-sex partners had to apply to adopt a child born within that relationship in order to become a legal parent.

Same-sex couples were afforded the same rights to parenthood as heterosexuals with the introduction of the Human Fertilisation and Embryology Act 2008 when registering their child's birth conceived using donor sperm or embryos.

In October 2013 the court of appeal ruled that legislation that makes adoption by gay and unmarried couples illegal was unlawful in itself. Despite that, Stormont's health minister, Edwin Poots, responded by planning to go to the supreme court to overturn that ruling. While couples are having their own children by IVF, this law prevents gay and unmarried couples in Northern Ireland raising children who are already here. In the BBC story reporting this, the article mentioned the argument that 'children needed both male and female role models'. Poots himself cited a nebulous need for 'stability'.[47]

Despite these objections, the many recent legislative changes that allow and enable lesbians and gay men to have children, either biologically or otherwise, are seen as wholly positive by liberal-thinking people, despite the fact that some of the methods used to enable it – such as surrogacy – are ethically questionable. It is as though, because of the prejudice and discrimination experienced in the past (and, to an extent, present), gays hold the moral high ground however they choose to have children, and, indeed, simply by *having* them.

Into the mainstream

It's certainly true that these days gay parenting has permeated the mainstream. In 2011 and 2012 the 'Family' supplement of the *Guardian* carried a weekly column called 'The Three of Us' by gay soap actor Charlie Condou.[48] Condou and his partner, Cameron, parent their two children together. In his first column Condou wrote: 'I used to have a fantasy about being a father. It involved me gently lifting my sleeping child from the car and carrying her upstairs to her bed. I would imagine the small weight in my arms and the soft breath on my neck, even the feel of her hair on my face.'

Condou shares responsibility for parenting not just with his partner, but with the children's mother, his friend Catherine Kanter. They had agreed that if she did not find a suitable partner by the time she was 40, they would have a child together. 'Catherine and I had the conversation I'm sure thousands of women have with their gay friends, a sort of plan-B act – to have a child together should Mr Right not appear.'

Lesbian and gay parenting are becoming the norm. In fact, Kanter's father was understanding of the situation because he'd already heard a similar storyline on *The Archers*.

Same-sex parenting is not just featured in national newspaper columns and radio soap plotlines; there are now publications and even a magazine targeted specifically at lesbian parents.

When Hannah Latham was pregnant, she felt as if she and her partner, Rowena, were the only people in the world in their situation. So she started up *We Are Family* to help other LGBT families feel less isolated. 'I always felt the desire to have children, since I was very young. I didn't see why being a lesbian should prevent me from fulfilling my dream,' said Latham. 'I do want to be able to make it easier for gay couples to have a family, though.'

I asked Latham to elaborate on why she thought there was a need for such a magazine.

'As lesbians, we needed a guidebook on parenting. I could see from Mumsnet that lesbians were crying out for information, but there was nothing out there.'

Certainly we know the numbers of lesbian and gay couples who are raising children or have them within the relationship are on the rise. Adoption is on the increase, and lesbians and gay men are swelling the numbers. It would seem that, since the introduction of civil partnerships, couples are, as is traditional, completing the heterosexual equation by adding children. Indeed, Condou faced criticism of this sort, saying that one friend 'accused us of trying to fit into some kind of heterosexual stereotype'.

There has yet to be research into whether the introduction of civil partnerships has led those couples who enter into the contract to be more likely to have children, but certainly it makes sense that it does.

It was not always like this. In the old days of the GLF its members developed a critique of the nuclear family and its trappings. As Peter

Tatchell recalls: '[Having children] is a really good indicator about how social mores and expectations can affect your behaviours and desire. In the days of the GLF I can hardly recall any LGBT person who wanted to have children, hardly any. They weren't against children, but just didn't want to have them. But now it's gone full circle. A very sizeable portion of LGBT people think that without children they are not complete and having children makes them a proper family. This is really a statement of the extent to which the LGBT community has imbibed heterosexual norms and values.'

Did he see that there were any intrinsic problems with heterosexuality as it was functioning then, or was it just a desire to have more options and choices?

'We saw heterosexuality and the traditional family as a problem, as an issue, as something that needs to change for the benefit of both the LBGT people but also for straights as well. Our view was that the word "equality" hardly ever passed our lips; we were predominately concerned with liberation and that meant transforming society; we never wanted to be part of what was. We wanted to change the existing laws, values and institutions to liberate everybody, whatever their sexuality. We were highly critical of the nuclear family, marriage and monogamy. In our view, if we merely argued for equality, we would in effect be accepting the status quo and merely seeking our place within it, so to the GLF that was not liberation, that was conformism.'

Maybe the recent gayby boom is partly an unconscious reaction against bigotry, particularly the painful fact that many bigots consider gay people unsafe around children? Or is it simply down to the fact that the mechanics are now easier?

Patrick Osborne is 42 and works in financial services. Australian by birth, Osborne currently lives alone and is involved in a number of LGBT campaigns within his working environment.

'Twenty years ago it would have been seen as really naff to be for gay marriage, but now it is like a badge of honour to be seen to be into it, for gays and straights,' says Osborne. 'But something I have seen really change in my lifetime is gays having kids, and I think it is due to IVF.'

Television programmes also reflect the shift in norms. In *The Good Life*, there were two childless couples and it was never mentioned.

In *Man About the House*, babies were equally never discussed. By the time we get to its spin-off series, *George and Mildred*, all of a sudden there were several baby-hungry props, for a woman who is nearly 50. A few years later, after the invention of IVF, having a baby became a consumer item because you could pay to have it.

'We are far more judged now for not having children than being gay,' says Osborne. 'There is something wrong with you if you don't have them. I find very small children extremely uninteresting. Lots of men want to know how to live a heterosexual life as opposed to "How do we live as ourselves?" These men with kids want a slice of patriarchal privilege. I see the people at work with photos of their kids on their desks. If it is a man, he is a good and responsible dad. If it is a woman, she is a lightweight.'

Equality in legislation still often has the result, then, of being expressed just as it ever was in a patriarchal society.

Parents versus non-parents

So it seems it's children who drive the biggest wedge between us these days. Do we divide more naturally into 'parent/non-parent' camps than 'gay/straight'? The responses to my survey seem to bear this out. I asked the heterosexuals who had said they don't have many gay friends why this is so and had the following responses:

- 'Have children now, so fewer gay friends' – male heterosexual
- 'Because we had children. Used to be more before' – female heterosexual
- 'I'm a new parent, which has moved us into straighter circles. Also, my workplace is rather conservative' – male heterosexual
- 'We tend to meet people through the school playground via our children; as such, our friendship groups have a bias towards "traditional" heterosexual family structures. It's also a middle-class area of the Midlands where same-sex couples are less likely to raise their children' – male heterosexual

These responses show how children are the key to entering the more traditionally conservative strands of society; without them, it is much harder to be accepted.

Sasha Roseneil believes that the most discernible difference in people's lives today is not between being gay or straight, but whether or not we have children.

'Lesbians and gays who have children – what is the difference between their lives and straight people who have children? The "procreative norm" seems to be one of the most unchanged factors – unlike gender norms. What's changed is how people might procreate, but the imperative to procreate and the fact that to reproduce yourself remains vitally important.

'You are now much more judged for not having children than for being a lesbian. People feel sorry for you, whereas they don't tend to feel sorry for you any more for being a lesbian. Most people are too polite to say it, though. It is being exchanged unconsciously. The non-reproductive person of working age is the least worthy. The lesbian couple is at least a couple.'

Roseneil goes on to explain how this has changed in the last 30 years. 'There was a non-monogamy politics in the 1980s and the couple was seen as oppressive. Coupledom was the worst thing.' I recall exactly what Roseneil means by this. For example, at Greenham Common, the women's peace camp, those lesbians who lived there in couples were assigned to an area known as 'Monogamy Mountain', and would face good-natured but robust teasing by the others. And the 'cat-free room' in the Women's Holiday Centre in Horton, North Yorkshire, supposedly for those visitors with allergies to cats, often provoked passionate debate about the exclusivity of monogamous relationships because it was almost always co-opted by lesbian couples wishing to have privacy away from the other guests in the dormitory. Feminist activists wrote about they 'tyranny of coupledom' in newsletters such as *The Revolutionary/Radical Feminist Newsletter*[49] (published between 1978 and 1990) and *Trouble and Strife* magazine.

Roseneil believes that today (single) gay men and lesbians can feel stigmatised and be seen as 'failures' in the same way that heterosexuals are, and yet it has long been a principle within lesbian feminist politics that people in couples should not be privileged.

'A certain group of elite people are obsessed with gay marriage – it was the only thing left to fight for,' says Roseneil. 'There is a young generation of lesbians and gay men entering civil partnerships [who] had grown up in a post-New Labour world. They have a desire for ordinariness. Civil partnerships and marriage are offering them that.'

I am sure there are lots of people who feel totally excluded now that many TV programmes feature lesbians or gays in established – increasingly married – couples. Even for heterosexuals, once you get older there is a stigmatisation to being alone because now we too can be left on the shelf.

Does this mean that the new 'tolerance' of gays is conditional on our behaving as close to straight as possible? Does it mean that the mainstream gay community is no longer accessible to or representative of more radical gay and lesbian activists or members?

Maureen Duffy, having lived through the period of time when there was almost no choice for straight women but to marry, is disappointed – not that women have more freedom, but that so many of us are madly keen to celebrate marriage. Duffy's first openly lesbian novel, published in 1966, was *The Microcosm*, set in the lesbian club Gateways in London.

'At the end of *The Microcosm*, Matt (the main character) says: "I could walk out into society and just be myself and society must accept me and I must accept society." But I didn't mean by that that we have to duplicate straight marriage and have children. OK, lots of people want children, fine; if they want children, that's OK, but it should not be seen as a necessary imposition on all relationships.'

Wedded bliss?

For me, the average gay wedding is merely a straight copy of a heterosexual wedding, but there is an assumption by many that because lesbians or gay men are marrying, it somehow subverts the narrative. Roseneil believes, for example, that marriage shifts and adapts as it opens up to those it had formerly excluded, and that the sight of two women partaking in the ceremony is, in and of itself, radical. At a public debate in November 2013 on 'Lesbians in the Media' hosted by Women in Journalism, the broadcaster Alice Arnold, who is in a civil partnership with the sports presenter Clare Balding, argued: 'Because there is no script, and we have a clean slate, we are able to organise these events [gay weddings] differently. That is what is so nice about it.'

But the majority of same-sex civil partnerships reported in the press, as well as those I have personally witnessed or heard about, appear to follow the usual wedding format. Either way, the break-up is every bit as painful as in heterosexual relationships.

Tess Joseph was one of the first lesbians in the country to sign the civil partnership, with her girlfriend of 11 years, on 21 December 2005 at Camden town hall, along with nine other lesbian and gay couples that day. They appeared in the *Camden Journal*, resplendent in traditional wedding dresses and holding bouquets of flowers.[50] Signing the register to Dusty Springfield's 'The Look of Love', the couple treated their guests to bagels and champagne. Other publicity included mentions in the *Observer*, the *Jewish Chronicle*, the *European Jewish News*, *Marie Claire* and a part in the massively popular fly-on-the-wall TV series *Wedding Stories*.

Five years after that groundbreaking day at Camden town hall, Joseph and her partner began divorce proceedings after the latter admitted she was having a sexual relationship with a man.

I ask Joseph why she was so keen to join in civil partnership. She tells me there were 'a million reasons: some practical, some romantic'. Joseph cites health issues, joint property ownership, the desire to have a child together and because she 'fell in love at first sight'.

The couple met in 1994 at a World Aids Day conference, ironically on the offensiveness of lesbian and gay families being described by the proponents of Section 28 as 'pretend' family relationships.

What did it mean to Joseph as a lesbian and a feminist who had previously been critical of the institution of (heterosexual) marriage to be entering into a civil partnership?

'I am conscious that many people do not have that choice and are forced into unions not of their choice or are barred from being with the person they love, or if they are with them against the wider society's precepts, they can be subject to stigma or their lives can be at risk. I am fortunate that I was born at a time and in a society that has developed a rare gift of choice and has improved the civil rights of LGBT people.'

Joseph had been very much part of the change. She was on the management group of the late Camden Lesbian Centre, involved in the 'Stop the Clause' campaign (against the introduction of Section 28), and worked to prevent hate crime towards LGBT people, both informally and through paid work.

'What matters to me is having the choice. It enables society to be more open. I don't recall how many conversations I was part of where straight friends were talking about marriage and I was invisible – a bubble inside. How can I celebrate if it is a love that dare not speak its name? What gives me validation?

'The critique of marriage as an unequal power dynamic, the patriarchal values … yes, these worry me, but are we able as individuals to construct and reconstruct the structures that we build?

'The experience of becoming civil partners on 21 December 2005, being part of the first-day club, as I like to think of it, was extra-ordinary. Making the decision to be one of the first couples was about stepping up, taking the flak and doing it anyway. I saw it as an extension of human rights and I was massively proud to be part of that moment.'

As I write, it has been nine years since the introduction of same-sex civil partnerships and we are beginning to see the statistics on divorce. In 2012 there were 794 dissolutions of civil partnerships granted in England and Wales, a 20 per cent increase on the previous year, and 60 per cent of those were of lesbian unions. By the end of 2012, 3.2 per cent of male and 6.1 per cent of female civil partnerships in England and Wales had already ended in dissolution.

It is of course positive that young people can now go to weddings of same-sex couples within their families, and perhaps it will help dissipate fear and prejudice of gay folk among the younger generation. And while there is no doubt that civil partnerships have brought an air of respectability to lesbian and gay relationships, things are not always as they seem. Those lesbians and gay men who argue that full and equal marriage is nothing short of a revolutionary act may well be simply wishing for a quiet life away from the barricades. A few months before same-sex marriage became legal, the actor Sophie Ward, who was planning to marry her long-term partner, Rena, as soon as the law permitted, wrote in the *Observer* in January 2014 about what being able to marry Rena would mean to her. Describing an embarrassing scene in a phone shop where she was asked if she was 'divorced, single or married', she observed: 'Had the Marriage (Same Sex Couples) Act already passed, I could have chosen the correct designation at the phone shop that day without coming out or lying.'[51]

As the gay wedding planners rub their hands in glee as they anticipate a flood of couples shelling out large amounts of money for legal recognition of their relationship, there are lesbians and gay men desperately campaigning for the right to be visibly gay, and for the right to come out with pride. Meanwhile, the lure of marriage is contributing to the assimilation of lesbian and gay identity and autonomy.

Buying into the status quo with white weddings and babies will not advance us any further. We have gone as far as we can by swapping shame for same. We need to get to the root of why so many of us pander to those who cause us harm, rather than return to a more revolutionary method to liberate each of us from the pressure to conform.

The support for gay marriage and adoption

There is often a divide between the views of lesbian feminists and gay men on the issue of civil partnerships and marriage. Gay men tend to think that gay marriage epitomises true liberation, whereas feminists think the abolition of marriage is one more step towards dismantling patriarchy.

Results from my survey aimed at lesbians and gay men show a widespread support for equal marriage and little critical analysis. Of those who responded to the question 'To what extent do you agree with this statement: "The legalisation of gay (equal) marriage is a significant step towards full equality for lesbians and gay men"?' 84 per cent either strongly agreed or agreed.

Further to that, almost half (49 per cent) of the respondents to that survey supported the institution of marriage, which is alarmingly high support for a flawed institution from a demographic that has a history of radical politics. This is demonstrated by 93 per cent of the respondents saying they were aware of the arguments that 'marriage has historically been a transaction between men in which a woman is purchased' and 'marriage is a harmful and outdated institution that has no contemporary relevance'. So despite the fact that most people claimed they were aware of the feminist critique of marriage, most people uncritically embraced the institution.

There were a number of different results in my survey when asking homosexuals and heterosexuals about their views on adoption by same-sex couples. Some expressed outright rejection of the idea, and others reported problems they had seen with the process. Here are two examples, the first from a gay man: 'I am atheist; however, I agree with Islam about opposing adoption! I think adoption must be only trusted to a mini school-family. I also think that every child has the right to be raised in a family with (something very close to) a dad and a mum.'

And the second from a lesbian: 'I was with my sister when she was inseminated in a very nice Danish clinic. I then watched the excruciating process she had to go through when she told friends and family she was pregnant. The obvious thought "Did she sleep with a man?" written all over faces, "What about the father?" and "What if the baby is Chinese?" (My gran said that.)'

However, some respondents felt far more positively and had experiences from their life that supported their feelings that same-sex adoption was a positive development. One gay man responded on his experiences: 'I have a two-year-old son with a straight friend – and I never thought that would happen as a young gay man. My family, friends and colleagues are nothing but supportive.'

There was also a positive response from a lesbian who found that children were happy to be around same-sex couples and were good examples for adults to follow: 'Children are very accepting of same-sex couples. My son knows he has two mothers, and pupils I teach freely talk about their two mums or two dads. I wonder how we can harness this acceptance so that the children can teach some of it to adults.'

There were other mixed responses, displaying a degree of scepticism and possible bigotry. This gay man appears to subscribe to gender norms and to accept the institution of the straight nuclear family as an unassailable ideal, with gay adoption only preferable to foster homes and institutions that are linked to abuse and unhappiness in children: 'I support the right for gay people to have children and enjoy time with their children. But I think children benefit more from living in a home with gender complementarity – ie with a mother and father. Gay adoption is preferable to foster homes or institutions, because it can provide long-time stable support and a loving environment, so I would not rule it out entirely. However, there's more to parenting than a few androgynous personality traits. I really believe that every child deserves a mother and a father.'

Beyond the opinions on same-sex couples adopting, there is also the matter of civil partnerships themselves. In 2007 acclaimed gay-rights activist, journalist and author Paul Burston entered into a civil partnership with Paulo, whom Burston refers to as 'the husband'.

For Burston, there is no contradiction between being a 'good gay activist, a good feminist and marriage'. 'I support equal marriage because I believe in equality – and because sexual politics isn't only about who you have sex with, but about who you love,' he says. 'Bigots always try to frame discussions around homosexuality in terms of sex, ignoring the fact that we're as capable of love as anyone.'

Burston and Paulo have every intention of 'upgrading' to full marriage 'as soon as possible'. 'Civil partnerships were a step in the right direction, but they aren't equal. There was a two-tier system, with one law for heterosexuals and another for same-sex couples.

'I understand why some people – gay and straight – aren't interested in getting married. And that's their right. I don't think we should distinguish between "good gays" who opt for marriage and "bad gays" who don't. Neither is morally better.'

Similarly, the writer Stella Duffy and her partner, Shelley Silas, fully intend to get married. During the 23 years they have been together, they have had a pre-civil partnership ceremony, in which they declared their love in front of family and friends, and then the year that the law changed, a full wedding-type civil partnership ceremony.

When the law allowing same-sex marriage was passed, Duffy blogged: 'It will be too late for me to have either of my parents at my wedding. It will be too late for me to have my nephew at our wedding. It will be too late for my wife to have her only sibling, her sister, at our wedding. I will be 51 before the law will allow me to marry. It will be too late for me, or my wife, to be a "blushing bride". We will be, we are, middle-aged women. It will be too late for the dozens of friends and family who were alive when we first wanted to marry, 23 years ago, who supported us in our love and who are now gone.'

I ask Silas and Duffy, who refer to each other as 'my wife', why marriage is so important to them.

'Civil partnership is not equal to marriage, and I want true equality,' says Duffy. 'I also want to be able to say the word "married" and know it is within a legal context.

'We call ourselves married now, wife and wife, but I look forward to hearing broadcasters saying: "Shelley and Stella were married," and calling us each other's wives, not civil partners.'

I struggle to understand the difference, for a lesbian feminist couple, neither of whom is particularly religious, between civil partnership and marriage.

But opposition from feminists towards marriage still exists. Feminist academic lawyer Nicola Barker is the author of the prize-winning book *Not the Marrying Kind: A Feminist Critique of Same-Sex Marriage*. When Barker began to explore the issue of equal marriage, she had an American partner who had no visa to remain in the UK.

'I started to think: "Wouldn't my life be so much easier if we got married and she had a visa?" At that stage I was almost coming out in favour of gay marriage, but then I looked at the feminist position.

'The question has always been "Should gay people be allowed to be married?" but my view is not against equality but against marriage.'

People dismiss feminist criticisms of marriage by arguing that modern marriage is not as it was, with the breadwinner and the woman doing the housework, but it still is, albeit to a lesser extent. Studies have demonstrated that men still earn more money for doing the same jobs as women, are more likely to be given better-paid jobs, and women are still more likely to do the majority of the housework in the household. The radical feminist perspective on marriage is that men uphold patriarchy through marriage and the family.

'[Supporting gay marriage] is a very conservative ideology,' says Barker. 'It doesn't subvert anything about the institution of marriage, but it does challenge some homophobic assumptions through visibility. However, there are better ways of doing that.

'It allows people to say: "I am not homophobic. I support gay marriage. I just don't like those men that go shagging in the park."'

Perhaps the option of normalcy is radical for lesbians and gay men. Having been labelled freaks and outcasts, been accused of being potential child abusers, told that our relationships are invalid and unnatural, it is easy to see why the blueprint of the nuclear family is so attractive to many. But it is all too easy to forget that heterosexual family life is not a successful model, at least not for women.

'There was someone during the parliamentary debate that said: "I don't have a problem with gay people, but isn't it better if they are in a stable couple?"' says Barker. 'We have given up on this idea that we can do families differently. "Alternative families" are not alternative at all.'

The negatives of civil partnership legislation have been ignored by Stonewall and individuals who appear to feel a need to defend it in its entirety. For example, people in couples who are on benefits, the poorest in the community, lost out. Since 2005 if you live with a partner, you are assessed in the same way as married heterosexual couples, whether you have signed the civil partnership or not. Each couple will have a drop in their monthly income by at least £20.

Stonewall recognised this as an issue but argued that 'equality works both ways'. But the key arguments, aside from romance, were all about inheritance tax and pensions. The positives were going to the richest, and the negatives were going to the poorest.

Once the wedding gifts have been broken, and the photos delivered via Dropbox to scores of folk who won't even open them, reality sets in. Many will have tied the knot because they could, from those in long-term relationships who have been bored for years to those new lovers mad with excitement and passion.

That lesbians are divorcing more quickly than gay men so far does not necessarily mean their relationships are less solid, but maybe that they don't see the point in hanging around after bed-death when they can do it all over again by logging on to Pink Sofa. Thirty-odd years hanging around with lesbians tells me that we tend to enter into committed relationships quicker than men, so maybe it makes sense that we also get out sooner?

I have seen a fair number of lesbian couples have children over the decades, and many who, with the help of a sperm donor, have one each but bring them up as full siblings. During discussions with such couples, I have often asked if the mothers have a particularly close or distinct relationship with the child they gave birth to, only to promptly have my head bitten off. They have all, without exception, informed me that they love both children equally and how dare I suggest favouritism? Funny, then, how every single time such couples split up, each takes the biological child to live with them. These days lesbian couples could, if they opted for a commercial service, decide on an egg swap, so that one half of the couple could carry the other's baby, but this option is still rarely taken. Once more, conservative attitudes are expressed not just entering into and during a marriage, but in its fallout too. So much for the alternative family.

So with marriage, babies, mortgages and pets, the lesbian and gay community, at least those who are privileged enough to be able to afford such trappings, are becoming indistinguishable from their straight, coupled counterparts.

Karen Wesolowski and Martha Padgett both gave birth to twins, using IVF, a sperm donor and eggs from Padgett. Padgett said: 'We wanted to have a really strong family bond.' This suggests, for this couple at least, that their view of a family is as conservative as their sexual persuasion allows them to be.

Married to conservatism?

If 10 years ago someone had suggested to me that today a Tory prime minister had, despite much consternation from a number of his colleagues, pushed the issue of equal marriage towards legislation, I would have been both disbelieving and disheartened. Yet not only has this happened in the UK, but several countries around the world are also bowing to pressure from the gay rights movement and looking to introduce equal marriage: Cuba, Finland, Uruguay, Nepal, Denmark, Brazil, Australia and Colombia are all in the process of scrambling aboard the marriage-wagon. This all sounds good on the one hand – any unequal treatment towards lesbians and gay men denotes prejudice and, ultimately, a violation of human rights – but on the other hand, the fact that it is with marriage that the international gay and lesbian community has chosen to draw the battle lines of social reform points to a deeply conservative tone in the movement that is more in step with traditional views than we have perhaps acknowledged.

Paradoxically, it suits the patriarchal anti-gay bigots far more to see us all in nice, legally sanctioned couples than it does living the gay outlaw lifestyle that so many of us over the age of 40 used to favour. I had a great time living in squats with other lezzers and their kids, being non-monogamous (being in an open relationship) and frightening heterosexuals by drinking, fighting, getting tattoos, converting as many women as possible to lezzerism and displaying our hairy armpits and extra fingers. Today it would seem that all lesbians aspire to is to be in a couple, get married, have children, a mortgage on a nice house and neighbours who will share the school run with them and invite them to BBQs on Saturday afternoon. How transgressive.

The whole issue of gay weddings and safe, secure couples is a shtick that suits the Tories down to the ground. It keeps us away from any of the really 'barmy' notions such as that heterosexuality is bad for women, or that conservatism is bad for absolutely everyone. If gay men are now tolerated in the workplace, the appeal of voting for low taxes becomes more attractive to them than realising that vote also oppresses women and other minorities. So long as we are aping the heterosexuals, we will toe the line and be kept quiet, satisfied that we are being tolerated. Of course we need to demand equality and refuse to allow discrimination of any type to affect our lives, but this cannot come at the price of our becoming, however subconsciously, the Stepford Dykes.

There are some lesbians and gay men, however, who do consider the normalisation of same-sex parenting a pressure as opposed to a liberation. One respondent to my survey, who identified as a 'female queer', said that she felt under pressure to reproduce by those within the community as much as from those outside of it: 'I don't have kids. It's a very conscious choice I've made, and I'm very happy with my decision. But I'm fed up of either having to explain it to people or being seen as "selfish", or not a "proper woman", or as a waste of some good old maternal instinct material. "Oh, but you'd make a lovely mum," some say. I feel like I'm suffocating under the weight of a load of "Straight Expectations", ones that involve motherhood and its endless grind, which is only made possible by being a certain kind of a woman, it would seem, and I don't feel like that kind of a woman.'

Maureen Duffy says: 'I think society could lose by this homogenisation. I mean, there should be places for people who do not want sex at all and who wish to live an entirely single life. When we were a radical movement, we stood out from the crowd, whereas now we've sort of become a little bit like them. It was a way of saying there are other ways of being.'

Conclusion

I am conflicted with many of the arguments and tactics used by those supposedly defending my sexuality. I don't think having children *or* accessing fertility treatment is a 'human right'. This was being argued in a case reported in Pink News, as I wrote this book, about a lesbian couple deciding to take legal action against a hospital that denied them IVF.[52] The notion that marriage be extended to lesbians and gay men as opposed to abolished gets my feminist hackles rising, and being 'tolerated' is less attractive to me than being despised.

IVF, surrogacy and the commercial baby-making business are being given a boost by lesbians and gay men, and yet, in many instances, this amounts to this oppressed group of people choosing a service that can lead to the exploitation of others – namely the poverty-stricken women in India who carry the babies for relatively rich westerners, or the children in local authority care who could do with a loving family but are being rejected in favour of a bio-baby. Does this reflect, I wonder, the continued erosion of the politics of the lesbian liberation and gay rights movement of yesteryear?

The cynic in me wonders if David Cameron and other Tory supporters of equal marriage have their eyes on revenue rather than rights: equity over equality. In January 2013 an article in the *Evening Standard* claimed, according to government ministers: 'A surge in gay marriages could boost Britain's ailing economy by up to £18m in a year.'[53] The figure was based on the prediction that 3,000 lesbian and gay couples would opt for marriage, additional to the roughly 6,000 civil partnerships that take place each year, and that the weddings would pull in money for local businesses.

It would also encourage tourism from countries without equal marriage, and a number of those already in civil partnerships would get married. In response to the statement that equal marriage is good for business, mayor of London Boris Johnson said: 'I have no doubt marriage equality is of benefit to our economy, and that in itself is a good thing.'

And they say romance is dead?

In the next chapter we look in more detail at how profit has trumped politics in the lesbian and gay community.

CHAPTER 6
THE BUSINESS OF BEING GAY

Amelia and I are shopping online for sperm. It is
disconcertingly easy. We choose some; we add the vials to our
"shopping cart" and press "buy". Cost so far: £3,940 (sperm,
£2,340 for nine vials; storage of sperm, £300; postage of
sperm, £300; family fee – to reserve one of 10 "family spaces"
that each donor is allowed – £1,000).

Rachel Arthur, 2013[54]

A recent survey into gay and lesbian spending habits indicates
that gay consumers can offer a new revenue source at a time
when consumer spending is slowing. It indicates that lesbians
and gay men can offer tourism suppliers significant new
marketing opportunities. With their earnings of over
£81bn in 2007, the 3 million gay men and lesbians
in the UK spent £7.1bn alone buying goods online.

Carol Southall, 2009[55]

I argued in the previous chapter that lesbians and gay men are
increasingly seeking access to a normalised, traditional family
life and that this quest for sameness has resulted in the growth of
commercialised services aimed at producing children for same-sex
couples and lesbian and gay individuals. Often these businesses, and
others aimed at the lesbian and gay population, present themselves as
helping the community rather than as profit-making enterprises.

Today lesbians and gay men can mean big bucks for businesses,
both for gay and straight entrepreneurs. There are sperm banks and
IVF clinics, dating websites, cat and dog rescue services, phone sex
lines, porn sites, clubs and restaurants. Popping up too, in recent years,
are wedding planners, hen-party organisers and travel agencies. We can

even buy bespoke insurance and arrange mortgages through lesbian-friendly brokers.

Gay male culture has long been defined by sexual practices and has been driven by pornography. A key aspect of being a gay man is having access to a sexual hypermarket. Because there is money in sex, it is no surprise that the gay community has had more support from business than other social justice movements.

When, in the 1980s, lesbians began to emulate gay male sexual behaviour, the commercial market began to target us, prodding us with sex toys and pornography. Towards the end of the 1980s the UK saw its first sex-toy business aimed at lesbians, an anthology of 'erotic' lesbian fiction and the first lesbian sex magazine, *Quim*. In the 1990s at least one lesbian club in London, the Candy Bar in Soho (which closed in January 2014), began to advertise strippers and pole dancers, and now there is a range of sex-based businesses aimed at lesbians. Lesbian publications drum up revenue from baby-making businesses, drinks companies and the latest lesbian fashion outlets. All these enterprises ape the gay male models that came before them. This commercialisation of our sexual identity has been massively instrumental in shaping the lesbian culture and lifestyle that are dominant today.

But does business lead gay culture, and is it influencing our identity as a result? Or is the way we choose to dress, socialise and live our lives simply providing new opportunities for entrepreneurs to service us? Is the supply creating the demand or vice versa?

In recent years gay charities such as Stonewall have been courting corporate sponsors, but are the businesses that sponsor gay charities and events doing this for altruistic reasons, or are they just targeting the spending power of the lesbian and gay community? They would be shortsighted not to see the business potential. Despite the growing numbers choosing to have children, gay men in particular tend to have more disposable income than their heterosexual counterparts. Gayby boom aside, the majority of lesbians do not have children, which means their money can be spent on holidays, cars, fashion and other luxury items.

Pretty much every aspect of our lives has been commercialised, and corporate sponsorship – from banks, airlines, restaurant chains and other large companies – often being used at lesbian and gay events that in the old days would attract no one more important than the DJ. How did this happen, and is it a good thing?

The lesbian Rupert Murdoch

I first met Linda Riley, founder of a gay publishing empire and a number of other businesses, at a glitzy Stonewall event in 2008. She has, over the years, turned a considerable profit on the back of gay culture, but she is also known as an extremely generous charitable giver. She is perhaps the best contemporary example of a member of the lesbian and gay world who combines caring with capitalism, and charitable work with cultivating corporate clients.

I affectionately named Riley 'the lesbian Rupert Murdoch' and was immediately impressed by her genuine rags-to-riches story. Riley began her career while still at school in 1977, selling DVDs on Portobello Road market, and today she is continuing to build her empire by concentrating on securing high-profile sponsors and spokespeople for her events, such as the Alternative Parenting Show and the European Diversity Awards.[56] At the same time she promotes and supports a number of LGBT charities and causes, such as Stonewall and the Albert Kennedy Trust, which provides supported accommodation through lodgings, fostering and specialist housing schemes to homeless LGBT young people.

In 2004 Riley formed Square Peg Media with Sarah Garrett to take over the business of *g3*, a magazine aimed at lesbians that was set up by Garrett in 2001. Two years later Riley added to the stable and launched *Out in the City*, the first pornography-free magazine for professional gay men, which was, in 2008, voted Publication of the Year by Stonewall. That same year *Proud* magazine, the ultimate guide to Gay Pride events, was added, with all three titles proving hugely successful in bringing corporate and blue-chip companies, such as property developers, employers and lifestyle brands, to the gay market.

Riley went on to launch *Out at Work* in 2009, aimed at bringing together recruiters and LGBT graduates. Then there is *Outclass*, produced for young people to advise them on gay-friendly universities and careers. The magazines are distributed in bars, clubs, libraries, charities and even prisons.

Square Peg Media is now one of the UK's largest LGBT companies and employers. Following the success of her magazine stable, Riley developed a brilliant formula of hosting large exhibitions based on themes relating to lesbian and gay lifestyle, such as the Diversity Careers Show, launched in 2009, an LGBT recruitment event that attracts over 5,000 graduates and jobseekers. Over the years her other businesses have included London's first women-only courier company, back in the 1980s, and a burger van called Hot and Hunky, based outside the Vauxhall Tavern in London. In 1990 she began buying and selling property in east London and Marylebone, and by 2001 had a 20-property-strong portfolio.

But is all this business enterprise a good thing for the gay community? Is there a way to reconcile hard-headed business instincts with the goal of addressing the issues facing lesbians and gay men?

Riley thinks so, and her own charitable giving suggests the two can go hand in hand. But she also believes that much of the gay media is lacking in integrity and concern for the community it is supposed to serve. 'I don't know why other gay media outlets do not campaign for gay charities and causes,' she says. 'We should all be doing that when we make money from the people within the LGBT community.'

One example of a clever merging of gay community values and canny moneymaking is the Alternative Family Show (recently renamed the Alternative Parenting Show), launched by Riley in 2009. 'I had twins with my partner and we kept being stopped and asked about how we parent, how my partner conceived and whether we had considered adopting, so we decided that there should be an event that explores all these issues and more,' she says. 'It brings people together who are planning on having kids outside of a nuclear heterosexual set-up.' More than 2,000 people attend the show each year.

Of all her gay-themed creations, her personal favourite is the European Diversity Awards, launched in 2011. 'We saw how much companies were doing to improve their diversity policies and that no one was getting to know about it in the wider community. One good example is Abercrombie & Fitch [a clothing company], which used to have a poor record. Now they are fantastic. We have helped them up their game.'

But is it OK to seek endorsements and give awards to companies that are saying and doing the right thing in terms of gay equality, but doing the opposite with other issues? In May 2013 it was reported on CNN[57] that Abercrombie & Fitch CEO Mike Jeffries said, in response to being challenged about the company refusing to stock clothes to fit larger people: 'Candidly, we go after the cool kids. We go after the attractive all-American kid with a great attitude and a lot of friends. A lot of people don't belong [in our clothes], and they can't belong. Are we exclusionary? Absolutely.'

The ethics of commercialisation

Square Peg Media deserves its success, and Riley is a great business role model, but how beneficial to the lesbian and gay community is a lesbian Rupert Murdoch?

Similarly, how healthy is it when commercial interests creep into charity campaigns? These days big business can often be seen playing a pivotal role in gay rights organisations, even to the extent of sponsoring their campaigns.

The financial benefits to both parties in such sponsorship deals are considerable, in terms of the actual cash changing hands and also the free publicity associated with this kind of arrangement. These sorts of relationships between big business and charity must be entered into very carefully. Never mind being grateful that big businesses want to be associated with us gays – perhaps we should be asking whether we want to be associated with them.

Stonewall is a well-off charity and has its ethos shaped by that of a big business. In September 2013 it teamed up with Paddy Power, an Irish bookmaker. On its website Paddy Power advertised its collaboration with Stonewall as such: 'Paddy Power, in association with leading gay rights charity Stonewall, today sets out to tackle homophobia in football by distributing rainbow-coloured football boot laces to every professional player in the UK.'

Stonewall did not directly receive any money from Paddy Power for the laces campaign. However, the bookmaker had recently joined the Stonewall Workplace Diversity Champions programme that promotes best-practice workplace policies on diversity and equality issues. Members receive one-to-one advice from Stonewall on how to do this. Membership is £2,500 per annum.

In December 2013 Paddy Power attracted criticism from Amnesty International for sponsoring the former US basketball player Dennis Rodman's trips to North Korea, a military dictatorship. And in March 2014 the bookmaker caused further controversy, this time over an insulting and insensitive advertisement regarding the outcome of the murder trial of South African Paralympian Oscar Pistorius. In the *Sun on Sunday*, the ad showed an image similar to an Oscar statuette with the face of Pistorius, next to text stating: 'It's Oscar Time. Money back if he walks. We will refund all losing bets on the Oscar Pistorius trial if he is found not guilty.' The Advertising Standards Authority (ASA) received 5,525 complaints, the most ever for a UK advert, on the grounds that it was seen to be trivialising the death of a woman, and also disability. The ASA ruled that the advert be immediately withdrawn. Paddy Power said it was surprised and sorry it had caused such widespread offence. Ruth Hunt from Stonewall defended the association: 'Effective campaigns need to reach new audiences and that means forming some unexpected alliances. Sometimes that works to great effect – the Paddy Power campaign was seen by 26 per cent of the adult population, many of them people who wouldn't normally be interested in gay and lesbian equality. Each unexpected alliance raises questions and we won't always get it right but we must take risks in order to drive an agenda.'

All this is emblematic of conservative and superficially unorthodox business leading a relatively conservative charity – certainly not a radical one. And you can hardly blame it. The whole gay community, not just its charities, is led by business. The sponsorship of Pride, the production of pornography, the proliferation of dating sites and clubs in our towns and cities are all examples of our progress becoming about profit.

There are some very rich men in the gay community and a number of them spend a lot of money acquiring sex. Sex sells, and because we are identified and defined by our sexual practices, we are just as good a target for adverts and business as anyone else.

As we saw in the previous chapter, in recent years a massive amount of money has been spent by lesbians and gay men on acquiring children. Those selling embryos, sperm, IVF, surrogacy services and so on have targeted and encouraged us to have the latest accessory – children. Reproduction is a big money-spinner. Heterosexuals have never been so directly led by a commercial pull to have kids.

Lesbians and gay men want to be seen as 'normal' and this can be sold to us like conformity is sold to everyone. It used to be considered horrific to be a lesbian mother, but now, thanks to the fact that money can be made from it, it gives you credibility. Having kids is good for capitalism, as it ties you into all the stuff you tend to buy when you have them, and the need to work to provide for them.

Recently, when switching on a mainstream TV channel, I was genuinely surprised to see that we even now appear in an advertisement for a bank, no less! NatWest has obviously seen the earning potential of same-sex couples and features a smooching lesbian couple to promote one of its generic commercial services. Apparently, now that it is assumed that lesbian and gay couples are joined together officially, we are even respectable enough for a large banking corporation to use us to advertise its services. Some will hail it as a great stride towards full equality, and an indication that we are now so mainstream that even banks are representing us respectfully in their promotion. This advert is certainly living proof that businesses can no longer overlook the spending potential of a large number of gay women. But how depressing it is that there are still barely any positive lesbian role models in the media and arts, yet there we are in a bank commercial.

'So we're now being exploited through that capitalist treadmill,' says Maureen Duffy. 'I don't see it as particularly positive. I'm glad that men are not prosecuted and sent to prison; I'm glad that on the whole people do not lose their jobs. Occasionally people are still spat at on the street; now they are bullied over Twitter and Facebook – so it has not gone away, but now we are desperately trying to conform to be accepted and are being encouraged to conform.'

Conforming, however, appears not to be as effective as the liberals hoped. In November 2013 Ikea, a favourite of domesticated lesbians and gay men all over Europe, pulled an advertisement from a Russian magazine in case it broke the anti-gay Russian law and replaced it with a story about a designer living in China.

How things have changed. In the early 1980s when I volunteered on Lesbian Line in Leeds, we hired the upstairs room in a pub once a fortnight and charged a small entry fee to raise money for the phone bills. There were one or two lesbian-run micro businesses, such as plumbing, removal services and vegetarian catering. No one was ever going to win Lesbian Entrepreneur of the Year for those efforts.

The value of the pink pound

The 'pink pound' is a phrase usually used to describe gay male spending power, and in general terms, they tend to be higher earners than lesbians for the simple reason that men, despite almost 40 years since the Equal Pay Act came into force, still earn on average 15 per cent more than their female counterparts. But as we grow, both in terms of being 'out' and in confidence, advertisers would be daft not to look to lesbians as the next best thing to target. More than half a million LGBT folk attend the annual Pride event in London, and big brands such as Coca-Cola Enterprises, AussieBum underwear and Sixt car hire rock up to flog their wares.

It is no wonder that many big businesses tapping into the lesbian and gay community have found it to be a gold mine. In 2005 research by Barclays Bank, based on a survey of 1,000 lesbians and gay men, revealed that gay and lesbian people have a greater disposable income than heterosexuals, amounting to up to £10,000 a year. In some ways, at least, it's good to be gay.

Companies of every ilk are now to be found chasing down their slice of the multibillion-pound pink economy. According to a 2006 report on the online press release distribution service PR Web, 'For the first time new research, released today in London, reveals just how much the UK gay market is actually worth. Britain's 3 million gay and lesbian citizens last year earned over £70bn. This income – along with fewer children in gay households – leads to higher disposable gay incomes that are now attracting the marketing attention of some of the UK's biggest companies.'[58] Another 2007 survey put the figure even higher, at £81bn.[59]

Barclays Bank is holding a series of seminars in cities where there is a significant gay population to explain the financial implications of civil partnerships to existing and potential gay and lesbian customers. The bank has paid for 300,000 copies of *Get Hitched!* – a guide to 'gay weddings' – to help explain the rights and responsibilities involved. Barclays Bank also gives funds to the gay rights group Stonewall and never fails to fund a float at Pride.

Many other businesses have already responded to the new markets opening up. In 2012 Hilton Hotels began the process of persuading gay couples to hold civil partnership celebration parties at its 70 branches across the UK; some are licensed to hold the registration ceremony itself. The Hilton Avisford Park in Arundel, West Sussex, held its first 'gay Christmas' break over the holiday period for £599 a head.

Meanwhile, L'Oréal is targeting its advertising at the gay male market. In heterosexual publications such as *FHM* and *Loaded* its Hydra Energetic Daily Anti-Fatigue Lotion for men shows a picture of a man beside the words 'You think you look the business. She thinks you look overworked,' while in publications such as *Attitude* and *Gay Times*, the 'she' has become 'he'. As Rob Robillard of L'Oréal Paris says: 'The gay market is important to L'Oréal and our success with gay men is a key priority.'

The effect of commercialisation on our culture

Naturally, all this marketing has an effect on our culture. As a result of increased targeting, the face of lesbianism has changed in the last 20 years. Jay Hunt, the broadcaster and fashion stylist, and partner of Conservative MP Margot James, said in an interview with the *Independent* in 2005, which was hilariously but aptly entitled 'The L word: Lesbian. Loaded. Loving it': 'In my 20s lesbians used their clothes and haircut to make a political statement. Everyone was very dismissive of the lipstick lesbian movement. Now you can have pretty girls, girls who follow fashion, girls who don't follow fashion. It's much less judgmental, so women feel OK about saying they've bought a Prada jacket or that they went down to Portobello Road and found a fantastic vintage top.'[60]

Even our activism has been commercialised. At the Women in

Journalism event in November 2013 on 'Lesbians in the Media', Alice Arnold advised her friends that coming out could be lucrative, as they would be eligible to earn big money doing a speech at one of the many diversity shows.[61] There was once a time when we would have done that sort of thing for free to help our fellow sisters.

In 1996 the radical gay rights activist Peter Tatchell wrote a blog entitled 'The gay community is doomed' in which he argued: 'The last two years have been a turning point in gay history, marked by a fundamental shift in values and attitudes. The idealism, solidarity and activism that [were] so significant in the first 25 years of the post-Stonewall gay psyche [are] now being superseded by a new gay zeitgeist of consumerism, hedonism and lifestylism. This shallow, vain, frivolous, amoral, self-obsessed, commercialised trend in gay "culture" is not a pretty sight, and no amount of glamorous beefcake in Calvin Klein underwear can disguise its essential ugliness. Moreover, it threatens to politically disarm a whole generation of lesbians and gay men. Who, then, will complete the unfinished struggle for queer freedom?'[62]

Surely one of the clearest manifestations today of the way in which our sexuality has been subsumed in this 'zeitgeist of consumerism, hedonism and lifestylism' is the advent of the gay dating app. When the GLF published its manifesto in 1971, its rejection of monogamy for all proposed to pave the way for gays and lesbians to 'question society's blueprint for the couple' and reinvent the old heterosexual order of the nuclear family. One imagines that Grindr was not what they had in mind.

The most infamous progeny of the new, smartphone-driven gay dating companies, Grindr uses your location to show you all the sexually available gay men in a certain radius. Grindr is the most popular service of its kind, with over 4 million users in 192 countries (including, apparently, the Vatican). Users post photos of themselves or their bodies (or a specific part of their body) in the hope of luring nearby prospective hook-up partners. As one gay friend of mine put it: 'Grindr is common as the clap. You're probably likely to get them both together.' The lesbian version of Grindr is not yet on the market, but I am sure, given time, it will be.

While there is nothing wrong with people using Grindr and the army of similar apps that have risen up since its creation in 2009 to facilitate quick and convenient sex, the popularity of services of this kind speaks to a fundamental shift in the way in which we express our sexuality. Far from the radical politics that underpinned the GLF's opposition to compulsory monogamous relations, the commodification of gay sexuality through apps like Grindr has depoliticised sex entirely.

But more than just replacing the political structures of our sexual practices with consumerism, apps like Grindr are also isolating. Such products implicitly promote the notion that gayness is a hermetic characteristic, just another market to be catered for, one that can be comfortably slotted alongside traditional conservative heterosexuality rather than presenting an active radical threat to its structures.

Just one year after Tatchell's denouncement of the 'new gay zeitgeist of consumerism', James Collard, editor of *Attitude*, the glossy magazine aimed at the gay market, said: 'Gay men have a lot to be grateful for in the way lesbians worked with gay men on Aids, way beyond the call of duty. But we're part of a bigger community now. Gay politics used to be about radical fucking; now it's about radical shopping. We want to buy exciting brands, like Black Label Smirnoff, or go partying.'[63]

When the corporations get it wrong

The idea of radical shopping may well sound like a bit of a paradox, but from one angle the shifting position of the gay community in relation to the mainstream economy can have radical implications. If the increasing market interest in the lucrative promise of the pink pound is threatening to depoliticise what it means to be gay and lesbian, it has also forced corporations to become more political themselves. And it has also shown them the consequences of what happens when they get it wrong.

In November 2013 James Arthur – the latest corporate musical offering pumped out from Simon Cowell's mediocrity machine – discovered the hard way that anti-gay bigotry can be commercially disastrous. In the midst of a rap battle with the rapper Mickey Worthless, the 25-year-old singer called his opponent a 'fucking queer' who 'probably wants to stick [his] dick' in him.

Arthur's subsequent, and slightly bemusing, claims that his comments were 'not meant in any way as a reference to homosexuality' did little to heal the commercial wounds that the episode inflicted. As well as being unceremoniously booted from the righteous bosom of SoundCloud, the singer saw his eponymous debut album, which was released just days before the slur, plummet from No 1 to No 30 on the iTunes sales chart in a matter of days. While it is unlikely that sales dropped so significantly solely as a result of lesbians and gay men refusing to buy Arthur's music, it cannot be denied that the lucrative pink pound has forced corporations to be more wary about condoning bigotry and discrimination for fear of losing the lifeblood of gay and lesbian disposable income.

Our American cousins have always taken pride in their ability to do things bigger, and, as recent history has shown, corporate anti-gay bigotry scandals are no exception. In 2012 Dan Cathy, the COO of the US fast-food chain Chick-fil-A, highlighted the influence of the pink dollar when, following reports that the company's charitable arm had been funding anti-gay groups, he publicly declared that same-sex marriage proposals were 'inviting God's judgment on our nation'.

The comments saw Boston mayor Thomas Menino, Chicago mayor Rahm Emanuel and San Francisco mayor Edwin M Lee declare that they would not allow Chick-fil-A franchises inside their cities. Meanwhile, Northeastern University's student senate passed a resolution cancelling plans for an on-campus branch of the chain. The fiasco also saw the Jim Henson Company end its licensing agreement to include its toys in Chick-fil-A children's meals.

While the bigots came out in force, lining up in their thousands at Chick-fil-A branches around the country to support the company's stance, the economic pressure proved too great. In September 2012 the company announced that it had 'ceased donating to organisations that promote discrimination, specifically against LGBT civil rights'.

Our establishment as a market – and voting block – with money and influence may be sapping radicalism from gay and lesbian culture, but it also forces the establishment to take our concerns seriously. The capitalists – quite literally – can no longer afford anti-gay bigotry.

Sex sells

According to Sheila Jeffreys: 'What happened in the late 70s and 80s of course was also the development of the pink pound, and pink consumerism and the development of a lesbian and gay culture. During the time of being in the closet the only options for socialising were the mafia-controlled bars, where it was all about heavy drinking and was very oppressive.

'But by the late 70s and 80s it was all much more commercial. It may not have been mafia-controlled, but there was a huge commercial gay scene,' says Jeffreys. 'And the socialism and radical politics fell away.'

Before the 1980s lesbian sex was innovative, imaginative, self-taught, low-tech, did not cost any money or provide any sex industrialists with an income. In the 1980s this changed and a lesbian sex industry developed. In order for a lesbian sex industry to be profitable, it was necessary to transform lesbian sexuality so that it would take the objectifying form necessary to construct lesbian sex consumers, consumers not just of mechanical products but of other women in pornography and prostitution. Suddenly lesbian sexuality began to attract the attention of entrepreneurs, sex therapists and pornographers.

Over the last 30 years or so the sex-toy industry has developed to the point where it has become mainstream – as evidenced by the phenomenal success of *Fifty Shades of Grey* in 2011– and now it appears that the industry is experiencing a lucrative financial rise thanks to online gay sex stores.

Online gay sex stores are, as the name suggests, intended solely for the gay community and offer the gay public sex items that can be bought and sold online. The unfathomable success of such websites has caused some people to think the internet is in fact 'saturated' with online gay sex toys.

In an article on gay sex toys for the Business Highlight website, Bei M commented: 'Gay people really take time and effort and spend money to order online gay sex toys from websites. As a matter of fact, some businesses are already getting envious to such operations because they seem to actually keep the market rolling. Other online sex-toy sellers are finding it hard to build their niches. That is not the case for online gay sex toys.

'When translated into actual figures, how much are online gay sex toys making? It would be hard to quantify at the moment, but what is important is that it is actually definite that businesses make easy and flooding money from trading and selling online gay sex toys. That is a clear explanation why such online materials are actually enjoying huge patronage and popularity.'[64]

Gay tourism

But it is not just a question of businesses making a few quid by selling strap-ons to lesbians. Now whole countries are climbing on to the gay bandwagon, with the arrival of gay tourism.

As well as profit, gay and lesbian tourism also brings with it a steamier side. The commercialisation of gay and lesbian sexuality has seen the wholesale rebranding of the most insidious elements of heterosexuality, reproduced for the gay market.

Back in 2008 I wrote a piece for the *Guardian* recounting my experiences on the Greek island of Lesbos – the mythology of which has long made it a popular lesbian holiday destination.[65] Locals informed me that, eight years previous to my visit, controversy had been sparked by a cruise-load of British lesbians on a trip organised by London's Candy Bar. Flyers advertising a 'wet pussy party' flooded the island, prompting the then mayor of the village to try to stop around 100 British lesbians from disembarking from their cruise ship for a stop-off. Behaviour was lewd and loud, and to make matters worse for the islanders, the group was accompanied by a film crew from Channel 5, making a fly-on-the-wall documentary called *Lesbians Go Mad on Lesbos*.

'We are still recovering from that,' I was told by Anastasia, who works at the Parasol bar, which is perched on the seafront. 'Some of the women were like men. They were shouting things to women that few men would dare, such as "Lovely tits".' One, she tells me, had a 'full beard'. What disgusted Anastasia most was that they had brought their own stripper, to entertain them in the evenings. 'We would not tolerate local men doing such things, so why would we put up with lesbians behaving like pigs?'

The behaviour is hardly out of character for the denizens of Soho's still iconic Candy Bar (which closed in January 2014). The basement area of the bar was well known for its striptease and pole-dancing nights. I have interviewed strippers and lap dancers. Some of them are lesbians, but none enjoyed their work, and all of them despised their customers, whether seedy, horrible men or equally seedy women.

Speaking in November 2013 on a panel at a recent event organised by Women in Journalism and *Diva* magazine on the media's treatment of lesbians, I was greeted by a decidedly lukewarm round of applause from the predominantly lesbian – and (almost) entirely female – audience when I denounced Candy Bar's abhorrent practices.

Is this OK just because it is women doing it to women? Is domestic violence acceptable if lesbians are knocking hell out of their girlfriends? No? Then why is sexual exploitation not stridently condemned in our so-called community?

This gradual acceptance of a lesbian sex industry began in the US (San Francisco, of course) in the 1980s, alongside the emergence of lesbian sadomasochism, porn for lezzers, such as the nasty magazine *On Our Backs*, and other such atrocities. It was around this time that Les von Zoticus set up a prostitution business aimed at femme lesbians. In an attempt to justify her business ethos, she said: 'The sad yet pervasive notion that the feminine should always be at the service of the masculine and never the opposite disturbed me to the core of my feminist sensibilities. The only viable solution I could find was to offer myself as a sexual object and become a butch gigolette.'

Lesbians, it would seem, are being sold – with a terrifying degree of success – the very social apparatus that drives the patriarchal oppression of women. Ironically, they are being sold the same sexist oppression that forms the cornerstone of anti-gay and lesbian bigotry.

The birth business

As we touched on in the previous chapter, another area in which the gay community are proving themselves to be a lucrative market is that of surrogacy services. In the US in 2010, the first year the US census counted gay couples and their children, one quarter of same-sex households were found to be raising children. Many surrogacy firms have seen a rise in wealthy urban homosexual couples seeking IVF treatments and surrogacy.

Commercial surrogacy is currently prohibited in the UK; however, this has not prevented a veritable litter of companies offering – for a fee, of course – to facilitate gay couples heading to jurisdictions more friendly to commercial surrogacy. Organisations like the British Surrogacy Centre, which was mentioned in the previous chapter, Circle Surrogacy and Brilliant Beginnings all provide services to allow gay couples to head across the pond in search of a womb-for-hire, a process likely to set them back upwards of $90,000 (£53,500).

Whatever the motivation, the love, sex and family industries are receiving an influx of capital from the gay community. It is a thriving business area, as wealthy homosexuals are willing to spend huge amounts of money to achieve domestic bliss.

When the *Guardian* food writer Yotam Ottolenghi wrote in the paper about 'coming out as a gay father', readers could have been forgiven for assuming the article was about him challenging the closet and anti-gay bigotry, but rather it was the tale of how he and his partner had purchased expensive surrogacy services in the US.[66] It was, in fact, another example of how gay commercialism is often dressed up or misunderstood as gay rights or campaigning.

But the cost of this newfound yearning for suburban nirvana is more than monetary. Just like the Candy Bar lesbians jumping on the bandwagon of patriarchal porn culture, the gay surrogacy boom is a symptom of the deeply regressive values that have seeped into gay culture via commercialisation. The Drewitt-Barlows of the world are more than content, it would seem, to condone hiring out the bodies of – usually economically disadvantaged – women in their quest to adhere to traditional heterosexual ideals of family. The commercial aspects of gay culture are often at odds with feminism.

Moreover, gay entrepreneurs are often mistaken for gay rights activists when they are in part at least motivated by profit. Ivan Massow set up a business in 1990 selling insurance to gay men who were being penalised by other insurance brokers for being thought to be at risk of Aids. Massow launched Massow Financial Services (MFS) from a squat in north London, and by 1997 it became one of the 10 biggest financial advice firms in the UK, valued at more than £20m.

In 1987 MFS became the first corporate sponsor of London's Gay Pride, which set the scene for the event to become one massive commercial party. Massow has made donations to gay charities in the past and spoken about the links between good business acumen and charitable giving. As with Riley, no one is denying the fact that charitable giving is welcomed by those in need of financial assistance, such as small campaigning groups and direct service providers, but it is also clear that both entrepreneurs are both viewed and view themselves as campaigners rather than capitalists.

The money in marriage

As well as insurance, the gay wedding industry has blossomed. As the public support for gay marriage has increased, so too have the economic possibilities that gay marriages can create.

Even the conservative US is now waking up to the monetary potential. 'The gay wedding market has grown nationally, creating,' as the *Denver Post* notes, 'new business opportunities for wedding planners, photographers, vendors, hotels, resorts and caterers – as well as financial planners and attorneys.'[67]

'It's a big business,' Bernadette Coveney Smith with the Gay Wedding Institute told the *Post*. 'There is definitely room for all of us to benefit financially from gay weddings.'

As we saw in the previous chapter, it's not just in the US that gay marriage will prove fruitful; according to an article in the *Evening Standard* in 2013, it is believed that in the UK the rise in gay marriage could boost the UK economy by £18m a year.[68] On the basis of the details contained in the article, a sceptic might conclude that the introduction of equal marriage was more about revenue than rights. While it is increasingly evident that the homosexual community is commercialising the areas of love, sex and family, there seem only to be benefits for the economy.

According to the article, the government 'estimates that these extra ceremonies could each lead to an additional £4,750 spending in the economy, on average, or £14.4 million in total'. It is also estimated that many same-sex couples who are already in civil partnerships will marry. With gift shops, hoteliers, florists and caterers expected to rake it in, the estimate of a £3m injection to the economy, according to the article, may be fairly conservative.

I spoke to Andrew Jackson, who runs the UK Gay Wedding

Planner, about his business. Jackson set up the business after planning his own civil partnership back in 2010, when he and his partner realised there were limited resources and suppliers aimed predominantly at the same-sex wedding industry, as opposed to the traditional wedding market.

I ask Jackson if trade had significantly increased after the passing of the new legislation for actual marriage and press him for answers on other aspects of the business, but he tells me he has not noticed a growth as yet.

'I think a lot of couples are only just starting to get engaged after the new legislation was passed,' he says, 'so the lead times for planning a wedding may mean that we notice an influx next year.'

The average spend on a civil partnership ceremony is £18–20,000, says Jackson, and all of his customers have been from middle-class backgrounds.

I ask whether this type of spending feeds into the wider economy.

'Definitely. During an average civil partnership ceremony and reception, a couple will be connected to approximately 15 to 20 different key suppliers who help to create their day, such as the florists, cake maker, venue dresser, musicians, catering team, etc.'

After years of radical politics, consumerism has turned gay men and lesbians into predictable couples like everyone else. Even honeymoons now have their own specialist companies providing bespoke services for the gay and lesbian market. Liberally sprinkled with saccharine images of lesbians in matching white dresses, or men in identical tuxedos, their websites make perfectly clear that the lifestyle on sale is one very much rooted in conservative gender roles.

With horrible irony, one such company, Perfect Gay Honeymoons, offers gay and lesbian newlyweds a luxury honeymoon experience in the iconic Trump Hotel in Las Vegas. Donald Trump, it would seem, has no problem cashing in on the pink dollar while publicly declaring that '[gay marriage] is not my thing one way or the other'.[69] Commercialisation allows the bigots to profiteer from the gay and lesbian community without ever having to concede any real social ground.

Only one way to be gay?

Another industry making huge gains from the cash injection provided by the pink pound is cosmetic surgery. A survey of 1,000 gay men carried out by the *Gay Times* in 2008 found that 22 per cent had already undergone cosmetic medical procedures, while a further 69 per cent stated they would like to have some form of cosmetic surgery.[70] And an article in online US magazine Slate in January 2014 reported: 'Gay men are said to be the fastest-growing client base in the cosmetic surgery industry, with liposuction being a common request.'[71] It may be interesting to ask why.

And what of the dominance of sex ads in our media? What effect does the advertising of pornography and escort services have on the lesbian and gay community? With print media shrinking, it has never been harder to make a magazine aimed at the LGBT market viable. The free scene magazines have always made a significant amount of their revenue from escort ads. Sexual imagery dominates – often to the exclusion of anything that promotes other ways of 'being gay'. Once editors go down the sexual advertising route, it is reduced to just that – more mainstream advertisers and brands are reluctant to work with them. Gucci does not want to be placed alongside adverts for sex toys.

Alex Hopkins is a journalist and executive editor of *Beige*, a quarterly magazine aimed at the LGBT market. He is a rarity as a young gay man, as he has written extensively about the negative consequences of commercialised sex within the gay community.

'Certainly in my experiences editing publications that have a strict "no sexual advertising or imagery" policy, it makes things tougher – there's no doubt about it – but as an editor, I believe I have a social responsibility to set an agenda that reflects the diversity of gay life,' says Hopkins. 'Gay men are more than what they do in the bedroom or sex club.'

So why, then, is there barely any concern or critique about the amount of pornography and prostitution services advertisement in the vast majority of publications aimed at gay men in particular but also lesbians?

According to Hopkins and other gay activists, such as *Time Out*'s Paul Burston, there is a link between the sexual imagery used in gay magazines and wider issues such as unsafe sex and drug use on the gay scene.

'The issue is a complex one, but I believe magazines have a responsibility in setting the agenda and in addressing cultural norms,' says Hopkins. 'Many gay magazines sell us a myth about how we should look, behave and what we should aspire to. Frequently, the "porn star" is sold to us as being the ultimate "idol" – it's he we should look up to for advice on the type of sex we should have. Anything less than "porn-star sex" is seen as a failure.'

According to Hopkins, the majority of gay publications shun any social responsibility by chasing the quick, easy commercial win and in the long term this has a negative impact on gay culture, which is becoming over sexualised to the exclusion of almost anything else.

'If an alien came to London and landed in one of our gay bars,' says Hopkins, 'and picked up a gay scene magazine, what would he/she think? That we lived in a 24/7 orgy devoid of any consequences, that's what.'

Living the dream

So how should we feel about the increasing commercialisation of our lifestyle? Heterosexual women have long been led to believe that they need a lavish white wedding before they can live happily ever after. A similarly empty promise has been made to lesbians and gay men in recent years. We have been sold the idea that having the wedding, honeymoon, baby shower and picket fence symbolises true liberation. It does not. While we should have every right to consume as well as campaign, there is no doubt that the businesses targeting the lesbian and gay population are selling the idea that it is possible to buy our way to emancipation.

Feminism has never had corporate sponsors. The extent of business support for feminist projects seems limited to some backing from the Body Shop for Refuge, the domestic abuse charity, and little else. Because radical feminism focuses on the destruction of existing institutions as much as it calls for constructive actions, it is not an easy sell. The status quo is profitable, and we are a demographic that can be affordably ignored. Doing the right thing is attractive to business only when it comes with a promise of good press and better sales. Gay and lesbian consumerism has blunted our politics, and our politics are essential to advance the cause of feminism, and together with that to improve society beyond a materialist spectacle.

While there are those who argue that the fact big business is courting us and using lesbian and gay iconography to shift its products, we must not forget that, for many of the money-makers, human rights and notions of equality will play second fiddle to profit.

On 29 December 2013 a story on Pink News demonstrated this perfectly, revealing how Coca-Cola, one of the major sponsors of the Sochi Games, published photos online of a group of gay rights activists in Brighton who had disrupted its Christmas advertising campaign with a demonstration against its decision to sponsor the Games in Russia. Coca-Cola's motivation for publishing the photographs was to criticise the activists. The company had not made any critical statement against the Russian anti-gay laws, or a positive one about the gay community. When business is threatened, lesbians and gay men will be thrown to the wolves. But wait! Coca-Cola was nominated by the *Out in the City* and *g3* Readers' Awards as Brand of the Year 2014.[72] You may remember from earlier that *g3* is part of Square Peg Media, which is jointly owned by Riley and her partner, Garrett. After mass protest by readers of both publications, however, *g3* dropped Coca-Cola because of its sponsorship of the 2014 Winter Olympic Games and 'its unwillingness to express any explicit criticism or concern about the new homophobic legislation in Russia and the wave of homophobic violence there'.

How could, one might ask, a gay publisher nominate a company for an award when that company has such a disgraceful record towards gay rights? Is sucking up to a mega-rich corporation in these circumstances more to do with hoping for sponsorship than truly believing that Coca-Cola deserves its place among organisations that challenge bigotry?

Coca-Cola put out a statement in response to being pulled, saying: 'We have long been a strong supporter of the LGBT community and have advocated for inclusion, equality and diversity through both our policies and practices.' But what does that mean?

On paper the company has sparkling credentials. It was one of the first US companies to support the proposed Employment Non-Discrimination Act, which would protect employees from discrimination due to sexual orientation. In 2000 it funded an LGBT employees association through its human resources department. But quietly taking care of your employees, invaluable as that is, is not the same as speaking out publicly in favour of gay rights and running the risk of upsetting anti-gay customers. The fact that Coca-Cola chose to sponsor an event in a country that has seen a sharp rise in violence towards lesbians and gay men, provoked – it can be argued – by the disgustingly anti-gay legislation, surely calls into question the limits of those in-house policies that got it shortlisted for a gay rights award in the first place.

Being gay is no longer as controversial as it was, so there is little or no stigma attached to businesses giving to same-sex causes. The pink pound is powerful. Diversity careers events are beneficial to the corporations that support them because they want rich gay men to endorse and buy their products and services.

Mark Palmer-Edgecumbe is head of diversity and inclusion for Google. His role is to promote the reputation of the business or corporation with regard to ensuring anti-discrimination and inclusive policies for employees and customers. These mega-rich bodies get to enhance their relationship with the gay charities and, via that route, rich gay men and lesbians. Their donations and sponsorship are tax-deductible, and because gays have become so respectable and toothless, straight customers will not lose sleep over the association.

Why does Palmer-Edgecumbe consider Google's relationship with the gay community important?

'I believe that working with the lesbian and gay population is a critical part of any commercial organisation's business strategy, and the link between business, philanthropy, charity and campaigning within that particular community has proved to be strong and highly effective.

'It is no longer "shameful" to be either a gay business or a gay consumer, and for me, sponsorship, tacit support and endorsement of lesbian and gay causes delivers a positive benefit to both the business and the community itself.

'Historically, society has attempted to stereotype lesbians and gay men, but gay community is as diverse as society itself and follows no monolithic political or even cultural standard – they may vote Conservative, Labour or not at all; be from every race and creed; be capitalists or campaigners, have children or not. Google's support merely demonstrates the true diversity of both the community and the corporate worlds respectively.'

Conclusion

Gays are a good bet for corporate sponsors, unlike black and minority ethnic causes, or feminism, because they have money and are desperate to be accepted by respectable society. Not only have gays become Toryfied, the Conservative government recognises that supporting the gay community is good business sense. In turn, the gay community continues on the road to becoming further entrenched in the politics of greed, wealth, complacency and hedonism. One of the key issues today for the gay community is the acquirement of individual rights to choice. It is a rightwing free-market libertarian agenda. Therefore, the gay business model fits perfectly with how we are gay today.

With the increasing commercialisation of our sexual identities, the sponsorship deals being cut with big businesses with questionable motives and morals, and lesbians and gay men thinking more about pounds than politics, the question of where, as a movement, we are going next fills me with trepidation.

CHAPTER 7
HOW WE ARE GAY TODAY

*When we went on Lesbian Strength marches in the 1980s
we felt we were part of a political movement challenging
male supremacy. Calling yourself a lesbian was a radical
political stance. Now it is simply a lifestyle.*

Bren Dewhirst, 62-year-old lesbian, 2013

*I think it is time for the gay community to move on in
its attitudes! If you continue to present yourself as a victim,
you will always be a victim! Gay and lesbian people are
simply people with a different sexual preference. They are
no different from the rest of the population! Why make an
issue out of it? The wonderful people from the past
who broke the prejudices had a point. Move on.*

Heterosexual male survey respondent, 2013

In the early 1980s Mary Whitehouse came to Leeds University to
address a massive audience of critics, sceptics and Christians. She spoke
eloquently about the dangers of sex on TV and promiscuity, and of her
disgust about a poem in *Gay News* about a homosexual centurion's
love for Christ at the Crucifixion that was considered 'blasphemous'.[73]
Gays in the audience, including me, heckled, shouting out that we
were decent human beings and deserving of equal rights. In those days,
of course, as I demonstrated earlier, we had nothing of the sort.

Whitehouse was true to form during her talk at Leeds University,
blaming lesbians and gay men for the breakdown of 'decent society'
and for the corruption of young children. There were, as far as I
could make out, no straight allies in the audience, only those who
objected to Whitehouse's censorial approach to pornography and
sex on TV.

It is October 2013 and I am sitting in the debating chamber at Trinity College Dublin when it suddenly occurs to me that things have come almost full circle. The conservatives are arguing for equality, on their terms and using their definitions, and the marginalised and radical campaigners (like me) are arguing that gay marriage is not the answer and should be soundly rejected.

I travelled to the debate expecting to challenge standard anti-gay bigotry opposing gay marriage. I assumed that conservative gay people would argue that we should not be allowed to access the hallowed institution of marriage. However, those who are particularly keen to promote the cause of marriage for us are the most quintessentially conservative of the speakers: the straight, posh white men.

Their argument is that injustice for one is injustice for all, and that there is no reason that gay men and lesbians should be kept out of the process any more. The argument is that inequality should certainly be addressed by moving from civil partnership to same-sex marriage.

I had expected to put forward my feminist critique of marriage while at the same time negating standard conservative bigotry. It's a nuanced argument, one that must be made carefully to ensure that I don't give ammunition to bigots.

However, as a result of the meeker proponents of gay marriage, and the lack of hellfire offered to those who weren't of the straight persuasion, my speech focused on the drawbacks of marriage. Marriage supports traditional roles of gender. Marriage supports subservience to the patriarchal society we have now. There is nothing in marriage, same-sex or otherwise, that challenges patriarchy, because it encourages the idea that family comes first, then the Mondeo and then the mortgage. Equality is important, but it should be marriage for nobody, civil partnerships for anyone who wants them, and the rejection of patriarchy for the damage it does to women, lesbian or straight, every day.

The motion up for debate at Trinity was: 'This house believes the struggle for marriage equality has been a waste of time.' During the debate I found myself surprised that everyone on the proposition side were 'radical' sexual-outlaw types. Those opposing were, in the main, heterosexuals who believed that it is morally and ethically wrong to discriminate against the LGBT community.

I was invited to defend the proposition because, as a radical feminist, I have written and spoken about how marriage is a patriarchal institution that is deeply conservative and can have negative effects on women. I had travelled to Dublin, up against a particularly heavy writing deadline, in the hope and expectation that I would meet at least one speaker who was seriously anti-gay. I had visions of crossing over to the opposition so as not to assist a bigot in their argument about marriage equality. But that did not happen.

One opponent said she was not straight, but beyond that she was 'confused' as to her sexual identity, and spoke humorously and passionately about the 'ordinariness' of her lesbian parents and how being brought up by two women was 'no big deal'. The audience laughed when she said that the reason her two mothers were not in the debating chamber to hear her debate was because they were playing bridge, as they did every week. 'How boring is that?' she asked.

But the closing remarks of the chair, Max Kryzanowski, from the gay rights group LGBT Noise, also underlined how wedded the contemporary gay community is to 'equality' rather than 'liberation'. The equal marriage debate has not only brought the bigotry out from the woodwork, but has also highlighted just how much the majority of lesbians and gay men crave 'ordinariness'.

On my return home to London, I find I have a choice of things to do that weekend. I have an invitation to a gay wedding, another to a lesbian couple's baby shower or I could pop down to the Alternative Parenting Show (APS) run by Square Peg Media.

Gay parents are now the new 'respectable'. They are the ones who are increasingly school governors and generally pillars of the community. Over the past decade I have witnessed lesbian couples in particular gravitate towards straight couples for friendship and advice because they have similar-aged children. Time and time again I have bumped into lesbians I used to know pre-kids and barely recognised them in their newfound respectability.

So where does this leave us? What does the future hold for lesbians and gay men today? And to go further: what would an ideal world for lesbians and gay men look like? What would need to change in order for anti-gay bigotry to be relegated to a museum as an ancient relic?

Related to this we need to look back and ask how effective the combination of feminism and the gay liberation movement has been so far. Have we really come as far as we think? As recently as April 2014 it was reported in the gay press that a teacher at a secular school, Andrew Moffat, had resigned from his post as a result of opposition by religious parents to his book *Challenging Homophobia in Primary Schools*, which was being taught to 10- and 11-year-olds.[74]

And yet so many lesbians and gay men will say that their lives are free from bigotry and oppression. Maybe those people are not engaged with what is happening to other gay people around them and are merely focusing on personal experience. Perhaps, as I argued earlier, the battle fought by many gays to become 'ordinary' was a radical act that has ended in victory.

How far have we really come?

The quest for ordinariness and equality that I have highlighted throughout this book is demonstrated by some of the responses from both my surveys on levels of anti-gay bigotry, while others seem to think that movements towards equality are merely superficial:

- 'Overall, gay visibility and the climate of "being gay" feels better to me than it did 10 years ago. However, I worry that the focus on marriage and the pink pound is causing an increased normalisation of "gay lifestyles" to pull us in line with a heteronormative ideal. In that sense, the future of the "situation" of gay men and lesbians in the UK is exciting, but also potentially worrying, in that some of us might end up being marginalised from our "own" communities' – gay male
- 'I don't get a Met policeman call me "faggot" in my face any more' – gay male
- 'Out celebrities and sports people (except footballers) have helped to "normalise" the existence of gay people in society. I was particularly impressed with the way gay characters have been treated in reality TV shows – eg *I'm a Celebrity*, etc' – lesbian
- 'I think the LGBT community in general has had it easier in the last few years (which isn't to say that everything's wonderful –

it's not), but gay men still have privilege: they're not fetishised as lesbians or bisexuals are, and they generally are represented in the media a bit more' – lesbian

- 'On the surface things have changed, but scratch the surface and much prejudice is very much alive' – gay male
- 'Lesbians still exist mainly in fantasy. They are predominantly manifestations of hetero male gazes. Personally, gay men are far too over-represented in society. Not going into the whole "gay mafia" debate, but an over-representation in media, fashion, design, arts and communications (huge determinants of culture), education (teachers, lecturers, researchers) and politics. Where are the lesbians? The bisexual women? Not the ones in hetero men's mags who claim to have gone down on a friend in school – not titillating shite' – gay male
- 'It seems that it is easier to live openly as a LGBT person than it was before, largely because they are more visible in public life and the media' – gay male
- 'I think gay women are too invisible. There has been some acceptance and understanding of gay men in the wider culture, but women are victims of homophobia and sexism – pretty toxic. I would like to see more gay women in the media and in the public eye. I think it's good for all women' – female heterosexual

In response to both my surveys, there are examples from straight, gay, lesbian and bisexual people who feel that the movement has not come to its conclusion, despite the apparent progress that has been made. For example, one gay man identified that although things are plainly better, there are other obstacles still to be overcome or dismantled: 'I am amazed and heartened by the position we are now in. I had hoped that we would reach this point, but not in my lifetime. There is, of course, still some way to go, but I am sure that acceptance and equality will be exponentially achieved. It is now unfashionable to be homophobic, which to me seems extraordinary. The next challenges are to tackle the issue in schools and minority religions.'

One 'bisexual/gay' man believed that for all the celebration of equality and tolerance, the majority of work was still to be done in challenging attitudes of society and that many people were merely masking their bigotry rather than really changing their beliefs: 'The fact is, I am 18, bi/questioning gay and I hate myself for it because of what society has done with general attitudes. People are either homophobic outwardly/politely – ie it's harder to notice, but they call it a lifestyle choice. If there had been such leaps and bounds, I wouldn't be closet. There is still about 80 per cent of the battle to go for equality and that is a fact.'

The quest for ordinariness can, however, cause consternation for those gay men who seek public respectability but also like the thrill of unorthodox sexual practices. For example, in March 2014 a gay former soldier suggested the path to LGBT equality would be to shut down gay saunas. James Wharton said gay saunas are 'thorns in our side that mark our community as different for the wrong reasons'.

This is an example of conservatism bleeding into gay culture, and it should be noted that Wharton is a friend of Prince Harry, a fundamental part of the British establishment. Quite what is 'wrong' about gay saunas is left not quite clear, but he mentioned that in order to be part of the 'new normal', saunas should be shut down because they encourage promiscuity.

Could Wharton have missed the introduction of the pill and the increase in divorce and non-marital sex that straight people have access to? There's not exactly a shortage of it in pop music, television or real life. Why Wharton thinks that gay people should be denied lots of sex is also unclear, but perhaps he is embracing the idea that we should not 'ram it down anybody's throat'. This is not aiming for equality, but rather suggesting gay culture is kept invisible in exchange for being tolerated by the straight community. It is tacitly bargaining gay and lesbian erasure in exchange for allowing us to become just like everyone else.

By saying: 'If we don't [close saunas], we feed the haters and we hand the bigots who remain a vocal minority ammunition with which to attack us,' Wharton appears to be under the illusion that the bigots will turn their attention elsewhere so long as we behave ourselves.

The butch and femme lesbian and the leather queen were all the product of oppression. Some overexcited observers are even describing the introduction of the Equal Marriage bill as the culmination of five decades of campaigning. Those who were at Britain's first Pride parades in the early 1970s have apparently seen their dreams of equality come true, we are told. Really? Or is this just the overstatement of achievements by gay and lesbian campaigners who are too tired to fight any more or too conservative to want to dismantle the remaining oppressive structures? Is it, from the straight community, a rush to pat themselves on the back for being so gay-friendly, like David Cameron, former Conservative MP Louise Mensch and the Tory party commiserating the death of Nelson Mandela once they'd airbrushed out inconvenient truths?

Those early gay radicals were not remotely interested in getting married, or in winning equality, the only thing that today's conservative gay campaigners are interested in. The early radicals wanted to see the back of marriage, not to be invited to the party. The GLF that emerged out of the Stonewall Riots insisted that 'complete sexual liberation for all people cannot come about unless existing social institutions are abolished'.

It was pretty clear that one of the social institutions that would have to be done away with was marriage. *A Gay Manifesto*, an influential radical pamphlet published in 1970, described marriage as 'a rotten, oppressive institution'. In *Gay Is Good*, lesbian activist Martha Shelley's explosive and much-loved 1972 booklet, homosexuals were described as 'women and men who, from the time of our earliest memories, have been in revolt against the sex-role structure and the nuclear family structure'.

The gay marriage campaign of today, with its drab demand that homosexuals be granted equal access to the social institution of 'rotten, oppressive' marriage, represents not the fulfilment of early gay radicals' demands but the warping of them, the stomping of them into the dirt of history. It is a well-known fact that most radicals end up going straight, eventually donning a suit and tie, and accepting a fat wage packet in return for tempering their ideals. But the gay movement, in switching from loathing marriage to longing to enter into it, and from demanding that the state get out of their lives to pleading with the state to officiate their relationships, has performed an about-face that is unprecedented even in modern radical politics.

The vast majority (over 75 per cent) of all respondents on both surveys supported gay marriage, with 89 per cent of 'other than heterosexual' respondents supporting it. However, 75 per cent of all respondents on both surveys had come across opposition to gay marriage, with the majority stating that it was from the Christian church, followed by politicians.

One of the questions I have been asking all the way through is 'What is it that instils fear and loathing in the anti-gays?'

The answer is, of course, that we present a clear threat, even if that is not our intention, to patriarchy and male supremacy over women and children. Patriarchy dictates the norms of sex, even.

One thing we do know, despite the lack of decent sex education in the UK, is how regular heterosexual couples have sex. The mechanics of gay male sex is something that is discussed rather more frequently. The widespread revulsion at 'sodomy', cruising and public, outdoor sex has created a folklore around it.

To the ignorant and the bigoted, lesbian sex is deviant and mysterious. What do they do, it is often asked, without a penis? Do they actually have sex at all? Do the butch ones have secret equipment with which to send the feminine lesbian into ecstasy? Can manly lesbians recruit and brainwash straight women? Do they have sex with their cats?

It appears that patriarchy means that most people cannot even comprehend of penisless sex. This is an example of the profound fear of lesbians, who deviate from patriarchy by kicking men out of the bedroom, and of gay men, who also deviate from the patriarchal structure, which is totally reliant on heterosexuality.

Lesbians and gay men have spent decades talking about our sex lives and desires, and responding to inappropriate and ill-informed questions and comments about such intimate matters. As a rule, heterosexuals do not have to do this.

New demographics

The changes over the last 30 years have been so dramatic that whole new demographics have opened up. There is now a second generation of children of lesbian and gay parents. And for the first time in history we will soon have a population of out lesbians and gay men reaching the end of their lives.

Many of my generation have begun to think about what will happen to us if we find ourselves living alone in later life. As blueprints, there is the Carefree Cove in western North Carolina and Marigold Creek in Arizona.

Gay retirement homes offer safety in numbers, but according to an article in the *New York Times* in 2007 entitled 'Ageing and Gay, and Facing Prejudice in Twilight', those living in nursing homes or assisted living centres 'increasingly report that they have been disrespected … or mistreated in ways that range from hurtful to deadly, even leading some to commit suicide'.[75]

There have been stories of staff wearing gloves to make beds for fear of contracting HIV, of assumptions that residents have no offspring and of women being mistaken for men and being accused of being butch and predatory by heterosexual residents.

But despite the problems with the existing facilities, the idea of gay housing communities is attractive to many lesbians and gay men for a number of reasons, such as independence from biological families, being part of a larger community of people with similar interests and lifestyles, and increasing social opportunities in a community obsessed with youth.

From Huffty to Clare Balding

Another change we have seen in recent years is the idea of gay role models, who many gay people seem to believe will magically rid us of all bigotry. These days it would appear that so long as you are famous and have come out as gay you are automatically assigned the honour of being designated a 'role model', whether you've done anything notable or not.

Similarly, the APS ambassadors are both conservative: Charlie Condou, mentioned earlier in this book, who is best known for playing the gay character Marcus Dent in the ITV soap *Coronation Street*, and actor Sophie Ward, also mentioned earlier, who was 'outed' by the *Daily Mail* after she left her husband and fell in love with a woman. Both have two children and are raising them in same-sex relationships. I know and like both Ward and Condou, but they are anything *but* alternative. Respectable, middle-class, well-behaved folk in monogamous couples raising well-behaved, respectable kids. In one way, Ward and Condou are great ambassadors because they reflect the new generation of lesbians and gay men who see the cause to which they have aligned themselves as one of striving to be accepted, and being allowed to have the same rights as their heterosexual counterparts. However, for me and many others of my generation, part of the fun of becoming a lesbian was being able to proudly and happily reject heterosexuality.

The Stonewall Awards also tend to honour a significant number of heterosexuals for being nice to the gays. That doesn't seem worthy of an award; it is something that should be a basic expectation of everyone.

Further to these examples, there are alternative lists such as the World Pride Power Awards. All these seem to do is heap praise on those who give corporate sponsorship and develop equality policies for highly paid professionals. It's an example of how boring gay rights is now that we have our own corporate jollies, when corporations are what we should be fighting against.

In the 1990s we had Huffty, who was regularly featured on *The Word* and was a butch, working-class lesbian.[76] Today it would be unthinkable to see someone so obviously lesbian in the way Huffty was on TV. Now we have to be polite. For example, we now have Clare Balding, afforded national treasure status because of her reporting of the London Olympics in 2012. Balding is in a civil partnership with Alice Arnold. She is a 'good gay', unthreatening and, largely, the acceptable face of lesbianism when it is not just a feature of porn for men.

In the past there were no 'good gays', but now there are many. They are the married gays, discreet lesbians (whereas now radicals are more likely to be discreet). and gay couples with children. Huffty would not have been seen as a 'good gay'. The gay movement has lost both its teeth and its marbles, and appears to be totally elitist.

In the past anti-gay bigotry stemmed from the fact that gay people did not live as they were supposed to do. But today much of it comes from how the gay movement behaves. There is an argument that some bad feeling has been stirred up by presenting a superiority complex, aping the cliche of the 'magical black' with the 'magical gay', such as *Priscilla, Queen of the Desert*. There is even a new strain of anti-gay sentiment because of the superiority and smugness of some of the spokespeople.

Some of these people are so conservative and cosseted that they argue that, since equal marriage and all the other legislation has been introduced, it means the end of discrimination for lesbians and gay men. The lack of empathy perhaps explains the rise of the gay Tory vote. If things are fine for you, then you have a selfish reason to be Conservative. This attitude ignores wider facts.

As we saw in chapter 2, a poll commissioned by Stonewall in 2013 showed that one in six gay or bisexual people in the UK has been the victim of 'homophobic hate crime' or abuse in the past three years. Compared to other types of hate crime, such as racism, the proportion of 'homophobic' incidents is on the rise. In 2009, 9 per cent of all UK hate crimes were classed as homophobic, rising to 10 per cent in 2010 and 11 per cent in 2011.

In the more liberal capital, statistics from the Metropolitan police showed homophobic crime had fallen across London by 12.7 per cent from March 2012 to March 2013 – however, several London boroughs recorded a rise.

Hate crimes are on the rise and yet not all law-reform campaigns are radical. Stonewall does important work, but it has predominantly been a law-reform organisation pitched on the mantra of equality. Even by its own standards, however, it has fallen short. Stonewall agreed with the Labour government when Tony Blair gave religious organisations qualified exemptions from the laws protecting LGBT people against discrimination in the workplace. An equality law that came with its own insult.

The Equality Act 2010 specifically states that protection from harassment legislation shall not apply on the grounds of sexual orientation or gender identity. Stonewall did not campaign against this exclusion and argued that there were other laws protecting LGBT people against harassment.

But today, increasingly, campaigning focuses on us being invited into the status quo. For example, Olivia, a 26-year-old law graduate, tells me it is extremely important that priests be allowed to bless a same-sex union because her faith is as significant to her as her sexual identity.

'It's important to remember that priests and vicars have often known their parishioners since the day they were born and play a role in their lives – sometimes from cradle to grave. My priest back home in Aylesbury recently passed away, and I'd known him for about 15 years. So, in that respect, I think it's important for same-sex couples to receive confirmation or approval of their marriage from somebody who has played a formative part in their growing up.

'Another more metaphysical reason is that a blessing (if not a full Catholic or C of E wedding service) would be a sign from God, I suppose, that the wedding was valid, and accepted. I think that's very difficult for an atheist to understand, but it goes like this: marriage is important, religion and God are important equals a connection between the two is important.'

Olivia has genuine concerns about having the right to secure validation of her same-sex relationship from the church, but for some lesbians and gay men, striving for approval from an institution that has historically excluded, maligned and vilified us is the wrong approach.

The equality law-reform agenda took over particularly strongly in the early to mid-80s, even before HIV struck big. It was partly because of the demise of the radical gay liberation politics following the fragmentation of the GLF that people went into many projects like *Gay News*, London Lesbian and Gay Switchboard, more mainstream politics.

I asked Peter Tatchell, veteran campaigner and critic of the liberal reformist approach developed by Stonewall, about his views on whether reform has taken over revolution.

'Quite a lot of people that were in Gay Liberation Front said that they had tried the revolutionary approach to transform society, it didn't work, so let's try and see what we can do in the here and now. But, of course, my response was, "Hang on to that vision, and do the here and now stuff – that's fine – but hang on to that vision and keep working towards that vision."

'The early 80s was the period when equality became the big match. Then HIV and Aids compounded that trend because faced with this death and destruction all around, people were clutching at straws, anything to get acceptance, and so people were desperate and felt that any argument that could be used *should* be used to deal with this crisis.'

There were reasons, then, for the focus on equality law reform, but it no longer needs to be the aim of the whole community, and certainly not as the apex of our achievement.

A day in the countryside

My research for this book took me to a lesbian enclave in the Calder Valley, West Yorkshire. I wanted to see how far lesbians really are accepted among the general population in Hebden Bridge, the lesbian capital of Britain. With a population of 5,000, there are an estimated 800 lesbians in this market town. It has even been claimed by some residents that lesbians outnumber their straight sisters by six to one.

Before I interview some of the lesbian inhabitants – most of them known to me from former years and through the network of contacts I have built up after more than three decades in what is still a very small world – I have a look at the businesses run both by and for the lesbian community.

A shoe shop named Rubyshoesday catches my attention. It advertises its wares as 'sensible shoes'. I can see a rust-coloured pair of Doc Marten ankle boots in the window, but there isn't a stiletto in sight. Further down the road, there's the Organic House cafe, selling an array of gluten-free and vegan cakes. My personal favourite, though, is a lesbian-run plumbing business named Stopcocks.

Now, I am a lesbian of 35 years standing who loves a good night out with the girls in Soho; I cannot get to grips with the idea of living in a small town in the countryside. I like a Martini, a multiplex cinema, being able to eat in restaurants serving everything from Peruvian to Parisian, and do not suit either walking gear or trekking through rough terrain while discussing the impact of *The Killing of Sister George*.

The reason I'm in Hebden Bridge, however, is to discover whether it represents the political, social and sexual utopia that I dreamed of when I fought on the barricades of the women's movement in the 1970s. Is this a vision of the future of lesbianism – a blueprint for a different way of life? My suspicion is that it is in fact a parody of itself – liberation stifled by woolly liberalism and every cliche about lesbians coming horribly true in an atmosphere of small-town cosiness.

How odd that such a town is more notorious for the sexual preferences of many of its women than anything else. Sir Bernard Ingham, Lady Thatcher's former press secretary, is a Hebden Bridge native – and is perhaps in part unwittingly responsible for the high numbers of lesbians here.

In 2001, when census figures revealed the gay ways of his beloved town, Ingham wrote in his column for the local paper that the fact so many lesbians had moved there did not 'say much for the men of Hebden Bridge' and pondered on what life was like 'BL' (Before Lesbians). Such was Ingham's distaste, he persuaded the BBC2 current affairs programme *Inside Out* to highlight the lesbian influx in a documentary charting his horror at the 'ruination' of this fine part of the country.

Ironically, all this publicity resulted in many young, isolated lesbian couples moving to the area, who for months after the programme was aired could be seen holding hands while peering into estate agents' windows. It brought good business to Hebden – obviously not quite Ingham's intention.

Part of the reasons lesbians had migrated to the area in the first place, in the late 1970s and early 1980s, was cheap housing. The former mill town suffered terribly when mills closed and the decaying textile town was left somewhat abandoned, with people unable to afford to stay. Hippies, followed by lesbians, began to move there, attracted by the alternative lifestyle and the chance to build communities almost with their bare hands.

I passed by a number of lesbians, obvious to me not because they necessarily conform to stereotype – after all, in a hippy enclave like Hebden all the women have, by default, an easier time eschewing the feminine trappings such as makeup and dresses – but because of some instinct that many of us develop over the years that enables us to spot 'our own kind'. I also met up with some lesbians introduced to me by a friend of a friend who lives in Hebden.

Sarah Courtney lives in Hebden with her partner, Tamsin, and their four-year-old son, Frankie. Courtney, 47, moved to the town 10 years ago, having previously lived in Todmordon, another lesbian enclave, in Calderdale.

Courtney tells me she advises new inhabitants that the easiest way to meet other lesbians is in the Co-op. Tamsin recalls a woman from New Zealand who approached her in the street and said she had come to Hebden to meet other lesbians and was wondering where she should go to find them. 'I told her we are everywhere.'

Courtney and Tamsin have lived together since 2007, and two years later Tamsin became pregnant by sperm donor insemination through a fertility clinic. The family is well embedded into the mainstream community. Courtney is a governor at Frankie's school and tells me it is 'an easy place to be lesbian parents. I don't think our son will be bullied here for having two mums.' Indeed, one of Frankie's school friends has a lesbian grandma, and there are always other gay women in the playground dropping off and collecting their offspring. Many of the lesbian mothers I encounter in Hebden tell me how important it is that their children meet those from as wide a range of family types as possible.

It has often been suggested that there might be a slight irony that so many lesbian mothers mention the positives of children mixing with children from different backgrounds when, for example, the monthly disco down the road in Todmordon is women only.

Personally, I don't think so. There is no women- or lesbian-only commercial venue in Hebden, with the lesbians being happy to mix with anyone who accepts their way of life. There may well be many lesbian-run businesses in Hebden, but the rest of the country could learn from its inclusivity – there is no sense of segregation from the mainstream population at all.

Many of the women have moved from Leeds and Manchester and run their own businesses from home, such as therapy, homoeopathy and manual trades. Burst a pipe and you are more likely to get a lesbian with an oversized tool bag clipped to her 501s than a geezer scratching his bald patch. Hebden also boasts the first ever cafe for dogs, Lamppost. Serving cakes and treats for canines (made with no sugar, salt or preservatives) and more decadent snacks for humans, it is run by Kate Henderson and Claire Gray, both 35 and lifelong best friends. They share a love of dogs and strong family connections, but not a sexual preference. The Lamppost is another popular spot for lesbians – many of whom have pets – to gather and socialise, as well as being popular with other locals.

'The other day we were pretty full up with kids, single mothers, families, old people and, of course, lesbians,' Henderson told me. 'Everyone was chatting away about their pets and I realised that dogs really bring people together, whoever they are.'

There is a lesbian choir, walking group and birdwatchers' society in the town. Inhabitants with a taste for rambling are catered for with plenty of North Face and Millets outlets flogging gear. The monthly women's disco is the social highlight of the Hebden Bridge lesbian community. There is little glamour at the disco, although its reputation for fun is such that women from miles away flock to it on a regular basis.

There is not usually such a wide choice of socialising for lesbians in other towns or even cities. I have no doubt it would be beneficial to have such a focal point for lesbians elsewhere, so those new to town need never feel isolated. Not all the women are in relationships, and there appear to be a number of single women who move to Hebden at least partly to find a partner.

I ask several of the women if there is a vibrant dating scene and I am told it has its moments, although there are certainly a number of women who share the town with several ex-lovers. Some of the lesbians in Hebden are of the young, lipstick variety, and many are old-school who knit their own yoghurt, sleep on futons and make organic muesli. At least 98 of the lesbian couples in the district have undergone civil partnership ceremonies.

Despite my cynicism, I found attractive aspects to Hebden. Who would not love a candle shop run by gay men where you can find cupcakes and swans made from scented wax? The men who own the Yorkshire Soap Company used to run a hardware store called Home-Oh! until it was flooded last year.

I also love the lack of stress among the women I meet, as well as the absence of the ghetto mentality I have become so used to as a lesbian constantly dodging nasty reactions. Importantly, according to a number of straight and lesbian people who know Hebden well, the kids just love growing up in such a beautiful town. Indeed, many of the women, and indeed the wider community, move to Hebden to start a family.

Marianna Shapland's six-year-old daughter, Rose, also goes to the local school. In her class almost a third have lesbian parents. 'Hebden is a much better environment for bringing up kids,' said Shapland, when we meet in Nelson's, the lesbian-owned wine bar in the centre of town.

Shapland moved from Bradford six years ago and had only ever lived in cities prior to the move. She said she felt increasingly unsafe in Bradford and worried that some of the men on her street were trying to find out what the type of set-up was in her household. 'I became more concerned for my kids,' she said, 'so it was good that we decided to move here.'

I have a strong suspicion that the cliches and stereotypes in evidence here, in terms of the names of the shops and other businesses, are gently poking fun at the old prejudices about lesbians rather than perpetuating them. It at least provides a context in which these women can live their lives as they wish without fear of reprisal.

I loved meeting the lesbians of Hebden and felt welcomed and included. There is no question that the indigenous population has benefited from seeing these women as whole human beings, rather than the negative stereotype so often peddled in much of the media. Children are growing up in an environment that is healthy and positive about difference. But for me, who loves the buzz of the city, living in Hebden remains as appealing as a tent in Greenham Common. I would balk at the wheat- and gluten-free organic vegetarian cafes in Hebden, and anyway, would rather live in an area without an obvious and visible lesbian community, so I can benefit from mixing among a wide range of folk, none of whom expect me to join their gang.

In Hebden Bridge, because of the influx of hippies in the past, the culture there is one that would be a counterculture anywhere else. The residents are used to seeing the unorthodox, so lesbians fit right in. However, to stay on the right side of the straight community, the lesbians seem to be the ones who bend over backwards to fit in.

Professor Darren Smith is somewhat of an expert on Hebden Bridge and its lesbian community. A social population geographer, Smith investigates contemporary migration flows and population restructuring. According to him, social class is of more relevance than sexuality in terms of the assimilation and acceptance of lesbians in Hebden Bridge.

'It is an example of a town where lesbianism has become normalised,' says Smith. 'Hebden represents, possibly, the biggest change in the gay community in 30 years. But in order to truly fit in with the wider population, it is probably necessary to be the sort of middle-class, slightly hippyish, alternative type and preferably have children. Class has trumped sexuality in Hebden, it would seem.'

The town is definitely a great place to be in a lesbian couple and raise children. The notion of lesbian families has become embedded within public services in the town, and that has resulted in an inflow of further migration. These women feel a real sense of entitlement these days, whereas previously they felt they had to fight for everything. There is a sense of acceptance about the lesbians in Hebden that has led to the lesbians there to become further entrenched within the wider population.

Is Hebden Bridge, and enclaves like it, the future of lesbianism? I doubt it. Lesbians are everywhere, which is why visibility continues to grow, despite the ongoing prejudice towards us. What would be the point of folk in certain towns and villages having a relaxed attitude to same-sex couples and those elsewhere being shocked at the sight of us?

Also known for its large and vibrant gay community is Brighton, the well-known seaside town on the south coast. Brighton is the gay male counterpart of Hebden Bridge, but notably different. Despite sharing a gay-friendly reputation, it is nothing like Hebden. Brighton is more popular with gay men, as well as a younger, clubbing crowd of lesbians. And although a night out is more expensive and cosmopolitan than in Hebden, it's definitely less friendly. There are more gay men than lesbians, and the two groups don't necessarily mix. Many of the Hebden women tell me that Brighton is far more orientated towards clubbing and picking up sexual partners. Whereas Hebden lists dog-friendly cafes and vegetarian cafes, Brighton advertises 27 'Brighton Gay Cruising Areas' on one popular website that recommends beaches, parks, libraries and other venues and areas in the town where gay men are known to look for a sexual partner.[77]

That is not to say that all the gay men in Brighton are single. Data on same-sex couples from the 2011 census found that Brighton and Hove had the highest number of civil partnerships in the country, at 3.1 per cent (2,346 individuals).

But how much does the existence of gay-friendly towns and cities, and the number of sex couples who have entered into civil partnership actually tell us about how liberated the contemporary lesbian and gay community actually is? Nothing much at all, I would argue. Are Hebden and Brighton not merely gay ghettoes, separated by cultural attitudes as well as kilometres from the villages, towns and cities in which isolation, bullying, violence and oppression are material realities in the lives of lesbians and gay men? There may be safety in numbers, but how does this support others who are still confined to the closet?

What about the rest of the world?

There are more than 80 countries that still criminalise homosexuality in the world, and out of those 10 still impose the death penalty.[78] The cute story about the so-called lesbian penguins in an Israeli zoo, containing the line 'Israel is famously tolerant of its gay community', masked the fact that anti-gay bigotry and violence in Israel are rife, especially among the Orthodox religious communities.[79]

As outlined in chapter 2, a number of legislative gains are being repelled in some countries around the world, such as India, Russia, Uganda and some states in the US. This backlash against gay rights is at least in part because culture is way behind legislation. It would be like imposing the ban on smoking in public without having done all the awareness raising, education and research beforehand.

In India, the government recently outlawed homosexuality, and as I write, in December 2013, we have just passed the anniversary of the death of a 23-year-old student in Delhi who was murdered by a brutal gang rape. Anti-gay bigotry and the oppression of women still go hand in hand.

In Germany, the *Guardian* reports on an expanding business for non-traditional lesbian wedding suits and dresses for the decidedly traditional practice of marriage. Further east, in Russia, the actor Ivan Okhlobystin, who wants to become a presidential candidate, told an audience that gay people should be burned alive in an oven. The contrast between those fighting for gay marriage and those fighting public incitement to be burned could hardly be more stark.

In December 2013 Uganda passed a law that banned the promotion of homosexuality. It also criminalised those who conduct same-sex marriage ceremonies and carries a three-year prison term for failing to report suspected gay activity to the police. The law was first introduced in 2009, when it advocated the death penalty, but after a worldwide outcry, that was removed from the final version. The most draconian element of the legislation is the fact that it will apply to Ugandan citizens who engage in homosexual liaisons while abroad.

Quoted in the *Guardian* on 20 December 2013, senior religion and sexuality researcher at the US-based thinktank Political Research Associates Dr Kapya Kaoma said that the measures had to be understood in the wider political and geographical context. 'It is part of a larger trend. The persecution of sexual minorities in other African nations such as Zambia and Zimbabwe has been especially severe in recent months.

'Also, we have to consider that the actions of Russia's Vladimir Putin to criminalise both homosexuality and reproductive freedom in Russia may provide cover as well as courage to human rights violators.'[80]

Dr Kaoma also suggested that the 'active involvement of American conservatives' was a major issue, as having lost public opinion in the US, they 'have determined to take their culture war crusades abroad'.

These laws are no less terrifying than those targeting Jews under the Third Reich, and it is clear that legislation in one country affects a much wider population. Who would have thought that Russia would adopt such horrific anti-gay policies?

But what, in the main, are we doing in the UK to support our sisters and brothers living under such fascist regimes? Very little. We appear to be too busy buying confetti and nappies. Some of the more privileged gay men and lesbians seem to have become smug, complacent and apathetic to others facing far more extreme prejudice outside the western world. Rather than focusing on imitating the heterosexual norm, surely it would be better to prioritise supporting oppressed and persecuted lesbians and gay men around the world.

Not everyone sees this global horror as an indication of a growing backlash against lesbians and gay men, however. Ian Birrell, who worked as a speech writer for David Cameron during the 2010 election, put a positive spin on things in a column in the *Guardian* under the headline 'The Tide is Turning against Homophobia'.

'We are in the midst of a worldwide revolution in which the tide is turning against homophobia,' wrote Birrell, having skipped through current legislative atrocities in India, Uganda and Nigeria, to name but a few.[81]

Turning blue

On the same day as Birrell's article appeared, another comment piece in the *Guardian*, headed 'Gay Voters "More Likely" to Favour David Cameron', outlined the results of a survey by Pink News that found that Tory support among gay people has increased since Cameron backed same-sex marriage and that around 30 per cent of those surveyed said they would vote Conservative, compared with 11 per cent at the last general election.[82]

We used to almost all be on the left. Indeed, a gay Tory was as rare as a Scottish one. But increasingly, alongside the depoliticisation of gay identities, lesbians and gay men are voting in the way that most people do – for the party that will directly benefit them the most. With many gay men and lesbians entering highly paid professions, having children and buying homes, that party is increasingly Tory.

Despite the controversy caused by Ken Livingstone's statement in 2013 that the Conservative party was 'riddled' with homosexuals, he did in fact have a point. The party has a surprisingly high number of both gay members and gay supporters. In an article published in the *Guardian* in April 2012 entitled 'Glad to Be Gay, Glad to Be Tory', the gay broadcaster Evan Davis ponders on why so many gay men wish to be involved with a political party that has been the least gay-friendly historically.[83]

'It was one of those strange phenomena that when the Conservative party appeared nationally to be at its most homophobic, at the very heart of the organisation were all these influential gay men,' wrote Davis.

Davis does not give an answer to his own question as such, but he raises various possibilities, such as internal self-conflict, a preference for the Tory 'camp' aesthetic and a belief in the myth that gays are 'created' within the private school system.

None of these answers felt particularly convincing to me. But why, then, *do* so many lesbians and gay men choose to support a party that seems not to support them? Could it be because many are traditionalists and their conservative views are being supported and reflected back at them by the Tories? A gay couple who vote Tory, own a home, send their well-brought-up children to school in a leafy suburb are no threat to their heterosexual counterpart. It's a shame that just because we were for so long excluded from the Mondeo Man dream, we jumped at the chance for it as soon as it became available. Having been marginalised for so long, you would have thought we could have come up with some more attractive alternatives to stick to. We shouldn't be longing to join straight society; straight society should be longing to join us.

Perhaps the change is because the Tory party, although seemingly anti-gay in the abstract, is well mannered in its treatment of the individual, and this kind of personal open-mindedness may make it easier than thought to be gay and Tory.

Matthew Sephton, who runs LGBTory, the Conservative LGBT group, told the *Guardian* that he has never experienced hostility as an out gay man at a local party level in his 10 years as a member. In the same vein, Ben Furnival, chairman of ParliOUT, an LGBT group for people working within the houses of parliament, speculates that the Tory party's acceptance of eccentricity might have made it appealing to many a gay man.

The modern-day gay rights movement, if it remains obsessed with marriage, families and respectability, will actually assist the Conservative party to remain in power. But there should be no surprise in that. We have been persuaded by the Conservatives, and the essentially conservative New Labour movement, that we should aim to be like them, flattered by the offer of equal marriage, thinking that will be the end to bigotry, or the culmination of a campaign. That is no success when we are still oppressed across the world, and women in particular are still disadvantaged and physically and verbally assaulted from the day we are born by the institutions we are born into without choice.

The rise of social conservatism in the west grows alongside gay rights. This is no coincidence – indeed, the new gay rights is all about social conservatism. As Tim Montgomerie wrote in *The Times* in his controversial column on abortion in December 2013, 'Forty years after the so-called Culture Wars began – when the US supreme court legalised abortion – America is becoming much more liberal on gay rights but is also becoming more concerned about abortion.'[84]

Conclusion

There is still a need for a cultural revolution. It might be better to come out these days in big towns and cities, and in secular communities and households than it was when I came out, but there are people whose experience will still be as painful as mine. Indeed, when people are still murdered for being gay, it might actually be worse than it was for me.

Rather than a new resistance and emergence of revolutionary politics, we are witnessing almost an erosion of our identity. Take, for example, the way that 'bisexuality' appears to be increasingly used as a soft substitute for lesbian or gay.

When I came out, like many others of my generation, I was tempted to describe myself as bisexual in order to soften the blow. It was a handy transition to admitting that I was, in fact, a full-blown lesbian.

While accepting that some folk are bisexual, why do we assume and label a woman as such simply because she was in a relationship with a man prior to leaving him for a woman? Do we impose the label 'bisexual' on the 'yestergays' and 'hasbians' who begin having straight sex? In doing so, we assign them the special privilege of remaining a member of the club despite their rejoining heterosexuality. Does this matter?

Most people say that it is far easier to come out as lesbian or gay these days, but perhaps they are kidding themselves. If we are to look at some of the so-called gay role models of late – such as the diver Tom Daley, singers Lady Gaga, Madonna and Jessie J – they all seem to be concerned with reassuring the general public that they are still attracted to the opposite, as well as same, sex.

As Rebecca Holman wrote in the *Telegraph* in an article critiquing the lesbian film *Blue Is the Warmest Colour*: 'Female celebrities are falling over themselves to, if not explicitly identify as bi, then admit they've had sexual relationships with women in the past.'

You might say this, and the popularity of *Blue Is the Warmest Colour*, is an indication of the increasing normalisation of lesbianism. Except the film can be viewed as soft porn for straight men, and women wishing to brag about their bi-curiosity may well see it as a sort of recreational activity, and a fashionable 'temporary lesbianism'.

Culturally, lesbians are either sexualised or made to be invisible. Leisa Rae, standup comedian and proud lesbian, points out that Clare Balding is now appearing on TV looking more and more traditionally feminine, with high heels and skirts, while Sue Perkins is presented as asexual. For Rae, 'in-your-face, unapologetic lesbianism is as threatening as it ever was, even in the world of alternative entertainment such as the Edinburgh festival. I remember when I had to go to Edinburgh and there were loads of comedians that year who just said the word "lesbians" and everyone fell about. I mean, that was the joke!'

Broadcaster Alice Arnold, whom I met when we shared a panel at the Women in Journalism event on 'Lesbians in the Media', believes that part of the problem in terms of the way that lesbians are represented is because of the preoccupation with what we do in bed.

'Being gay is about so much more than sex,' says Arnold. 'It is about love and the freedom to share your life with your chosen partner. If we focus on sexualising our lesbian role models, we fall into the worst traps of the straight world. We should be above that.'

So what do we focus on? We have the exploitation of the bisexual empire to provide titillation to the straightest of men and use it to airbrush what radical lesbians really look like. We focus on same-sex marriage when the majority of society still can't even fathom what our wedding night would actually look like. Even in our lesbianism we are forced to live our lives centred round the phallus, defining ourselves as if we're missing out on one rather than benefiting from it.

There are lesbians such as Linda Riley, the entrepreneur extraordinaire, profiting from lesbian and gay culture, and we have all kinds of ways of being exploited by adoption agencies and others crassly chasing the pink pound when they evidently don't care about pink politics. And our politics is rotten. We have gone from the excellent role model of Huffty and shifted it to Clare Balding, who protested the abuse of gay and lesbians in Russia by ... going to the 2014 Winter Olympics in Russia. We have gone from radical pink politics to the most boring grey politics imaginable.

Balding, the UK's most treasured lesbian, who came second in the Pink List and fourth in the World Pride Power List 2013, refused to boycott the Sochi Olympics because, in her words, 'I will be presenting from Sochi for the BBC. I will do so because I am a sports presenter who happens to be gay. I think the best way of enlightening societies that are not as open-minded as our own is not to be cowed into submission. I intend to stand proud, do my homework and my job as well as I possibly can – as I would for any other sporting event.'

Perhaps Balding, like many other lesbians in the public eye, realises she treads a fine line between being seen as a national treasure and an object of ridicule, as evidenced by the debacle with AA Gill calling her a 'dyke on a bike' and the boys on the all-male panel of BBC Radio 5 Live show *Fighting Talk* having a laugh about how to turn her straight.

Gay men, too, are accepted but forced into a court jester role. They are used like accessories by writers such as Caitlin Moran, who seems to find the whole idea of gay men having sex hilarious – she recently used fan fiction to make Benedict Cumberbatch and Martin Freeman pretend to be gay at a BFI event, purely for laughs. Gay men are used in their cliched roles almost exclusively – fashion experts or a shoulder for the straight women to cry on, or to share in the objectification of men, or, often, women – such as Gok Wan.

The legislation is there, but the world we should be living in is not, and that seems to be enough for most people. We are so far away from the vanguard of radical politics that nothing short of a revolution is needed.

CONCLUSION

When I came out, in 1977, lesbians and gay men had few legal rights and were regularly the victims of verbal and physical abuse. At that time the idea of being accepted as 'normal' was pretty attractive to many. Life was extremely hard, and things could go badly wrong for any of us who spoke out.

Things are now both better and worse. In terms of what is better, there are some huge legislative victories. Section 28 has been repealed. Gay men and lesbians can adopt and have access to IVF, we can become civil partners, and we can be married, both in church and in secular society. It is illegal to discriminate against us in the workplace, and there is an understanding that many institutions have moved – and some still need to move – from a point of institutional anti-gay bigotry.

Many more heterosexuals are relaxed about the existence of gay men and lesbians, and happy to celebrate diversity. The accepted wisdom in the UK is that being gay is OK.

But all this is a qualified success in my eyes. Some people see a victory, but this was never what I was fighting for with my radical friends, colleagues and fellow lesbians. We didn't want admission to the status quo; we wanted to overthrow it. We have been granted acceptance to the capitalist set-up of mortgage, marriage and children. Despite the fact that the lifestyle on offer was once critiqued by the left and by those seeking a way out of the status quo, many lesbians and gay men now appear to be standing at the front of the queue, seeking normality. We appear happy to be bought off with it.

Legislative equality is necessary, but the fact that it has come as a sop to replace a radical overhaul of the nuclear family does not make it a change for the better. Our work is not yet done. Outcry over anti-gay actions has not eradicated all thoughts and practices that will subtly or otherwise undermine or damage the lives of lesbians and gay men. The prejudiced boss, vicar or politician can still do damage.

There is plenty in my surveys to back up my argument. The following account from a respondent makes for depressing reading: 'So many times I've experienced situations where people use the word "gay" in an entirely negative sense, normally to describe something – whether a person, action or situation – is bad, stupid, rubbish, etc. It's also interesting that while people proclaim *not* to be anti-gay as such, they feel the need to distance themselves from homosexuality by declaring: "I'm not gay or anything," or other similar phrases, usually when stating an attraction to someone of the same sex. It feels as if society is saying: "It's OK for you to be gay, but I wouldn't want to be," and I feel this is something which needs to be addressed.'

Another respondent, a teacher, felt that it was not possible to be out, because his relationships with male friends may be 'compromised', because of 'an association of paedophilia with gay males'.

The threat of isolation and violence is ever present. As one survey respondent stated, 'My town is full of white cisgendered heterosexual Catholics and they think it's funny to throw water at me and scream "dyke" at me from their cars while I walk home from the bus. Most students think being gay is gross and that I'm going to hell.' Another male respondent said he chose not to be out because he didn't want his 'windows smashed'.

One lesbian respondent recalled the time 'a man was waiting outside a lesbian bar and attacked me and then my girlfriend'. And a gay man told of the occasion he 'was punched in the street, dragged down an alley and kicked and punched by three men all calling me a "faggot"'.

There was also a deep concern that legislation is not always terribly effective in practice. As one lesbian respondent commented about her decision to not come out at work: 'I want to keep my job and I don't believe I would be able to by coming out. Jobs can force you out, will claim other reasons.' Legislative equality has not meant practical equality, and some respondents are concerned that the legislation is not always enforceable.

There were some who justified their decision not to come out with arguments that don't quite hold up. For example, as one respondent said: 'Only some people need to know. I'm a private person and wouldn't be offering information on my sex life to the others even if I were straight.'

This may, very possibly, be true, but there are precious few straight people in the world who don't acknowledge the existence of a personal life when they are in the office, the pub or anywhere else. This argument also denies the political need to be out and assertive. If people are still thinking that their homosexuality should be hidden, then it is obvious that society does not really accept us at all.

As another respondent commented, 'I wanted to be true to myself. I struggled for years trying to repress my feelings and thoughts, trying to be "normal". When I came to terms with my sexuality, I could finally live honestly.'

If there were no such thing as anti-gay bigotry, labelling our sexual preference would be unneccessary. But in our imperfect world we do define ourselves as lesbian or gay because of the political meaning of not toeing the heterosexual line. It is necessary to do so because of the prejudice we face as a result of daring to be who we are.

While so many gay men and lesbians settle for legal equality rather than social and political liberation, I think about women under patriarchy in the UK today. In 1970 the Equal Pay Act was passed, and five years later, at the height of the gay liberation movement, the Sex Discrimination Act came into effect and the Equal Opportunities Commission was established. Since then we have seen several new pieces of legislation, from the provision of improved maternity leave to political representation in parliament and laws to eliminate gender-based violence.

But despite the legislation and equality in the eyes of the law between women and men, two women a week are still murdered by former or current male partners. According to the Crime Survey for England and Wales, each year on average around 404,000 females are sexually assaulted. Women are paid less than men for doing the same job, do most of the childcare and domestic tasks, and are less likely to be promoted into senior and management positions. They are excluded from the boys' club established in private education and cemented at Oxbridge.

However, it is easier for gay men than it is for lesbians. As one lesbian survey respondent said: 'I think there's a lot more prejudice against women in society in general and as a result it's harder for lesbians. Even in the gay community they come in for a lot of stick for not always conforming to our idea of what a woman should look or behave like. I find this really sad.'

Gay men still have the privilege that comes with being a man, but they also face the oppression that comes with being gay. Gay men are still mocked for not conforming to the most boring of stereotypes. They still face violence and other prejudice. But gay men's culture has been adopted into the mainstream in a way it hasn't for lesbians. In fashion, gay men are prominent, if not quite entirely dominant. (Men still own pretty much everything, everywhere, and fashion is no different.)

Pop music demonstrates the difference between lesbians and gay men. Jessie J is supposedly bisexual, but the rumours and suspicion point towards the idea she is simply a lesbian marketed in a way so as not to alienate straight men. Gay men succeed in pop in a way lesbians don't. In pop music – see Britney Spears, Rihanna and Shakira – lesbianism is not for women; it's aimed at titillating men alone.

In the wider media, where gay men have *Attitude*, which often makes the mainstream headlines, lesbians have … ? Exactly. Lesbian columnists are a rarity compared to their gay men equivalents. In business, it's the same. Everywhere gay men are given the advantages that come with being male – celebrity, promotion and respect – that a lesbian will not get simply by being a woman. And there is a clear lack of lesbian 'role models' for want of a better term.

For gays and, particularly, lesbians living in the UK today, legislation simply does not reflect current opinion. Equal before the law does not mean liberation, or even equality. A similar situation exists for those of minority ethnic heritage. Since 1976 incitement to racial hatred has been enshrined in the criminal code of England and Wales, but in 1993 Stephen Lawrence was murdered by a gang of white racists. Legislation is a crucial component in any liberation struggle, but it is only a component. It would appear, however, that for many in the lesbian and gay community in the UK, we have reached the pinnacle of our struggle.

But we have been duped. We have been appeased. The crumbs were thrown and we were standing there with our hands outstretched, thanking the straight masters for giving. We were told: 'Have some of this – we are outgrowing it,' and we took the hand-me-downs of marriage and children, of respectability that have long proved to be a sham for heterosexuals.

The commercial market, as it expands, has taken ever fewer risks. The money is in becoming straight – not in terms of sexuality, just imagination and lifestyle. Money is funnelled into marriage celebrations that match straight couples', mortgages that are advertised to us along with straight couples, gym memberships, holidays and every other frippery that straight folk enjoy. The commercial market is driving gay culture. Gay culture used to be about rebellion, but the market is impelling us to accept the same as everyone else, merely using the 'find and replace' function on a PC to make sure it's inclusive.

There is no doubt for me that lesbians and gay men are almost as far from liberation as we were 10 years ago, despite the vast and important changes in legislation. In one respect we have stopped fighting for true emancipation from the tyranny of heterosexuality because we have been included in its rituals. We have mistaken being invited to the party for full inclusion and acceptance. We even use the word 'tolerance' as though 'putting up with' someone or something is the same as being welcome.

All women, not just lesbians, continue to suffer because gender roles are still left unchallenged. Had the GLF realised its aims and stuck to its guns, we could have seen a revolution unfold that challenged gender norms and dismantled patriarchy. Instead, we have marriage, IVF, surrogacy and as much, if not more, bullying in schools than we did when I came out.

Society as a whole is damaged by the lack of radical homosexual criticisms of the generally straight society, because most gay people have joined it. Whereas lesbian and gay men used to turn up to events such as protests and fundraisers in clothing and with hairstyles that in and of themselves were a challenge to prescribed gender roles, now any Stonewall event, for example, is filled with men in penguin suits and women in cocktail dresses.

A once radical community has now started aping not just straight people but the most conservative of straight people. Just because we can marry, it makes no good reason for us to marry. Marriage is no less a patriarchal institution, because the extension of marriage and civil partnership has led us to embrace traditional gender roles rather than question them. We had the chance to revolutionise the concept of marriage, but it appears we'd rather simply tie the knot and settle down.

Gone is the celebration of the liberty of being child-free; here is the celebration of getting to have children. In other words, being like everyone else. When it comes to children, we have swapped the goal of equality and started courting sameness. The radical basis of being gay or lesbian has been lost as we put down our banners and started changing nappies. Yes, we can be like everyone else, but why would we want to be?

Now we can have kids and get married, it doesn't mean that we have combated and defeated bigots. The overriding achievement is that we can now be sold tatty babygrows and wedding cakes like everyone else. Stonewall admits that it no longer sees the gay lifestyle as countercultural. Tolerance is one thing, acceptance is slightly better, but assimilation is a defeat for gay and straight alike. The culture we were (and some still are) opposed to is a pernicious and damaging one. It needs to be criticised.

Being so happy with the legislative changes also obscures the oppression that continues nonetheless. Bigots who harass, assault and even kill gays and lesbians will not be dissuaded from their actions simply by seeing us marry or adopt. Our efforts have been focused on nominal equality, and away from the anti-gay hatred that still continues in parliament, the street and places like pubs and B&Bs. And that is before we even consider the fate of gay men and lesbians abroad – it is not gay marriage that persecuted people in Uganda, say, are crying out for.

We are still being oppressed and attacked. People are still assaulted in the street for being gay, gay people who die are still vilified in the media and their sexuality is blamed as the cause, and gay men and lesbians are still more likely to be homeless than someone who is straight. In 1983, on my 21st birthday, I was attacked for being a lesbian, and there's still a chance it might happen again on my next birthday.

Violence against lesbians and other women happens because the gender roles have not been overthrown. Women are expected to be subservient to men. In mainstream gay couples, the gender roles are emulated and not rejected. In mainstream straight couples, the gender roles are still treated as the status quo. Gay culture used to challenge this. Radical feminists and lesbians are a threat to the traditional gender roles expected of both men and women, and if they were annihilated, it would lead to a reduction or elimination of rape, assault, oppression and misogyny.

Religion is a stronghold of bigotry. Fundamentalist Christians offer courses to convert us back to being 'normal'. Some members of organised religion refuse us access to services, pastoral or merely religious.

The media are often outspokenly bigoted. People like AA Gill and Jan Moir spit invective about gay men and lesbians, and even liberals like Will Self expose their ignorance about us.

We have equality legislation, and representation in the Tory party, and we're on television. We have lessons in (some) schools and talks in (some) workplaces stating why oppression and anti-gay bigotry are unacceptable. And yet there is plenty of evidence of residual or active hatred. Being gay is still an acceptable punchline. Parents are still given understanding if their child comes out. Gay CEOs are a rarity, and workplace discrimination is regularly reported.

This suggests that legislation does not celebrate us and it does not engage us as radicals; it tolerates us as imitations of what we used to campaign against. Are gay marriage and adoption a sufficient sop to us?

Once we used to, to paraphrase the bigots, ram it down their throats. We were out and proud. Now, we hide behind biology to excuse ourselves and to implicitly absolve ourselves of responsibility or, worse, blame. Being gay is, to me, a choice. And there is no evidence to persuade me or the general scientific community to think otherwise.

From the Nazis onwards the scientific search for a gay gene has come explicitly with the aims of curing us or removing us from the gene pool. Supposedly neutral studies are now held up as a way for parents to elect to erase us from their future. All this does is reinforce the idea that being born gay is still something negative, to be avoided if it can be helped.

If we protest there is a gay gene, then essentially we are asking for pity and tolerance. The radical quality of being homosexual has been lost if what we are demanding is pity, when once we demanded respect and asserted our way of life as not just equal but in many ways superior.

The search for a gay gene is nonsense and detracts from the greatest qualities of the movement I joined in the 1970s and refuse to see become any more blunted. Gay and lesbian radicalism has so much to offer gay men, lesbians and straight people. If we accept there is a gay gene – especially when there is no proof – we ruin the movement. The reason to celebrate being gay is because half the fun is in *not being straight*. No imposed gender roles, no expectation for a nuclear family, no voting Conservative, no to a lifetime of being a wage-slave.

Lesbian radicalism can offer liberation to *all* women. The society we live in is undeniably patriarchal. If we persuade people that sexuality is a choice, then we persuade people that they can opt out of patriarchy, and start to challenge for equal pay and an end of discrimination against all women. If we end discrimination and prescribed gender roles, we save women and make society fairer and more enjoyable for both sexes.

With gay marriage and adoption, and nominal acceptance in the workplace, we are being invited to join society as it is now and accept what it has to give us. Wiping children's arses, having coronation chicken at the wedding reception and paying a mortgage. What a gift. Instead of seeing what conservative straight society has to offer us, the really progressive, radical and superior option is to show lesbians, gay men and everyone else what they're missing out on by not joining us.

Until all lesbians and gay men are free from the oppression caused by anti-gay bigotry, I will continue to refuse to accept that having a wedding and babies renders us equal to heterosexuals and therefore free from oppression. Let's face it, marriage and children have not liberated heterosexual women from patriarchy, but further embedded them in it.

Rather than accept the cultural relativist line that, as one Stonewall spokesman said, 'parachuting into other countries' is akin to western cultural imperialism, we should be using our relative privilege to support gay liberation campaigns in India, Uganda, Nigeria and the many other countries in which gay sex is criminalised. We should be hitting out at the UK government for sending lesbians and gay men back to countries to face oppression, imprisonment and death.

My thoughts can't help but turn to the situation in Russia, and in particular Vladislav Tornovoy, a gay man who was tortured, raped and murdered by his 'friends', and Masha Gessen, a lesbian mother who was physically violated and now has to leave her country to save her family and to keep herself safe. The current atrocities in Russia prompted me to look back at Berlin in the 1930s. Prior to the Third Reich, Berlin was a liberal city, with many gay bars, nightclubs and cabarets. The rest, of course, is history.

I am not being over-dramatic when I worry that this is the way Russia is headed. Lesbians and gay men in Russia are under constant threat of bigotry, hatred and violent assault. Gay sex was decriminalised in Russia in 1993, but the rights of gay men and women are now being aggressively eroded. Their latest national law bans the distribution of 'propaganda of non-traditional sexual relations' to minors, which means anyone who shares information about lesbian and gay issues. In practice, that means not only fines for anyone who shares information about homosexuality but age warnings appended to any media articles about homosexuality. It also carries fines and imprisonment for the organisers of gay events and for speaking in defence of gay rights, and severe punishments for any 'demonstration of homosexuality in public'. This, unbelievably, includes holding hands.

A number of local initiatives designed to suppress lesbian and gay lives have been introduced, the latest being that lesbian and gay parents would lose custody of their children under a law proposed by a senior politician in the United Russia party.

Besides the actions of the police and courts in Russia, there is widespread acceptance of anti-gay bigotry and hatred, and the tolerance of attacks is growing among the general public. There is hideous footage of social media sites depicting gay men being tortured by neo-Nazis in Russia with passersby joining in.

Of course, we must not forget that things are just as bad, if not worse elsewhere in the world. In Iran, where homosexuality is criminalised, lesbians and gay men have been subjected to 60 lashes in public for same-sex kissing, and a number of gay men have been executed for being in a same-sex relationship. In Jamaica, another country where homosexuality is illegal, those convicted of buggery can be liable to 10 years' imprisonment and hard labour.

But Russia is currently up there among some of the worst countries in terms of state-sanctioned anti-gay bigotry. The victory for equal marriage in the UK should spur us on to campaign against the current horrors for our gay brothers and sisters. A vodka ban is not enough. We need to name the human rights atrocities for what they are and never rest on our laurels.

Clare Balding's refusal to take a stand by boycotting the 2014 Winter Olympics reflects the attitude of many other lesbian and gay public figures who benefit from being lauded at Stonewall-type public events and are assumed to be brave simply because they came clean when outed by the tabloids, as Balding was, but who refuse to put politics and principles before professional expediency.

At the time of Section 28, I honestly thought that Thatcher's government, paradoxically, had done lesbians and gay men a favour. So appalling was the message behind the legislation I had assumed we would rise up again as a movement and become the radicals we needed to be. Instead, we became a cowardly mass of apologetic sops, asking for sympathy and tolerance rather than demanding a revolution. We were told that if we became good girls and boys and assimilated ourselves into the straight lifestyle, we would be protected from nasty folk who wished to do us harm. But it does not work like that. The only ones truly protected are the well-off, coupled folk who quietly get on with their respectable lives. The rest of us are left with a stark choice: do we fit in or fight?

One respondent to my survey replied brilliantly. This is what we should carry on fighting for: 'What I'd actually like to see is for the state to recognise one type of spousal union (with no gender restrictions) and to cut the crap around the distinction between civil partnership and marriage. I suppose this basically means civil partnerships for all, and you can go to a church and get a priest to tell you you're married if that's what you're into. I support the right of same-sex couples to marry, but it's probably worth noting that I don't think I'd want to have a same-sex marriage myself. To me, it seems too much like buying into an institution with a lot of nasty hetero-patriarchal baggage – I'm queer, and I think I want queer relationships too, not to be assimilated into some approximation of the hetero-patriarchal mainstream.'

And there was one very concise response: 'Marriage is a crock of shit.'

Lesbians and gay men are at a crossroads. The year that all lawful impediments to same-sex marriage are removed is *not* the year that will be marked down in history as that in which anti-gay bigotry ended and lesbians and gays achieved full liberation. So what do we do next? Carry on fighting for an end to the bigotry that is prevalent around the world and that affects most severely those lesbians and gay men with the least privilege, or go shopping for a new wedding outfit and sperm donor catalogue? It is, of course, your choice.

ACKNOWLEDGMENTS

This book is dedicated to the early pioneers of feminism and gay liberation. We owe them our lives.

Several people helped and supported me through the journey of writing this book. Those who helped with research include Fiona Barry, Katherine Clementine, Susie Dickie, Ella Hayward, Julia Hilliard, Helena Horton, Tara Joshi, Anthony Lorenzo, Andy Love, Steph Mann and Marj Morgan, Helen Price, Lily Rae and Taylor Riley.

Thanks to Isaac Delestre and Alexander Netherton for tech support.

Thank you to those who agreed to give their time to be interviewed: Christine Bakke-O'Neill, Nicola Barker, Paul Burston, Maureen Chadwick, Jane Czyzselska, Michael Davidson, Barrie Drewitt-Barlow, Maureen Duffy, Stella Duffy, Rev. Giles Fraser, Daniel Gonzales, Rev. Kes Grant, Ruth Hunt, Alex Hopkins, Andrew Jackson, Sheila Jeffreys, Tess Joseph, Hannah Latham, Gia Milinovich, Brendan O'Neill, Patrick Osborne, Mark Palmer-Edgecumbe, Lisa Power, Qazi Rahman, Leisa Rea, Linda Riley, Sasha Roseneil, Adam Rutherford, Shelley Silas, Darren Smith, Patrick Strudwick, Peter Tatchell, Jane Traies and the lesbians of Hebden Bridge.

All those who completed the questionnaires, and to the *Guardian*'s 'Comment Is Free' deputy editor, David Shariatmadari, who gave my articles in which I outlined the themes of this book a good airing.

Friends such as Rose George, Patricia Holmes, Ashley Maguire, Denise Marshall, Sandra McNeill and Chris Root inspired and sustained me through the process.

My mother Maureen who saw a future for me before I did. She sacrificed the daily contact with me she would no doubt have had if I had stayed in Darlington and married a local boy. For Maureen, it was more important that I tried to make my mark in the world. She is the best of all mums.

A very special thank you to Harriet Wistrich who lived with this project from its conception and encouraged and believed in me, as she has done for the past 27 years. Harriet, you truly deserve a medal.

Julie Bindel, April 2014

BIBLIOGRAPHY

Barker, Nicola, *Not the Marrying Kind: A Feminist Critique of Same-Sex Marriage*, Palgrave Macmillan, 2012

Brooke, Stephen, *Sexual Politics: Sexuality, Family Planning, and the British Left from the 1880s to the Present Day*, Oxford University Press, 2011

Chitty, Clyde, *Understanding Schools and Schooling*, Routledge, 2001

Fine, Cordelia, *Delusions of Gender: The Real Science Behind Sex Differences*, Icon Books, 2011

Gottschalk, Lorene, *Genderations of Women Choosing to Become Lesbian: Questioning the Essentialist Link* (no publisher listed), 1999

Hamer, Dean, and Copeland, Peter, *The Science of Desire: The Search for the Gay Gene and the Biology of Behavior*, Simon & Schuster, 1995

Jeffrey-Poulter, Stephen, *Peers, Queers and Commons: The Struggle for Gay Law Reform from 1950 to the Present*, Routledge, 1991

Jeffreys, Sheila, *Unpacking Queer Politics: A Lesbian Feminist Perspective*, Polity Press, 2003

Komhiya, A, 'Britain Section 28', in Sears, James T (ed), *Youth, Education and Sexualities: An International Encyclopaedia Volume One*, Greenwood, 2005

Labour party, *Social Justice and Economic Efficiency: First Report of Labour's Policy Review for the 1990s*, 1988

Power, Lisa, *No Bath but Plenty of Bubbles: Oral History of the Gay Liberation Front 1970–73*, Cassell, 1995

Rubenstein, William (ed), *Lesbians, Gay Men, and the Law*, The New Press, 1993

Smyth, Cherry, *Lesbians Talk Queer Notions*, Scarlet Press, 1992

Vines, Gail, 'Queer Creatures', *New Scientist*, 1999

Whisman, Vera, *Queer by Choice: Lesbians, Gay Men, and the Politics of Identity*, Routledge, 1995

ENDNOTES

CHAPTER 1

1 www.totalpolitics.com/history/1783/where-are-they-now-maureen-colquhoun.thtml
2 Quoted in Power, p.64
3 Power, p.240
4 Carla Toney, quoted in Power, p.242
5 www.theguardian.com/uk/2005/dec/11/gayrights.immigrationpolicy
6 'The School Report: The Experiences of Gay Young People in Britain's Schools in 2012', Stonewall, 2013

CHAPTER 2

7 www.theguardian.com/commentisfree/2012/nov/27/homophobia-islamophobia-right-words-associated-press
8 This survey was carried out by YouGov and commissioned by Stonewall.
9 www.bsa-30.natcen.ac.uk/media/37580/bsa30_full_report_final.pdf
10 'The School Report', Stonewall, 2013
11 www.galop.org.uk/wp-content/uploads/2013/08/The-Hate-Crime-Report-2013.pdf
12 http://kaleidoscopeaustralia.wordpress.com/2014/03/10/homophobia-shaming-the-commonwealth-of-nations/
13 www.fmreview.org/sogi/bennett-thomas
14 www.spuc.org.uk/news/releases/2013/january15
15 www.archbishopofyork.org/articles.php/2919/same-sex-marriage-bill-committee-stage#sthash.7KtGn9c2.dpuf
16 See, for example, Melanie Phillips' *Daily Mail* column of January 2011, in which she claims that gays are the 'new McCarthyites' and went on to rage against the fact that it is illegal to actively discriminate against lesbians and gay men: www.dailymail.co.uk/debate/article-1349951/Gayness-mandatory-schools-Gay-victims-prejudice-new-McCarthyites.html. Also in the *Daily Mail* in July 2013, Richard Littlejohn poured scorn on the idea that prime minister David Cameron would concern himself with decriminalising homosexuality in Commonwealth countries: www.dailymail.co.uk/debate/article-2378260/RICHARD-LITTLEJOHN-Camerons-mission-export-gay-marriage-world-We-Call-Me-Daffyd-gay-global-village.html
17 www.independent.co.uk/voices/comment/the-return-of-section-28-this-cant-be-brushed-aside-as-an-oversight-8776017.html

18 www.independent.co.uk/news/uk/this-britain/the-exgay-files-the-bizarre-world-of-gaytostraight-conversion-1884947.html
19 www.beyondexgay.com
20 http://will-self.com/2006/01/12/the-island-of-doctor-moreau/

CHAPTER 3

21 www.apa.org/monitor/2011/02/myth-buster.aspx
22 McIntosh, Mary, 'The Homosexual Role', *Social Problems,* Volume 16, No 2, pp.182–192, Autumn 1968
23 Whisman, p.17
24 *Ibid.*, p.35
25 Camperio, Ciani, Andrea, S, Fontanesi, Lilybeth, Iemmola, Francesca, Giannella, Elga, Ferron, Claudia, and Lombardi, Luigi, 'Factors Associated with Higher Fecundity in Female Maternal Relatives of Homosexual Men', *The Journal of Sexual Medicine*, Volume 9, Issue 11, pp.2878–87, November 2012
26 Swaab, DF, *We Are Our Brains: From the Womb to Alzheimer's*, Allen Lane, 2014

CHAPTER 4

27 Title from an article in 'Comment Is Free', *Guardian*, www.theguardian.com/commentisfree/2010/jul/26/lesbian-gay-rights-portrayal-tv
28 Jeffreys, p.9
29 GLF manifesto, 1971. See www.awakeman.co.uk/Sense/Books/GLF%20Manifesto%201971.pdf
30 *Ibid.*
31 Smyth
32 www.thegayuk.com/magazine/4574334751/INTERVIEW-How-To-Survive-A-Plague-with-David-France-and-Peter-Staley/6993992
33 www.virusmyth.com/aids/hiv/iycultsero.htm
34 www.stonewall.org.uk/documents/prescription_for_change.pdf
35 Heaphy, B, Yip, A, and Thompson, D, *Lesbian, Gay and Bisexual Lives over 50*, York House, 2003, quoted in www.thelabrystrust.com/uploads/1/1/7/4/11743016/labrys_trust_research_report_march_2013_v3_for_pdf-1.pdf

CHAPTER 5

36 'Gay is the Word', *Guardian*, 12 April 1971
37 www.aclu.org/lgbt-rights_hiv-aids/overview-lesbian-and-gay-parenting-adoption-and-foster-care
38 www.britishsurrogacycentre.com/gay-surrogacy
39 www.nymag.com/thecut/2012/12/gay-men-christian-wombs-the-new-surrogacy.html

40 www.asianews.it/news-en/Thai-organisation-involved-in-trafficking-in-Vietnamese-surrogate-mothers-uncovered-20916.html

41 www.londonwomensclinic.com

42 www.telegraph.co.uk/news/religion/10283556/Vicar-refuses-to-baptise-baby-of-lesbian-couple-who-both-want-to-be-registered-mother.html

43 Roseneil, Sasha, 'Queering Home and Family in the 1980s: The Greenham Common Women's Peace Camp', talk given at the Queer Homes, Queer Families: A History and Policy Debate, British Library, 17 December 2012 (convened by the Raphael Samuel History Centre and the British Library)

44 See, for example, Feargha Ní Bhroin's paper, 'Feminism and the Same-sex Marriage Debate', April 2009, www.marriagequality.ie/download/pdf/feminism_paper_final_01.05.pdf

45 Quoted in Rubenstein, p.481

46 www.belfasttelegraph.co.uk/woman/my-two-mums-growing-up-with-lesbian-parents-28488408.html

47 www.bbc.com/news/uk-northern-ireland-24918026

48 www.theguardian.com/lifeandstyle/series/the-three-of-us

49 www.grassrootsfeminism.net/cms/node/580

50 www.camdennewjournal.co.uk/122205/cn122205_10.htm

51 www.theguardian.com/society/2014/jan/05/gay-rights-we-are-getting-married

52 www.pinknews.co.uk/2013/11/14/manchester-lesbian-couple-sue-nhs-after-hospital-prevented-them-from-accessing-ivf

53 www.standard.co.uk/news/uk/surge-in-gay-marriage-could-boost-uk-economy-by-18m-a-year-8471195.html

CHAPTER 6

54 So wrote Rachel Arthur in the *Times Magazine* on how she and her partner, Amelia, began their family.

55 www.insights.org.uk/articleitem.aspx?title=Gay+and+Lesbian+Tourism

56 www.alternativeparenting.co.uk and www.europeandiversityawards.com

57 http://edition.cnn.com/2013/05/23/living/abercrombie-attractive-and-fat/

58 www.prweb.com/releases/2006/01/prweb335713.htm

59 www.webwire.com/ViewPressRel.asp?aId=74423#.U0UOD1wkjmI

60 www.independent.co.uk/news/uk/this-britain/the-l-word-lesbian-loaded-loving-it-516111.html

61 www.standard.co.uk/news/londoners-diary/alice-arnolds-advice-on-coming-out-of-the-closet-8957551.html

62 www.petertatchell.net/lgbt_rights/gay_community/gay_community_doomed.htm

63 www.independent.co.uk/life-style/sexual-politics-in-the-90s-gay-and-lesbian--the-rainbow-alliance-comes-of-age-1262133.html

64 www.businesshighlight.org/business/the-rising-demand-for-online-gay-sex-toys.html

65 www.theguardian.com/world/2008/may/08/gayrights.greece

66 www.theguardian.com/lifeandstyle/2013/aug/03/yotam-ottolenghi-gay-fatherhood-parenting, accessed 1 September 2013

67 http://money.msn.com/now/post.aspx?post=601552a7-4497-4f28-847f-27137d413118?OCID=MSNNWS

68 www.standard.co.uk/news/uk/surge-in-gay-marriage-could-boost-uk-economy-by-18m-a-year-8471195.html

69 www.huffingtonpost.com/2013/02/07/donald-trump-gay-marriage-not-my-thing_n_2637646.html

70 www.cosmeticsurgeon.co.uk/blog/how-much-is-the-credit-crunch-affecting-cosmetic-surgery

71 www.slate.com/blogs/outward/2014/01/23/gay_men_and_plastic_surgery_why_so_much.html

72 www.outg3awards.co.uk

CHAPTER 7

73 http://news.bbc.co.uk/onthisday/hi/dates/stories/july/11/newsid_2499000/2499721.stm

74 www.gaystarnews.com/article/gay-teacher-resigns-after-parents-complained-about-him-teaching-their-children070414

75 www.nytimes.com/2007/10/09/us/09aged.html?pagewanted=all&_r=0

76 www.independent.co.uk/life-style/interview-the-word-according-to-huffty-the-end-of-the-current-friday-night-tv-series-is-nigh-just-when-shed-mastered-shaving-her-head-when-drunk-so-what-next-1429234.html

77 www.cruisinggays.com/brighton/c/areas

78 www.washingtonpost.com/blogs/worldviews/wp/2014/02/24/here-are-the-10-countries-where-homosexuality-may-be-punished-by-death

79 www.haaretz.com/news/national/.premium-1.564217

80 www.theguardian.com/world/2013/dec/20/uganda-mps-laws-homosexuality

81 www.theguardian.com/commentisfree/2013/dec/26/tide-turning-homophobia-gay-rights-humanity

82 www.theguardian.com/world/2013/dec/26/gay-voters-more-likely-favour-david-cameron

83 www.theguardian.com/politics/2012/apr/20/gay-tory-conservative-party

84 www.thetimes.co.uk/tto/opinion/columnists/article3958225.ece

INDEX

media:
  bigotry in 38–9, 201
  lack of decent
    representation in 9
  stereotypes used by
    44
Mensch, Louise 175
Messner, Michael A 101
Microcosm, The (Duffy)
  134
Milinovich, Gia 75
Miller, Maria 25
Mills, Bob 29, 39
Miss World 12
Moffat, Andrew 172
Moir, Jan 38–9
Molecular Genetic Study
  of Sexual Orientation
  78
Montgomerie, Tim 191
Moran, Caitlin 193
Morton, George 5–6
murders 45
Murray, Colin 39
MX 107, 108

Namigadde, Brenda 40
'nature vs nurture' 9–10,
  15, 43, 53, 61–91
  author's speech on 64
  readers' comments on
    79–80
  scientific research into
    71–9
  Strudwick's views on
    84–7
  survey responses to
    80–3
  Tatchell's views on
    68–9
NatWest 151
New Scientist 65
New Statesman 62
New York Times 84
Nigeria 1, 189
Nixon, Cynthia 61, 83–4,
  85, 87, 91
*No Bath but Plenty of
  Bubbles* (Power) 13
Nolland, Dr Lisa 46
'Not Born That Way'
  (Bindel) 64

Not the Marrying Kind
  (Barker) 140

O'Brien Keith 47
Observer 136
Okhlobystin, Ivan 188
On Our Backs 159
O'Neill, Brendan 65–6
Operation Spanner
  103–4
Osborne, Patrick 131,
  132
Ottolenghi, Yotam 160
Out at Work 147
Out in the City 147, 165
Outclass 147
OutRage! 107–8

Paddy Power 149–50
Padgett, Martha 142
Pakistan 40, 85, 90
Palmer-Edgcumbe, Mark
  166–7
ParliOUT 190
Perkins, Sue 44, 192
Phillips, Melanie 47
Pickup, David 88
Pilkington, Lesley 52
Pink News 79, 144, 165,
  189
'pink pound' 152
  see also LGB-focused
    business
Pistorius, Oscar 150
Pizzey, Erin 33
Poots, Edwin 129
pornography 44, 97, 146,
  159, 163
  and feminism 23,
    102
  for lesbians 103, 157
  see also erotic fiction
Portas, Mary 44
Positive Strength 106
Power, Lisa 13, 16, 99,
  100, 101, 103, 106
Prescription for Change
  110
Preti, George 79
Proud 147
Public Order Act 45
Putin, Vladimir 188

Queer by Choice
  (Whisman) 70

Rae, Leisa 192
Rahman, Qazi 74–5, 76,
  77, 87
Reagan, Ronald 104
Refuge 164
Reid, Beryl 21
Rich, Adrienne 24, 69
Riley, Linda 147–8, 149,
  165, 193
'Road to Auschwitz, The'
  14
Robillard, Rob 153
Robinson, Tom 90
Rodman, Dennis 150
Roseneil, Sasha 13–14,
  106, 126–7, 133–4
Russia 59, 151, 165–6,
  187, 188, 193, 203–4
Rutherford, Dr Adam
  75, 87

sadomasochism 103–4,
  159
  and handkerchief code
    102
same-sex marriage 1, 18,
  25, 26–7, 36–7, 37–8,
  46–7, 115–16, 124,
  126–8, 133–5, 136–7,
  139–41, 142–3, 175,
  202
  college debate on
    170–1
  and GLF 12
  held up as symbol
    liberation 40
  industry surrounding
    161–2
  other countries
    pressured to
    introduce 142
  and patriarchal power
    127, 137, 142, 170
  political opinions of
    41–2
  poll on 37
  readers' comments on
    42–3
  as smokescreen 57